FATE AND DESTINY
THE TWO AGREEMENTS OF THE SOUL

Illustration for Cover

Originally, "pity" and "piety" were very close with each suggesting aspects of affection, duty, and kindness. The idea of "having pity" on some poor soul came much later. William Blake considered Pity to be a divine attribute in the eternal realm; but on earth, like many other things, pity becomes divided. Here, the image of Pity represents the distinction between fate and destiny, for those two energies can also be seen as unified in eternity, but fatefully divided once the soul is born on earth.

Contents

Stories

EX MALO BONUM

Out of bad comes good; but also out of fate can come a destiny.

INTRODUCTION

Fate is an invisible thread woven though all the things of the world and through all the events of time. Fate is a mysterious presence found in each life and in all serious undertakings. Fate involves those things which are woven into the fabric of our soul from the beginning. Fate and the soul are woven of the same threads and fate includes the strange twist that makes each soul unique and each life unrepeatable. Denying all sense of fate and limitations in life also means denying any sense of inherent uniqueness in the soul. Our "uniqueness" is woven exactly where the thread of destiny entwines with the twists of our fate.

Fate refers to our deepest sense of subjectivity, where we are subject to mysterious limitations and open to surprising potentials. Fate can be seen as whatever limits, restricts or even imprisons us; and fate is where we must go if we are to awaken to our own destiny. In seeking to live our destiny we inevitably encounter the obstacles of our own fate. Fate and destiny are an archetypal pairing within each soul; they form a dynamic tension that makes each life meaningful and purposeful. With the loss of fate, we tend to feel less purposeful, less aimed at life, less convinced that our souls could be leading us somewhere.

There is an old connection between fate and fame that is preserved in the words themselves. *Fate* comes from *fata*, an old Latin word with root meanings that include a "sentence of the gods" and "to be spoken of by the divine." There was an old sense that the human soul was touched by the divine and that the gods were interested enough to have something to say about each of us. Fame comes from another direction as *fama* means "to speak and to tell," but especially to "tell rumors and to report on the reputation of others." Our fate revolves around what the gods first said about us, while any fame we might acquire refers to what others say about us during our lives and after our death as well.

Destiny is the hidden thread that connects the old notions of fate and fame. Destiny can mean being seen standing together with one's genius or life spirit. Living out one's destiny reveals the divine word set within the soul and also causes others to recognize our true value and speak well of us. In this older, deeper sense, becoming famous meant something closer to being "known well," rather than simply becoming "well known." The true sense of fame and the true issue of fate involve more the quality of one's life than the quantity of one's renown.

The opposite of fame is *infamy*, meaning "not famous" or more often, famous for the wrong reasons. Infamy involves a subversion or perversion of the true spirit in one's life, a reversal and undermining of the aims of one's inner star and the purpose of one's innate genius. Infamy suggests being seen standing away from the true spirit and original aim of one's life. The infamous become famous for the wrong reason and become well-known in the wrong way.

Modern mass cultures seem to produce new forms of infamy as brief flashes of fame seem to substitute for genuinely discovering the inner spirit and true destination of one's life. Anyone can suddenly "be a star" and go from being an "unknown" to becoming "world famous" in a moment. More and more people seem willing to become famous "for no good reason" as if "sudden infamy" has replaced genuine notoriety. People desire their "fifteen minutes of fame" and by virtue of mass technology and mass communications, they may get it.

The greater life is found where destiny calls to each of us to become who we are in essence, to live far enough into life to reveal the inner story set within us. The older sense of fame depended upon moments of revelation in which the inborn spirit of life became recognized and celebrated as the soul approached the destination it was aimed at from the beginning and thereby reconnected to its divine origins.

TERRITORIES OF FATE

Fate inscribes an area or territory that we are bound to enter. Destiny involves finding a way out or a way through exactly those areas and aspects that constrain the vitality of our lives. Fate places us in specific contexts where meaning and purpose can be explored. Wherever we brush against the limits of our fate we also stand near the doors of our destiny. When we face our fate in life we also begin to move it and when fate moves destiny moves closer. Only from the ground of destiny does an individual life make sense. Taken together, fate and destiny are purpose seen from the other end of life.

We have an appointment with destiny but must suffer the disappointments of fate in order to arrive there. Fate would stop us in our tracks and strip us to the bone so that we might discover the essential imagination and sense of meaning and purpose that lies at the core of our lives. When we ignore the limits of fate and the hints of destiny we tighten the unconscious web of our lives. Eventually, we make our lives fixed, settled, and intractable. Thus, we seal our own fate and ignore our hidden destinies.

Fate can mean "it has been written," yet the inner story that our fate inscribes is a living text and breathing record that is open to interpretation and subject to change. Fate is the story of our lives unfolding from within us. When life is fully lived fate functions more as an oracle needing interpretation than a pre-determined outcome. Shifting fate and finding the destiny within it is part of the art of truly living and of living truly.

Fate and destiny are close woven within us and near them can be found the true genius of our lives. *Genius* refers to the inborn spirit and innate style of each person, the "spirit that is already there." The natural genius in us protects and reminds us of the innate gifts we carry and of a primary agreement our souls have made to deliver those gifts to the world. The soul arrives gifted and aimed and dedicated to fulfilling its first agreement with life. However the labor of being born and the necessity of entering the realm of time and expediency causes us to forget the divine errand that the soul agreed to fulfill.

This book is about the first agreement of the soul and its divine errand; it's about the mystery of fate speaking everywhere and the possibility of destiny appearing anywhere. It's a collection of stories both personal and mythical, for those are the texts that give texture and shape to the mysteries of fate and destiny. The idea behind the book is that it might help people find the ways that the threads of fate hold and aim them at the ground where destiny can be found.

As the book makes clear, I had my first conscious connection to the mysteries of fate when I was barely a youth. Since then, I have learned that everyone has at least one experience in which the inner pattern of their soul becomes revealed to them. Unfortunately, modern life tends to overlook, miscast or diminish the ways in which the soul tries to awaken us early in life. The stories gathered here are of the kind that people used to use to bring the essential experiences of the soul into greater awareness.

Meanwhile, it seems to be our mutual fate to be living during a time of great upheaval and sweeping change. Nature and culture used to be called the "two great garments of life." By now, the fabrics of both cloaks of being have become frayed and torn we are less woven into the world. There are many ways to view the dramatic changes that are well underway, but no easy way to see where life is going and how things might end.

It is on the ground of uncertainty and in the face of the unknown that the inner story of our souls becomes most pertinent and important. The soul requires an outer drama so that it can reveal its full imagination for life and its inner myth. There is no way to avoid the dramas and surprises, the tragedies and losses that characterize the modern era; but there may be no better time to learn the inner story that our souls carry.

When the story of the world becomes less clear, it is the unfolding of the inner life of the soul that might provide the best way to proceed. Myths, folk tales, and fairy tales most often depend upon great obstacles and impossible tasks to call forth the inner resources of the heroines and heroes of the soul. Fairy tales were once called "fated tales" as if to drive home the point that fate is waiting for us to enter the drama of life and learn what we are truly made of. No one has a small soul or a timid fate, but each will find obstacles that force the soul to grow.

For the past thirty years, I have worked with at risk youth and overlooked elders, with prisoners and homeless youth, with veterans and refugees. One thing they all have in common is that there can be no denying that they are in trouble and facing great obstacles. Of course, those are the exact conditions for generating change and for bringing the soul with its inherent genius and deep resources closer to the surface of life. I'm not wishing trouble on anyone, but I have noticed how trouble comes knocking at every door and how it knocks harder each time it is simply ignored or denied.

Trouble is another word for fate; what troubles us the most is what we are fated to one day face. What troubles us in youth will return at each crossroad in life because it secretly seeks to provoke a deep awakening to the unique way that we are intended to live. The stories gathered here are full of troubles and trials and threaded through with the surprising ways that the genius of life opens the way to change and healing and wisdom.

Some of the stories are "wisdom tales" that try to return genuine wisdom to a world that prefers information or common knowledge. Wisdom involves a darker knowledge as well as ways of finding uncommon illumination. Like mythic stories, wisdom combines a depth of knowing with a tolerance for trouble. The wise are those who find the inner thread and true gradient of their lives and learn the ropes from following the through line of their own destiny. The last section of the book has the title, The Return of Wisdom. There's seems to be less and less wisdom about more and more things and I'm trying to imagine ways that wisdom might return to common life. In the old sense of things, love is a secret part of wisdom as well as a necessary condition of the soul. Both learning and love require that the heart remain young and that we be foolish enough to become wise.

The middle section of the book bears the title, The Dream of Life. Without fully intending it, I have put a dream in the middle of the book.

Then again, there is a dream in the middle of each life; each of us a dream seeded in a soul around which the body is wrapped. The first agreement of the soul can be viewed as the dream that keeps calling us to a greater life. An old idea holds the place of awakening to be in the space between sleep and the waking world as the awakened soul serves both worlds and connects them together.

The first section is titled, The Book of Fate. It refers to the book of myths that I received by mistake on my thirteenth birthday. Of course, it wasn't a mistake at all, but something that was fated to happen one way or another. Fate appears in the accidents that aren't accidental and in the mistakes that turn out to be fortuitous and purposeful. I take aim at critical events in my own life in order to offer a sense of how fate has shaped and informed it. The personal tales keep slipping into myth, perhaps in the same way that myth keeps slipping back into life. This section focuses on the old sense of receiving a certain life sentence and specific "lot in life." *Lot* refers to our small allotment of all that is possible, but it includes a divine word that inscribes the inner text and living language of our soul.

ASPECTS OF THE SELF

Another way to view the sections of the book involves the way it considers certain aspects of the deep self. I imagine the deep self as the depository of the exact knowledge that we need for our lives to be purposeful and make sense. Under the old notion that each person is born with their own medicine, the deep self can also be seen to carry the antidote for what truly ails us. Throughout the book I contrast the deep and knowing self with the little-self or ego self. As happens in stories, self and soul often trade places and each becomes the vehicle for dreams to manifest and for spirit to awaken.

The first section focuses on the Gifted Self, how it tries to awaken during youthful encounters with fate; but also how it becomes crucial during later life. There are stories of the struggles of youth trying to find and use the god-given gifts of the soul. And, there are tales that describe the weird and wise ways of genuine elders. The initiations of youth involve an awakening of the inner sage and the rites of the elders require a renewal of the dream of life first encountered in youth.

The second part of the book focuses on the Golden Self as it tells tales of the birth of the soul and the life callings that bring the inner gold to the surface of one's life. The first agreement of the soul is described and contrasted with all other agreements that life requires. Tales of following the dream of life serve to remind us that the treasure hard to attain and the inner gold is within us all along. However, a genuine calling must be followed to find and uncover the golden self. The intimate relationship between our gifts and our wounds becomes critical for healing and growth as well as for understanding both what we fear and what we love.

The Awakened Self becomes the focus of the third part of the book as we move deeper into the territory of myth and take up old ideas from both the West and the East regarding the "inner disciple" of our lives. The search for the deeper self becomes a pilgrimage that leads to the pearls of wisdom, the pains of awakening, and the power of truth to counteract what can poison the soul. Distinctions are made between "big death" and the "little deaths" that take us to the middle of life and make rebirth and renewal possible. While following the path of the disciple we learn of the brilliance of the tiger-self, the "roar of awakening," and the many ways that difficult fates unwind into realizations of wisdom and destiny.

Taken together, the tales of the initiated soul and awakened self serve as a ground for considering the necessary troubles and essential callings that affect all young people. At the same time the stories mark the paths along which people of any age can find threads of meaning and hints of purpose. The text is populated by images of the wily teachers and wise guides that exemplify the soul's instinct and ability to serve both this world and the otherworld. There's an old thief who instructs misguided authorities, an old prostitute with critical truths to tell, a young woman who must approach a tiger to preserve love, a foolish dreamer who learns the alchemy of the heart, a holy man who falls in love and forgets his errand for god, and a village where the rotten aspects of life are cleansed and the inner gold of the self is polished.

The great marketplace of life appears in several forms and is visited by terrified servants and wandering disciples, lost dreamers and saintly thieves. Death makes an appearance in the middle of life as does Brahma, the Buddha, and the goddess Saraswati. All have something to say about the conditions of the soul, the importance of dreams, the dance of fate and destiny, and the secret unity that holds the two worlds together.

I

The Book of Fate

"We are hunting are fate and we are pursued by it."

CHAPTER 1

THE BOOK OF FATE

On the occasion of my thirteenth birthday I received a book that indelibly marked my life. It was my first conscious experience of fate and it involved a hint of destiny as well. It was the first hardcover book I ever received that wasn't a school book or a church text. In some ways it turned out to be both of those things for me, yet also more than either of them. The book came as a gift, but was also given to me by mistake. A twist of fate can work that way, turning one thing into another in order to reveal the inner shape of one's life.

My closest aunt had noticed that I read a lot and asked what most interested me. I told her that history intrigued me, how the stories of the past seemed to continue to affect the present. In order to support my interests and encourage my education, she went looking for a history book for me. She was kind-hearted and generous and she looked out for me and my sisters. She was also a notably short woman and that may have affected what happened next. In the bookstore she spotted a history book on an upper shelf. In reaching high above herself, she must have taken down the book next to the one she intended to buy. Unaware of the mistake, she purchased the wrong book and had it wrapped as a gift for me.

As I began removing the wrapping paper, my aunt could see that she had come away with the wrong book. She explained the mistake and quickly offered to return it. Meanwhile, I was having a completely different experience. For partially revealed behind the torn paper was the image of a winged horse with an archer riding bare-back upon it. Pulling off more of the wrapping, I could see that he had released an arrow aimed at something slightly behind him. Following the flight line of the arrow led me to the spine of the book. There, I found a stark mask emblazoned with a tangled array of snakes for hair.

Compelled by the images, I turned back to the cover to see the title of the book. It was simply stated: *Mythology* by Edith Hamilton. Through an accident or an unintentional accuracy, history had become mythology and I was instantly stricken. No way would I exchange this surprising gift; not for a history book, not for any other book, not for any other gift either. Something in me leapt to the image of the flying horse and understood the language of the images immediately. The arrow loosed on the cover struck something deep inside me. In one glance I found something I was looking for without even knowing that I sought for it.

Looking back, I cannot recall anything about that birthday other than the remarkable book and the effect it had upon me. It's as if a part of me still stands with that book in my hands, both standing for something essential in me and standing out from the dusky haze of the past. In reading history I was really looking for something older and deeper and more mysterious. Now, it makes a kind of intuitive sense that a book that contained and sustained the mysteries behind life would arrive in a mysterious way.

My aunt bought it by accident and gave it to me by mistake or else we were both moved and affected by the hidden hand of fate. Seen from the deeper angle of fate, it was the right book that fell into her hand; and, it fell to her in order to find its way to me. Given the way my soul was inclined, the accident was not accidental at all. It was a fortuitous gift as well as a mistake, the kind of accurate error that can occur when fate takes a hand in things and someone's life is about to change.

Many years passed before I could see how elements of fate and destiny were present in that moment that remains present in me. Unnoticed by my family, unseen by my friends and only partly conscious to me, I had been touched by fate and had found a thread of my own destiny. What I am calling fate has to do with the way a person's soul is seeded and shaped from within, like a story trying to open and unfold and become known. What I am calling destiny has to do with the direction and arc of the arrow of one's life. For each soul is secretly aimed at the world and inclined toward a destination that becomes uncovered in crucial moments and at turning points in life.

The elements of fate and destiny are intimate within us; they are closely woven to us, yet hidden from common sight. They are the intimations of the story our soul would have us live, both the limitations that must be faced and the destination that would be found. And, they are often found by what seems like an error or a danger or a surprise.

That night I read almost the entire text. Time stood still and the timeless realm of myth kept opening before me and growing deeper like the night. I pored through the stories and felt the world around me expand as if I had entered a remarkable territory that had been nearby all along. It was as if a void in my life suddenly became filled with stories and mythic images that turned the unnamed emptiness into a newfound abundance. I had received a true gift, something beyond anything I expected, yet something I was bound to encounter.

Years later, when I thanked my aunt for that gift, she could not recall the occasion. Yet that night, in the blind confines of New York City and amidst the confusion of my youth, I found something of my own purpose for being alive. The image of the flying horse, the arrow launched from it, and the word *mythology* all entered me together and altered me entirely. I later learned that symbols and myths work in that way; they grab one's psyche suddenly and fill it with ideas as well as with energy. They defy rational explanation and tend to affect each person differently, trying to draw inner meanings up to the surface of life. I felt invited and pulled into a world that was alive and brimming with ideas and living imagination.

Early in the text I encountered the idea that the early tellers of myth "transformed a world of fear into a world of beauty." I wanted to be part of that transformation. I was standing at the end of childhood and in the uncertainty of my unformed identity. I feared that I would be trapped in life the way most grown people seemed to be. I feared that the same forces that made my family and neighborhood feel confined and narrow would capture and entrap me. I knew that my father felt burdened by the repetition of days and years spent driving a truck through the narrow streets of Manhattan; each day spent loading and unloading freight like Sisyphus pushing rocks up a mountain only to find them waiting at the bottom again on the next day. I knew that my mother dreamed of some other life, one more luxurious and unencumbered with five children. I saw the barely hidden anguish behind the effervescent façade of the neighborhood taverns where all our parents socialized, either soothing their souls or else troubling them further.

Most of the time I liked the intensity of New York City, the palpable sense of life's "rough and tumble" and the feeling that we knew what hard reality was and could handle it as well. Yet, there was something diminished about the common reality and there was a persistent "meanness" in our lives. It wasn't just the dangers and edginess of the "mean streets," but a hollowness that could be felt just under the bare-boned surface of life. This other kind of meanness appeared to me as a "demeaned life" where people gave up on their genuine dreams, replacing them with a chip on their shoulder.

People talked of having to face the facts and deal with the realities of poverty as if that was the prime focus of life and a justification for some kind of collapse of imagination. Meanwhile, many people were mean spirited whether they were impoverished or not. Despite the local bravado, we lived under a mean rule, within a poverty that included the hollowness of actual hunger, but just as often a spiritual emptiness. By the age of thirteen I feared that what I observed in those around me was what I had to become. I loved my family, yet there was a double bind that went with the bonds of that love. Part of me was already looking for a way out of the family fate and the weight of collapsed dreams.

Both sides of my family had Irish ancestry and there were strong internal elements that came with that inheritance. There's an old notion of the "gloom and glam" that attends things Celtic. The sense of Irish gloom plays out in the great tragedies of the land and its people, in the ongoing "troubles" that trouble both politics and religion. For there is a dark side to Irishness, a rough music and heavy gloom that slips shadowlike down the back stairs of time passing from family to family, from parents to child.

The other side of the gloom is the "glam," shorthand for the old word *glamour* that meant not superficial beauty as much as a natural magic and an enchantment of life and love. The glam involves the very "spell of life" that combines the beauty and wonder of nature with the inspiration and art of culture. The glam appears in the grandness of the poets and musicians; it's in the "blarney" that turns everything into a story and in the tendency to seed common speech with philosophical questions. At its best the glam provides an imagination and an instinct to make everything and anything a living proof of the blessed, mythic, calamity and song of life.

My family had its share of both the glam and the gloom as well as a mixed attitude toward our Irish background. My mother could wear her Irishness as a badge; she was Irish and proud of it. She spoke of the Emerald Isle with great longing, yet we knew next to nothing of relatives back in the old country. We heard Irish songs on the juke boxes in the local pubs, but had no idea where we actually hailed from. Like so many ethnic immigrant groups, there was an intense desire to leave the dramas and questions of the past behind and join the American quest for a redemptive future.

There was some embarrassment about being less than American and an awkward memory of tragic displacement from the old country because of the great famine. There was an edgy humility as well as a potential for humiliation about the immigrant background that lingered like an indelible ring pressed into the blue collar of an old shirt. There was an attempt to leave the past behind in order to find a promised future that never arrived. There was a conspicuous lack of education and some shadowy mysteries held back behind the lace curtains intended to put a genteel veil over family things.

"Lace curtain Irish" was a term used for those who sought to rise socially in American life. The lace of the curtains allowed those within to keep watch on the outside while keeping others from seeing all the way in. The lace was also a metaphor, a filmy way to obscure parts of the painful stories of those who sought to cover over inherited poverty and the despair born of the "shanty towns" where many New York Irish dwelt for decades. The lace curtains both hid and revealed elements of our family fate and the ethnic threads that tied us back to history, but deeper yet to mysteries and myths of ancestry.

There was enough inner pride to claim some of the glam of Irishness, but plenty of the remembered gloom that caused folks to join the open-faced hordes of Americans voting to be all future with no past. The recent past of my family involved a crowd of quarry-workers and dock hands, longshoremen, truck drivers, and horse handlers. They were Teamsters and union men, many of whom married waitresses, seamstresses, and secretaries. If you listened carefully and asked the right uncles you'd learn that there were also some gangsters and hooligans that figured into the mix. My father was born and raised in Hell's Kitchen and something of those fires burned behind the lace curtains and smoldered inside the family and inside me.

AN ORPHAN OF THE STREETS

My mother made sure that her children felt the Irish bones within us. She'd talk about her grandmother as if the woman had brought the sod of the old country over with her. In my mother's eyes, the Irish speaking grandmother walked on holy ground. She had raised ten sons here, all the while dreaming of the rolling, green hills of mother Ireland. It was as if my mother clung to the earth of that story more than to the earth beneath her feet. The pieces and parts of that tale were right under my mother's skin and could be provoked from her by an odd word or an Irish song, or by a sudden shift of her inner mood. For she was taken to sudden and extreme moods and the mood of "dear old Ireland" was one I preferred as a child.

I liked the palpable longing in it and the sense that we came from somewhere that was magical and mythical and worth returning to. If anything characterized our family it was the sense of longing for something essential that was missing and wouldn't or couldn't be found in the moment. On one hand, there was an uneasy acceptance of the idea that redemption could be won by gaining an education and earned by dedication to hard work. On the other hand, there was an endless longing for the mystical mother Ireland that also involved my mother's long lament for a mother she never had.

My mother was the first born child with her sister coming along less than a year later. During that second birth something went wrong. The new daughter arrived, but as fate would have it, the young mother did not survive the birth of her second child. My mother never told us any details of what happened and I doubt if she actually knew. She carried the felt sense of the tragic birth, but offered no particulars about it. The same vagueness and mystery attended each of her own pregnancies, as not a word was said until the condition became evident and the time of birth was already near.

She did tell repeatedly how the two tiny sisters not only became motherless, but also felt abandoned by a father who never recovered from the devastation of losing the young wife he loved. Because the presence of the daughters only served to remind him of the wife he lost, their father had great trouble caring for them directly. He gave the little sisters over to their Irish grandmother, the one with the ten growing sons. She loved having the little daughters after producing the long line of sons, but she was already worn to the bone with the work of nourishing and raising so many. She did her best to love them, but her own heart longed more than anything to return to the green hills in the West of Ireland and rest herself near the holy, singing waters and wells of Saint Brigid.

Having lost her own mother early and lacking the love she needed as a child my mother absorbed the longing for mother Ireland as if it were breast milk. Inside herself, she mixed the loss of one mother with the longing for the other. And, in the mood of mother longing, she talked of the old country as if she knew it first hand. She also sought for the missing mother in the Catholic Church. She went to mass each morning and prayed to Mary, the mother of god and keeper of all children. She insisted that we attend mass each Sunday and go to Catholic school. In trying to plug the hole she felt within herself, she took the church and all its doctrines and dogmas as whole cloth, and she expected me and my sisters and brothers to do the same.

Part of what I call my fate involved being born into the womb of my mother's loss of her mother. I was partially mothered by a "mother-loss" and nurtured on longings that wouldn't be fulfilled. I call it fate because I had no control over it and because I felt constricted by it. It was as if each new thing had to first be passed through the unsteady womb of the family; it had to be doused in the waters of loss and then had to be approved by the mother church.

As a boy, I often heard my mother tell how she and her sister feared that they would be smothered by the heavy coats that their uncles would toss in a pile each evening or else trampled upon in the commotion of the household of ten growing sons. I could picture my mother and aunt terrified, like children in a fairy tale huddling close in a dark house of giants. As I grew older I realized that although the story of the orphan sisters was in the past, the effects of it were quite present. My mother, who could be a force of nature and could erupt with volcanic intensity, was also afraid of many things and at times childlike in her fears. I too felt smothered by something from the past, as if there was no way to escape the shades and glooms, the lost lands and missing mothers and disappearing fathers.

Each family has its own inheritance of fateful themes and inner woven stories that are passed down along with the DNA of the cells and shared body shapes. Each family has a womb of fate and a mixture of glam and gloom through which each child born must pass. For the past is never quite over; it clings to us and secretly asks us to solve and resolve the essential questions of life as well as the particular issues that pull our families together when they aren't driving us all apart.

My mom never recovered from her lack of direct mothering and fathering. At times she referred to herself as a "street orphan," describing how she was left alone and on her own as a child. She roamed the streets of New York learning to look out for herself. One side of that orphan feeling was loss and abandonment, while the other side was tough, independent, and resourceful, unless it was being resentful and punishing. She married my father despite and because her own father threatened to disown her for good for choosing an uneducated, rough-neck from Hell's Kitchen.

My father was himself the youngest of ten and had left school during the third grade. He was at school long enough to learn to read and write, but had to go to work in order to help his mother out. There were hungry mouths to feed and his father was never known to have taken a job. Throughout his life my dad continued to perfect the cursive script he learned in school. He would pen the address on bills as if he were continuing school lessons or carefully signing important documents. He had an elegant and careful hand with a pen, even if his hands were most often grasping freight or imitating his favorite boxer.

Inside, he longed to be a writer and carried western novels by Zane Gray in his freight truck. He had a photo of himself wearing a suit and holding a pen to paper while sitting at a copy desk at the New York Times. Someone had seen some latent quality in him and offered him an entry level job at the great newspaper. You could see his inner smile of delight in the photo, as clearly as the part in his slicked back hair. And, if you didn't know about the Second World War that killed the career before it began or the gloomy periods of joblessness that followed after, you'd think he was a bright young writer settled at his destined vocation.

My siblings and I were born into the archetypal and fateful arrangement of missing mothers, distant fathers, street orphans, and lost lands all waiting for some divine intervention or magical release. And, it wasn't just my father and mother caught in the gloom of lost dreams. The truth was that an inner lament haunted most people around us who only partially ever settled for the working class ethic and the vapid promise of material success that was being marketed so widely in the post-war world. A longing for heaven and an affinity for hell seemed to grow behind the curtains and set the stage for the children of the next generation.

MY LOT IN LIFE

I was born after my father was drafted and departed for the Second World War, leaving my mother and her sister in a fourth floor, walk-up apartment. They lived on food stamps and milk rations while trying to care for three young children. I was born between my two sisters who in many ways seemed to be reflected images of my mother and her sister. My brothers were born later, so for a time I was the only boy in a flat full of women and girls.

It was also my "lot in life" to fall into a particular shadow of disaffection as I was the second child born. As my aunt later told me, my impending birth triggered an array of fears and anxieties in my mother. She feared that she would miscarry, but dreaded more that she would die herself while giving birth to me as her mother had failed to survive giving birth for a second time. She would tell whoever might listen how I was her most difficult pregnancy and the cause of trials and great uncertainty from conception to birth. She would describe her long laboring through a winter night troubled with icy winds and driven snow and shaken with bolts of lightning. She thought that night would never end and that the pains of labor would never stop.

Finally, just at dawn or just after, depending on the version she was telling, I was born and she could rest. She would tell the tale with me in the room, all the while acting as if I weren't there at all. Listening to her caused me to experience a strange sense of power as well as a feeling of being unwanted. My mother carried her infantile fears of death and disaster as certainly as she carried each child god chose to give to her.

As my aunt told the tale, my mother seemed afraid of her new child so that when I cried she would hesitate to respond. Of course, that caused me to cry all the louder and that only pushed her further away. Apparently, I continued to be a fearful reminder of her early life loss, leaving me with little choice but to feel somehow at fault and somewhat rejected for a mysterious error. Later on, my Catholic education would seal the deal on that feeling with the notion that I was also somehow responsible for an "original sin."

Reflecting upon the family tales makes clear why my aunt took a kind interest in me and how she later became a crucial agent of fate and destiny on my birthday. The truth was that I had rarely received what I asked for on birthdays and holidays. As a small child I often asked for too much, being as yet unaware of how poverty could make gifts a secondary consideration. When there are too many mouths to feed you eventually learn not to ask for much; especially, you learn not to ask for what you really want. The simple act of asking brings up too many family shadows; it stirs too many ghosts and rubs against old and pressing pains.

Once it became clear that the desired gift would not appear anyway, naming the desire only served to make the shades of disappointment in the house more palpable. Not asking for anything seemed to reduce the depths of disappointment. Of course, the problem with that solution comes when failing to ask for what is wanted leads to not knowing what is most desired.

My aunt understood the family situation and tried to fill in the gaps for me and for my siblings. Out of her sympathy she knew that I felt misunderstood and overlooked and I was grateful for her kindness and care. But, with the gift of the mythology book something different had happened; some kind of mystery had developed. I had received something that I truly wanted without knowing what it was beforehand. I had casually requested one thing and had received another that was better than anything I could have asked for. The wrong-right book fell into my hands just when I was becoming able to imagine a life of my own.

The fact that the book of myths arrived mysteriously suggested a separate element of fate, a thread that did not originate within my family. It was as if I was secretly tied to something beyond the confines of history and family fate. I couldn't dismiss the strange occurrence as a mere accident or a fluke, for the myths themselves informed me that to scorn fate was an unwise thing to do. Remember old Oedipus? Before his birth an oracle announced that the child about to be born would one day slay his father. In order to avoid that terrible fate, the fearful father ordered the death of his newborn son.

Yet, as fate would have it, the servant given the task of killing the child could not abandon it to death. After being given to another family to be raised, a second oracle announced that Oedipus would both slay his father and sleep with his mother. Not knowing that the adoptive parents were not his natural mother and father, the worried son quickly left their home to avoid fulfilling the dark fate. Of course, in running from the parents who raised him, he has a fateful and fatal run-in with his actual father and falls into bed with his birth mother. Thinking that he will run away from the issues of fate, he runs right into them. Not understanding his true origins, he succumbs to the darkest aspects of his fate.

Oedipus fulfills the oracle blindly, slaying his father unknowingly and sleeping with his mother unwittingly. Afterward, he becomes literally blind and only then begins to see. We are each blind to our fate until we encounter it on the narrow roads where one thing conspires with another and we become unable to escape what was within us all along. We can not run from our fate any more than we can run from our family. Trying to run from the fate woven within us only leads us back to it. Fate involves aspects of life that aren't freely chosen and plot lines that were well underway before each child came upon the scene.

Moments of fate give shape to our lives and can initiate us into knowing more consciously who we are and how we are styled from within and woven into this world. Such occasions separate us from our daily entanglements; they distinguish us from others and mark us in indelible ways. In the crucible of life we can choose to learn about the fate within us or else live our fate unwittingly, encounter it blindly and live it out unconsciously.

Many myths begin with an oracle as if trying to remind us all that we arrive with an inner story that intends to be discovered and become uncovered. Fate is a kind of inner oracle that cannot be completely denied and that can intensify and harden the longer it is avoided. Fate involves the inevitable and indelible threads of family heritage as well as the unique and oracular inner voice of our own lives. Only in facing fate can the blindness within us be penetrated and the intended story and potential destiny be found and become known and be released.

THE SISTERS OF FATE

The book of mythology caused me to see the world in a new way. I read the tales voraciously and could see them vividly in my mind's eye. It was as if I entered the stories as they entered me. I wandered amidst them quickly forgetting all else. The felt sense of an array of gods and goddesses secretly populating the earth as well as the heavens stirred a feverous imagination in me. Rather than the church idea of a single god in heaven I could imagine the divine everywhere. There might be one god above it all, but the sense of immortals nearby and semi-divine figures like tree sprites and river nymphs made the world more alive and more meaningful for me.

Through the lens of stories and the eye of myth, I found myself in a world of meaning and true imagination. For me, the mythic stories offered more truth than anything else I had heard or read. It wasn't that all my troubles went away or that I knew exactly what to do with the rest of my life; far from it. It would be years before I could grasp what was grasping me that night. Yet, for the first time I felt, not just grounded in the world, but centered in myself. I did not understand it, could not have described it, and did not express what I felt. But, the occasion marked me indelibly and remains a sign post that stands out brightly when I look back over the path my life has taken.

Amongst the array of surprising figures described in the text were several sets of divine sisters. The first that struck me were called the Graiae. They were three gray cast sisters who had but one eye between them. In order to see anything they had to pass the single eye from one to the other so that as one began to see, the other two went blind. Somehow that made sense to me; it seemed to depict the amount of blindness in so many situations and the way that my family and teachers insisted upon a single view of the world.

The shaded sisters were said to dwell on the "farther bank of the ocean." There was no explanation of what the farther bank might be, but on the way there you might encounter another set of sisters called the Sirens. They lived on a rocky island in the open sea amidst some great longing that made them sing endlessly. The Sirens had beautiful and enchanting voices; but the Sirens' song most often lured people to their death upon the rocks of their lonely island. The Sirens were only known for their song with no visual descriptions given. They couldn't be described in any detail because no one who had seen them had returned to tell the tale.

As I imagined this wild geography of the unseeing and the unseen, the three Sisters of Fate were introduced as "very important but assigned to no abode whether in heaven or on earth." Their importance didn't involve where they resided unless you considered that they lived within people. Each sister was said to hold a part or a portion of a person's life and each contributed to the allotment of good and bad things that each soul received at birth. According to this old and mythic view, each one born is in the hands of fate before ever being held in human arms. Our fate in life may include aspects of our family, but it also includes unique qualities that are present before we are born into the world of time and place.

The sisters of fate were named and briefly described as if the long procession of mythic tales could not ensue without their presence. Clotho was the name of "the spinner" who first spun the invisible thread that ran through each person's life. Lachesis was the "disposer of lots" who gave each person born their positive and negative qualities and assigned to each a destiny. And Atropos, "who could not be turned," carried the "abhorred shears" that cut one's life-thread when the end of life's cord had been reached.

The Fates were formidable and essential and not to be discounted or scorned. They were a "mysterious power, stronger even than the gods." To refuse one's fate could bring forth Nemesis, a fierce, dark spirit who could cancel all good fortune and bring in its place dire retribution. The fates were the feminine side of the mystery of life as they shaped the womb that gave birth to the inner story as well as the specific inclinations of each one born.

I felt compelled by this trio of sisters so close as to hold parts of one's life, so strong that they could direct the gods. For me they represented an alternative mystery to the doctrines of the church and provided a sense of hidden potentials that were separate from familial and familiar conditions. If there were threads of an individual fate running through each life, then there could also be a destiny beyond one's inherited conditions. If there were ways of discerning an inner threaded story then life was not simply determined by one's birth or the family faith or local beliefs. For me, the images of fate and destiny offered a way out of predetermined ideas of the value and purpose of individual life.

HELL ON EARTH

From a young age I had been frequently warned that I could wind up burning in hell for my sins. But, in Greek mythology hell was called Hades, a mysterious territory that was always nearby. It was not just a place where you might wind up at the end of your life, but a place that you might fall into at any moment. I had felt that kind of sudden slip or eerie fall into a dark place. I felt it as moods that I suddenly fell into, not wanting to go out of the house and not knowing exactly why. Living in a big city I had seen people be attacked and beaten for being in the wrong place at the wrong time. I had seen many others simply living on the streets with no other place to be as if the pitfalls in life could easily become a living hell or a deep valley in Hades from which they could not escape.

One day I saw a man running through the streets on fire. I was on my way to school and suddenly saw a man engulfed in flames burst out and screaming into the street. He worked in a little car garage near the store at the end of our block. He must have lit a cigarette while standing too close to a gas can and it exploded. By the time people caught up to him and knocked him down, he was charred beyond recognition. I never saw him again, but I passed that garage every day. When I saw the men working in there covered in grease and oil and smoking away, I thought of Hades, how close it could be, how its fires could suddenly engulf a life. I didn't want to die in such a fateful accident and I didn't want to live in fear of winding up in eternal flames.

A few blocks away there was a junk yard with rusted old cars and shadows that didn't seem to move. It was guarded by a fierce dog on a heavy chain. It was clear that the dog was intentionally underfed and only barely held back by the links of the chain. You couldn't go near the place without it going wild with barking and snarling. Some of my friends would stand just at the edge where the chain held the dog back and taunt it as it drooled and snapped at them. I thought of Cerberus, the three-headed hound of Hades that could trap a person in the underworld and kept my distance.

For me, there was an increasing overlap between the common world and the realms of myth that could give meaning to each event and to each encounter in life. I could understand that there was a darker side to everything and that the Fates and Sirens could represent the shadows and uncanny elements that might erupt into the daily world at any moment. When, one night it turned out that the dog had slipped its chain, I was way ahead of everyone else when the race to outrun the hound of hell began.

I became fascinated by the description of the god Janus who stood at the beginning of each year and at the start of every enterprise. I was born in January and it was a birthday in that dark month that brought the book of fate to me. Statues of Janus had two faces with one being youthful and the other old. That's how I felt when sitting with the myths. I felt young like a child whose eyes were opening wider than ever before; yet also older somehow and more able to see behind the scenes and into the shadings and shadows of life. In a sense, I was slipping behind temple doors, peeking into ancient scenes and seeing levels of the world that had timeless meanings and a wild intelligence even amidst the modern dedication to facts and figures.

The temple of Janus had two doors, one facing East and the other West, for Janus ever looked both ways. One door looked back to the beginning where each day rose while the other opened to the dusk where each day ended. He was called the "god of good beginnings;" for what had a good beginning would likely come to a good end. I liked being associated with the god of beginnings and began to understand why New Year's Eve had to be celebrated even if people had forgotten the mythic origins of how life continually renews from a light hidden within the darkest time of the year. It seemed that destiny also was a light hidden in the darker threads and twisting ways of fate.

AN INNER FLAME

It was the onset of my thirteenth year and I felt I was at the beginning of something meaningful and fortuitous. Although I had no way to explain or share what was happening inside me, I knew that something had shifted and altered my way of seeing the world around me. I felt invited to the celebration of life and introduced to the unseen world from which life continues to emerge. When I later learned that the candles on birthday cakes derived from an ancient practice, I thought back to the book that fell into my hands and lit a flame inside me.

Birthday celebrations began as a way of recognizing the spirit that comes to life with each soul born. Originally, there was but a single candle representing individual life no matter what the age of the celebrant might be. The single flame symbolized the inner spirit and natural, shining genius that enters the world at the birth of each child. The flame of inner intelligence burns at the center of the soul and would light a path through this uncertain world. The single candle was lit to remind everyone of the invisible fire at the core of each life and birthday gifts were not given to the person, but to the spirit born within them.

In this old sense, a birthday serves as a reminder that each person is already gifted; each having an inner genius and some god-given gifts to bring to life. One's birthday involved a return to the mystery of oneself and a reminder of the inner flame of one's life. The point wasn't simply to make a wish, but also to consider what the candle of each life burns for. If the candle was blown out it was in order that the rising smoke could carry prayers for the spirit of the celebrant to the heavens above.

I felt that I had received a gift secretly intended for something that had been born with me and was just beginning to awaken. At some level, I could feel that this was not just another birthday, but also another birth. For me, the realm of stories and mythic imagination lit up the world around me and became as compelling as anything in the "real world." The stories spoke to me at the edge of life where childhood retreats and the turmoil of youth arrives along with stirring dreams, sudden drives, and burning questions. It quickened something in me that was there to begin with, just waiting to awaken. Unexpectedly, I had found a way out of the purely local story and a pathway into the ongoing drama and great mystery of the world.

I was repeatedly struck with wonder and transported beyond anything I had seen or heard before. I may as well have taken off on a flying horse myself, for I went back in time. I was carried back before time as it said in the book, back where "imagination was vividly alive and not checked by reason." The ancient stories arose from someplace before the march of history and for me they opened the doors of mystery. What I experienced wasn't an escape *from* reality; more of a case of finding what reality was to be for me.

I found myself wide awake and in awe of the world. Not the world reported in newspapers or outlined in textbooks, nor the world defined by the church. I felt fully connected to life for the first time in my life. I felt able to see in a new way and invited to learn what was behind the confusing foreground of life. For me, this was "it," a way of seeing and thinking that made immediate, intuitive sense of the chaos and confusion and vacancy of the world around me.

ANOTHER EDUCATION

It wasn't simply that I received the right birthday gift, but also that a kind of gift already existing within me became more present and palpable, even if it was only apparent to me. Like any wondrous gift it was complete as it was given. I didn't have to qualify to receive it because it was already tuned to something trying to awaken in me. I didn't have to wait until I was older to enter; I didn't have to believe in the tales or pass a test to gain access. Believing wasn't the point, for I could imagine it all. That was the point; a radical awakening of an imagination for life that somehow was waiting to be discovered.

The discovery was triggered by the book of myths, but the imagination for it was already in me. The gift within the gift involved the opening of an inner eye that changed how I looked at life. That was the point, the opening up of an entire way of seeing and being present in the world. For a time, I felt that the world was an open book trying to reveal itself to me, to anyone, to everyone.

By the hand of fate, I had become a disciple of myth, a servant of stories, and strangely a devotee of the notion that the soul is threaded through with a plotline from the beginning that aims at a destiny that might be possible to find before the end. I felt truly pulled into the story of life and felt that I had a meaningful role to play in it. Something in me knew how to be inside stories and how to feel them in a deeply internal way. It would take me years to understand it, but I had been touched by something essential and artful. Events may have gone differently if someone had confirmed what I was experiencing. Yet again, I have always tended to go my own way and rarely have taken direction from others.

If someone had suggested I look into mythology, I would have resisted. Having the myths appear accidentally seemed to be a right thing; it seemed similar to the surprises and sudden appearances that were essential to the mythic tales themselves. Looking back upon it, I can see that the die had been cast and the future path indicated even though decades would pass before I found a way to tell stories and live with them more consciously.

Meanwhile, the tales became alive for me, were even illuminated before me. The book of myths seemed to flip a switch that gave me an open-ended interior life. Whatever might be happening in the outside world, I could enter the stories and a light would go on. When I would read a story again different aspects of it would come to life as if the stories were responding to changes occurring in my life. Not only did they "speak to me," they seemed to offer guidance and alternative ways to view all aspects of my life. In the midst of the tales of gods and goddesses, in the heroic adventures of love and danger, I was no longer too young or too small or too poor to be fully in life.

Secretly, yet potently, I felt related to, even descended from mythic heroes. In the "wine dark seas" of imagination I followed the adventures of wily Ulysses who escaped so many dangers and the courageous Theseus who survived the labyrinth. I followed into the underworld where Orpheus searched for his beloved Eurydice and saw the strange fate of Psyche whose beauty caused great envy and left her exiled in darkness. Like Theseus following a thread through the maze, I had to learn to find my own way through each tale. I had to surrender and trust my own imagination and find my own way of understanding the world.

Like so many young people I experienced no outer confirmation or even recognition of what had been ignited within me. When I tried to offer a mythic image or tell part of a story, people didn't get it. Yet, something inside me took a deeper root and began to grow, however slowly. There was an inward branching that continued whenever I returned to the genuine reflection and musing that the stories caused me to experience. I felt more rooted in the world and able to aspire to a life beyond the life I had been given. I imagined that there were adventures that I could undertake and that could take me to places of meaning and beauty.

The notion that the soul was shaped from within and possibly aimed from the beginning cracked something open in me. I didn't know it then, but know it better now, that part of each person's birthright involves at least one revelation of the inner pattern of their life, at least one intuition of the innate gifts and natural orientation of their soul. The human soul is shaped in such a way that it carries in seed form something meaningful and valuable that cannot remain completely hidden. The revelation may be brief and may make no sense to other people. The inner pattern may conflict with the expectations of one's family and may be disturbing to the one having to carry it. Yet, the pattern would be known and if possible in any way, would have us follow it.

THE WELL OF TIME, THE ROOTS OF ETERNITY

After a long survey of the myths and gods of the Greeks, the book offered a short section on Norse mythology in which it returned to the theme of the Sisters of Fate. With no real explanation, the scene shifted from the orderly pantheon of ancient Greece to a wild creation story from northern Europe. The Norse stories began with a vivid cosmology in which the world was divided between a realm of fire and another of ice. When the extremes of fire and ice became separated the middle ground of the earth appeared along with the first humans. The original ancestors were not shaped from mud and bone but were created directly from trees with the first man coming from an ash and the first woman from an elm.

The entire cosmos also formed around a tree, a wondrous, eternal tree that supported the entire universe and everything in it. The world tree connected the under world, the middle earth and the heavens above. It served as a mystical axis that kept things in place and it provided nourishment for the gods, humans, and animals alike. This mythical and mystical tree connected all living things and represented all phases of existence from birth to death and renewal.

At the roots of the cosmic tree there was a well of white water, called Urda's Well or Urth's Well, although we might call it Earth's Well. Three sisters dwelt at the well at the center of the earth and protected the living waters within it. Each day they poured the life renewing waters from the depths of the well onto the roots of the great Tree of Life. The sisters were named Urda, Verdandi, and Skuld; names said to mean past, present, and future. They were personifications of the flow of time that ever comes from the ancient well of eternity as the past pours continually into the present and the future arises from the open moment before us.

Besides keeping the well of ancient wisdom and sustaining the flow of time, the Norns, as they were called when taken altogether, also gave each soul about to be born its individual shape and style. They carved each soul from the roots of the living tree that was also called the Stem of Stories. Each soul was uniquely carved and shaped and secretly rooted in stories connected to the Tree of Life. All living souls were related to each other by virtue of being rooted in the same tree; it was the "family tree" at one level, but also the ever branching tree that bears the seeds and roots of each individual's share of fate and destiny.

The story set within the soul of each person derives from the stem of all stories so that each carries a part of the eternal drama that is continually regenerated from the inexhaustible springs of the water of life. Each individual is connected to the human family that enacts the great drama of creation over and over again. And, each has its portion of fate to be learned and its thread of destiny to be found.

What the ancients called fate is there at the beginning and there at the end and it appears in the midst of the defining events in each person's life as well. Fate holds us in life as much as it ties us to death. Fate which seems to speak deterministically of the end of life also refers to the essential moments of renewal each life must find if it would continue. Fate involves the accidents that are not accidental, the mistakes that turn out to be fortuitous, and the curious twists that turn our lives around or upside down or back to where we started from.

Our fate involves us in the great mysteries of being and sets us on the stage of life with a meaningful part to play, a role in life that can only be learned by living it out. For fate is more a story line than a completed script, more a pattern woven into the soul than a fixation of the mind, more a drama seeking to unfold from the center of our lives. Fate is a thread that, much like life, seeks the unfolding of itself. Fate involves the core pattern and living story woven and set within us from before birth.

For life is an eternal story, a mythic drama that begins again each time a soul enters the world. In mythic terms, the whole story begins again as each one born is doused with the waters of life and touched by the hand of fate before being held in human arms. Without a "sense of fate" we lose touch with the great dramas of life. We live outside the compelling myths and soulful literatures where fateful twists and fatal flaws bring the human heart and soul to the very center of life's incredible story. Without a felt sense of how we are fated to be, we can't find or sort or draw upon the inner threads of our individual destinies.

Another name for the world tree was the Tree Book of Fate; it was a tree, but also a living book. The Sisters of Fate appeared at the end of the book of myths just as they had at the beginning. Now, they were described as being at the center of everything and at the roots of the cosmos. The Sisters of Fate represented the entire flow of time and the constant renewal of the universe. They had a hand in the beginning of each life and were present in the midst of each life change. And, they were also at the root of existence where they protected the living flow and handled the renewing waters of life.

The book of myths concluded with some wise proverbs from the ancient Norse poems or "eddas." The last saying stuck with me as it seemed to tie together what the mind might know and what the heart might love. It stated that "the mind only knows what lies near the heart." It seemed to me that the threads of fate and destiny might be part of what lies closest to the heart and might provide the very heart strings of one's life as well as the inner weaving that holds together our deepest thoughts and our greatest loves. What lies inside the heart of one's heart might be the inner text and living language, the story already set and woven within, only waiting to be stirred and awakened and followed all the way to the end.

CHAPTER 2

KNOW THYSELF

"Coming of age" involves coming upon what is ageless in a person. Not just the predictable hormone changes and awkward experiments of youth, but the unique twists and turns through which the individual soul encounters the universal themes of life and death. People are fascinated with youth partially because during youth each of us becomes exposed to and touched by the eternal. The touch of something eternal breaking through the ordinary is what makes youth both beautiful and vulnerable; both inspiring and dangerous, both purposeful at times and also completely lost. More than a specific age period, youth is an internal, eternal condition. The gift of youth involves its proximity to eternal things and its vulnerability to its own inherent gifts.

In coming of age a person comes in touch with that which is universal and deeply human, yet finds it in their unique way; in the way that their soul requires. During youth a blossoming and budding forth tries to happen from inside out as each young person encounters what is seeded in them and gifted in their soul. The inner garden of the soul sends forth shoots of imagination intended to take root in the world and become an anchor for the soul throughout life. The beauty of youth exists in those blossoming moments when the inner gifts become revealed and they become able to bring more life to life.

After a sudden blossoming however, the land may become silent; the seed of the soul may become obscured and be pushed aside by the demands and confusions of the world around. Then, the hidden beauty and seeded story must wait for another season to return to awareness and awaken again. For what is native and indigenous to one's soul will keep trying to manifest itself throughout one's life.

A great tragedy occurs in the modern world where mass cultures overwhelm the importance of the individual soul and the notion of a life lived in accord with it. The growing tendency to treat people as statistical segments and voting blocks, as interest groups and age categories serves to diminish the psychic fact that each is also a unique individual. In the blind rush to the future some things that were of primary importance to our ancestors have been left behind. In the effort to leave the past far behind and rise above the seemingly restricting notions of fate, many people have lost the sense of a particular purpose and potential destiny seeded within them to begin with.

Besides the job of instructing and socializing its youth, a genuine culture has a responsibility to assist each young person to find and develop the unique qualities already existing within themselves. No notion of collective freedom and no amount of good intentions can substitute for the felt sense that one's life has inner meaning, that one's soul is uniquely shaped, and that the inner spirit of one's life is aimed at something beyond mere adaptation and survival.

A society that fails to water the life-seeds of its members may be capable of instructing its citizens, but will be incapable of truly educating its children or wholly embracing its youth. Besides the development of governing laws and socializing norms, a culture forms to cultivate the unique qualities in each child. When it comes to issues of the human soul there is no normal condition; rather, each soul carries its own norms and seeks to manifest its own inherent style. Despite the growing pressure to blend with the collective will and submit to the leveling required by mass cultures, a community can only develop through the essential character and natural potentials of its individual members.

A community best serves itself when it truly serves the awakening of the unique story trying to come to life through each person born. Freedom of speech has a much greater value when those who speak have learned something of the language already written in their souls. The point of freedom isn't found in the simple permission to speak; rather it develops where the soul has something meaningful to say and finds ways to express itself fully. In the long run, the freedom that everyone seeks and needs most is the freedom to become who they already are at their core. For life is supposed to be a revelatory drama and it is the uniqueness of the individual soul that can never be predicted, that cannot be completely repressed or be fully accounted for.

What makes us each unique and therefore genuinely human is more vital than any dogma or doctrine and more creative than any ideology or system of belief. For the ideas seeded in our souls from the beginning confound all the ideologies and trump all the abstract systems. It is the spark of spirit within the individual soul that makes religion possible at all and that makes culture inevitable. It is the inner uniqueness that makes life meaningful at each stage, that makes love a possibility at any moment, and that makes each moment susceptible and vulnerable to the eternal.

We are the individual carriers of fate's unending plotlines and we enter the stage of life inclined to play specific roles and bring to life certain dramas. The comedies and tragedies of the endless drama of life are continually recast through us with the auditions occurring before birth. People take up the archetypal roles of sinner and saint, of tyrant and victim, of lover and outcast; yet each brings a unique twist and characteristic style to the plot. For that too is fate, the twist that makes each soul specific, unusual in some way, and ultimately unique.

What tries to awaken and become recognized during youth is the seed of the story sewn in the linings of the soul before birth. The uniqueness within the soul is the essence of the seed waiting to be cracked open by the pressure of growth and the pains of life. The specific struggles and surprises of youth are the twists of fate through which the seeded story seeks to unfold and reveal itself. For fate is less a fixed tale or predetermined text and more a living story-line with compelling twists and surprising turns, a tragic-comic libretto that requires some improvisation and allows some continuing innovation.

What becomes revealed at the end of a life fully lived is the story that was trying surface all along. Yet, like any compelling drama, specific limitations are needed to shape the plot and give it tension and intrigue. The dynamic tension for each living script grows from the limits of fate and the longings for destiny carefully set within each soul. Fate is the shell of the inner seed of one's life that must be cracked open in order to reveal the destiny hidden within it.

Just as the natural seed must first settle in some ground in order to grow, each child nestles within a certain family and social arrangement. When childhood comes to an end, life becomes more open-ended and a further identity is required as the inner seed tries to break through the earth of its origins in order to rise and stand on its own. Strangely, as we begin to hunt for our fate in life, we are also being pursued by it.

TELL A STORY OR DIE

The defining events of our lives always involve some sense of the mysterious and weird touch of fate. Often, such fateful events have the feeling of life or death; as if the revelation of who we are at the level of our soul is itself a "matter of life and death." While many believe that young people take great risks because they feel immortal, youth is also the time when we encounter our own mortality. Each person is a mortal body wrapped around a divinely gifted soul and both aspects must become revealed to some degree.

The same year that I received the book of myths, I began a practice of taking long walks through the city. Like many young people, then and now, I felt uninvited by and somewhat alienated from the culture I was trying to grow up within. I felt on the edge of some event that would change everything in the outside world the way the book of myths had opened the interior of my life. I was just starting high school and despite being the smallest boy in my class, I felt that something meaningful was about to happen to me. Having read many stories of great adventures, I expected that the real quest of my life would start at any moment.

I would walk the streets of New York City imagining that the mythic tales were still alive and that the young hero Jason would soon form the crew of the Argonauts again and begin the search for the missing Golden Fleece. I prowled through the patchwork of ethnic neighborhoods as if hunting for a doorway or threshold that would open to the greater world my soul imagined. Meanwhile, the streets themselves were becoming more dangerous. At that time there were gangs sprouting up in poor and working class neighborhoods all over the city.

Amidst the increasing density of population, a gang would form every few blocks. Most were just local youth trying to feel that they belonged somewhere and had some "turf" to call home. There was a kind of parallel to the story of Jason and the Argonauts in the sense that he formed a crew and undertook a dangerous adventure in order to reclaim his rightful realm. Strangely, in the street language of the times, newly formed local gangs were called "crews."

The crews were loosely organized and new sets and groups were always being formed. I decided to join a crew that hung out on a nearby corner and began to emulate the behavior of the older guys. I didn't fully resonate with the random and sometimes brutal gang fighting, but I was intrigued with the bravado and rebelliousness of being a "hood." I wanted to belong somewhere, wanted to be "cool" like the older guys and I liked the drama of the streets. At times there were glimmers of genuine bravery and even a little nobility. In some vague way I imagined that the recklessness and desire for danger might somehow turn into a genuine quest.

I had barely become a member of the corner crew when we managed to get cornered ourselves and it looked as if there was no way out. We had gone off to see a movie that was playing in a nearby neighborhood. After the film, we left the theater and began to walk back to our corner just as it was getting dark. We were walking along, talking about the movie; when we found ourselves surrounded by a gang of older guys. They had seen us inside the theater and wanted to send a message that the place was on their turf and we weren't welcome.

There were twice as many of them and they were bigger than us. They had weapons and looked ready to use them. There was no visible way out and no where to turn. I was figuring out how best to protect myself and preparing to take a beating, when one of the older guys from our corner walked up. He stepped right into the middle of the circle and stood with us. He wasn't very tall, but he was known as a fierce fighter and he had a certain way of walking and talking.

Without any preamble, he began to threaten them. It wasn't clear to me if he intended to fight them all or was warning them of retaliation if they attacked us. It all happened quickly. Despite all the odds being in their favor, they hesitated for a moment and he pushed right through them. Some energy in him just backed them down; you couldn't exactly see it, but you could distinctly feel it. He became bigger somehow and they couldn't seem to find their strength in the face of his. It was as if his spirit overwhelmed them and the fight was settled on another level.

Then, he pivoted on his heel and said: "Let's go!" We turned and followed him, too scared and mesmerized to do anything else. As we headed toward the safety of our neighborhood, our protector said: "Keep walking straight; don't look back, and we might live through this." That's when I realized that he was scared just like we were. The difference was that he knew something; he felt something and trusted the feeling. It wasn't just bravado; he wasn't simply bluffing. He would have fought with us, surprisingly fought for us. But, something else had entered the situation, something had come over him; and whatever had altered him had changed the entire situation and saved us from certain harm.

The truth was that I didn't even like that guy. None of us did. He never spoke to us; barely even acknowledged us. Yet, he suddenly risked being seriously injured for us and seemed heroic in doing it. For a moment, he seemed like one of the Argonauts willing to risk himself for the crew and for something beyond us all that remained unnamed. He never said another word about what had happened, didn't explain any of it; didn't even tell us why he was at that theater. The only thing different after that incident was that when we saw him down at the corner, he would nod to us as if we all understood something that would not be spoken of.

Maybe it was something that could not be spoken of; maybe we didn't have the language for it. It seemed to me that often there were revelations at hand, but the language for describing them had become lost and was just out of reach. In the absence of that clarifying or defining something, everyone just pretended that the local turf and the local beefs were the real issue.

For me, the quest for the Golden Fleece was more compelling. Jason, the hero, was a kind of orphan. He would have been the heir to a small kingdom, but an usurper had taken the throne just before he was born. As a future claimant to the throne he was a threat to the usurper and his life was in danger even as he took his first breath. So, his mother gathered all the women around the infant and had them raise the cry of grief so that everyone would believe that the child had been stillborn. Afterward, she sent him into hiding, later to be raised and educated by Chiron, the wise leader of the Centaurs.

Meanwhile, the Golden Fleece had been stolen from the realm and taken to a distant place. The mythical fleece was the symbol of the spirit of the ancestral land and the communal essence of the realm. Without the defining symbol and centering image, the people felt diminished and disoriented. When Jason became a youth and learned the story of his origins, he returned to reclaim the heritage of his family. The false king agreed to relinquish the throne on one condition—if the youth could find the Golden Fleece and return it to its rightful place, he would become the new ruler.

Of course, the king knew full well the great dangers that would be encountered on such an expedition and he never expected Jason to survive the adventure. Jason readily agreed to the deal; no questions asked. In fact, he seemed to prefer the quest itself to the throne.

Word went out that a crew was needed for a great quest and soon all kinds of characters appeared. Hercules with his great strength came right away, but also Orpheus with his divine gift for music. Castor and Pollux, the twin brothers of the great beauty Helen came, as well as two other brothers said to be descendents of the North Wind. Having gathered the crew and christened their ship, the "Argo," they all set sail for a distant land where the fleece was said to hang on a certain oak tree in an ancient grove that was guarded by an unblinking dragon.

I liked the idea that the orphan child was really of noble birth and secretly the heir to an ancient realm. If you met him, you wouldn't know the real story; yet the truth of it was there. I liked the sense that there was a missing inheritance and hidden nobility that could be sought for and be reclaimed. I identified with Jason and felt myself to be an outcast looking for a chance to correct the past and open the future wide. I loved the idea that there was something golden that was missing and needing to be returned to its rightful place. And, there was some subtle connection to the local gang and the sense of a crew of weird and unpredictable characters.

Meanwhile, the place where most people found their stories was the neighborhood movie theater. Our theater was just a few blocks from our corner, right under the elevated train that rumbled through on its way to the center of the city. The place seemed to fall right between our turf and the gang from the next neighborhood over. They had a reputation for being vicious; but they mostly left us alone because we were younger and seemed puny to them. For out part, we were both intrigued with them and afraid of them. We kept our distance and only repeated stories we heard about how dangerous they were.

The exception to this practice was a friend who had a fierce temper that could go off on anyone. On some occasion, he had encountered them and cursed and raged at them over some perceived threat or insult. When they came after him he escaped; but they were not finished with the incident, as I found out when they came after me to get at him.

We were in the theater for a Saturday matinee; that's when they usually showed the new movies that were aimed at teenagers. The place was packed with boys and girls and only a few ushers trying unsuccessfully to keep things in order. I had to go to the bathroom and began walking up the aisle while the film flickered against the dark innards of the theater. I noticed that two guys stepped right in front of me when I stood up, but didn't realize that I was surrounded until I reached the popcorn stand at the back of the theater. By then, there were seven of them, all older and taller than me.

They motioned me over to the stairs that went up behind the projection room to the men's bathroom. I was scared, but didn't see a way out; so I went along with them. Once inside the door I was thrown to the ground near the urinals. Looking up, I recognized some members of the crew from the next neighborhood. They had knives and wrenches in their hands as they glared down at me. The look in their eyes terrified me as they ranted about how my friend had insulted them and how I was going to pay for it.

I felt I might die right there, next to the dripping urinal while a film reeled on in the theater. Suddenly, I began to tell them a story. It wasn't a decision, more like something clicked inside me and a voice began to speak both despite and because of my fear. Whole sentences came out, paragraphs with a rhythm that didn't stop and only barely paused for breath. Words simply welled up and flowed out as if to stop time and dull the edges of the blades before my face.

I didn't know where the voice came from but knew that I had to trust that it would keep coming. Although I was speaking fluidly, I was not thinking in a normal way. It was as if something else was thinking and rapidly arranging words and even responding to reactions in the faces of the surprised listeners. The gang had become an audience. They kept listening as long as I kept telling the story as if we all had fallen under a spell.

It wasn't an episode from Jason and the Argonauts or the Seven Against Thebes that came pouring out. That would not have worked under the circumstances, being too foreign and complicated to shift the flow of events. I simply began to tell the story of my friend and why he was so out of control. I rapidly described how his father drank every night and regularly beat the hell out of him. Beyond that, his older brother beat on him too. Maybe there was something else wrong with him or else all the beatings had made him kind of crazy. You couldn't completely blame him. He wasn't really responsible for what he said or did. If he was sane at all he wouldn't threaten them. He didn't understand who he was fighting with; he was just fighting with everyone.

It was as if something in me had silently been considering the story of my friend's life, trying to make sense of his reckless behavior. There was some primitive diagnosis involved and an attempt to make sense of the seemingly senseless behavior; but the shape and style of describing it was clearly storytelling. I added details and embellished the tale without hesitation and in direct response to the feelings of my audience. Something keen and newly awakened in me could tell what affected them and how it moved them. The impromptu tale fluidly adjusted to shifts in their attention and changes in the mood of the situation. I saw their eyes soften as the tension in the air diminished and the weapons began to point down and drop toward their sides.

Suddenly, the leader of the gang spoke. He looked at me with some odd appreciation, the way you might look at someone giving you some interesting news. His eyes were steady and he spoke deliberately as if he wanted us to be clear with each other. He said that it made sense to call the kid crazy, otherwise why would he risk his life like that. Then, to my surprise, he said: "Alright, we're gonna let you go; but you tell your friend that if he even looks at us the wrong way… we're gonna cut him up. You got it?" Oh yeah, I got it and I got out of there as fast as I could. I hurried back to my seat and told my friends that we had to slip through the aisles and out the side doors… right now. Now! I was afraid the gang would change their mind and be waiting for us outside when the movie let out.

We snuck out and ran back to our corner. I described what had happened, how they had threatened me with knives and wrenches. Everyone became agitated, but also excited, exclaiming that they couldn't do that to us. We were a crew too, and we had older guys that would help us. Once the word was put out, everyone connected to the neighborhood would get involved. That theater didn't belong to them. It was time to teach them a lesson.

I tried to explain that the issue wasn't the threat to our neighborhood, nothing had really happened. Besides, there was a bigger point here. I wasn't recounting the story to provoke more gang fights. I was trying to wrap my mind around how it could be that telling a story was more powerful than wielding a weapon. To me, the point was that there was no fight, there was no damage when there should have been. To me, it was the story of what didn't happen that mattered most.

No one listened to the rest of my tale; they had heard enough to be motivated for battle. The threat was in the air and the atmosphere was turning red. That's how most turf wars begin and many bigger wars as well. Meanwhile, I was in a different place. Part of me was still in the movie theater trying to understand what had happened, especially what had happened inside me. Where had the sudden speech come from and how did I know what to say and how to say it? Why would those guys listen to me and forget to do their damage and exact their revenge?

Telling the story about my friend's family clearly struck a chord of recognition with them. The tale of his wounds and rage was the story echoing through most of our houses in one form or another. They were being beaten and neglected and mistreated as well. Hearing the common anguish as a narrative seemed to shift their rage to a kind of self-reflection. We were in an old story of the loss of nobility and the absence of a meaningful center. There was a tale behind the accepted tale of our lives. While some teen movie was being projected behind us, we had slipped inside the actual drama of our lives and were viewing our own pains and desperation.

In considering the fate of my friend we seemed to shift our own fates a little. Given the situation in that theater I should have been injured severely and they should have had more blood on their hands. And, that should have led to reprisals and the payback should have provoked more revenge and things should have played out the way they do in neighborhoods everywhere and throughout history. But, something else happened that seemed to loosen fate, and at least for me, provoke some destiny as well. In one sense, it was but a little shift; yet seen another way it set the course for a much greater adventure.

In the oldest version of the search for the Golden Fleece, the Argonauts sailed on a ship that had the gift of prophecy. When they became stuck at sea or threatened with danger and uncertain which way to go, the ship itself would know the right course because its hull contained an oak timber drawn from the sacred grove of Dodona. Something in the vessel of the deep self also knows which way the wind blows for us; yet such self knowledge only appears when the trouble becomes thick and life and death seem to hang in the balance.

GIFTS OF THE SOUL

I became a storyteller all of a sudden. When my thirteen year-old ego recognized that it couldn't handle the danger I was in, it retreated and left the battlefield. But, something life preserving and purposeful awakened inside me and it knew exactly what to do. Not necessarily what someone else would do; not even what Jason or the Argonauts might do. But, under great duress something deep within me knew exactly what I should do. In order to survive what felt like a life and death situation I had to become more myself. Anything else would have had a false ring to it and would have been more dangerous and damning. In the face of death something already seeded in my life responded intelligently, somewhat defiantly, but also artfully.

Something had come over me and soon came over those who listened to me. It wasn't the same as what came over the older guy who stepped up to help us at the other theater; it was different. This was a moment in the central drama of my life as the back of the movie theater became a sudden stage on which a strange debut was required. Having no alternative and reaching the last resort, an innate and unexpected capacity in me suddenly in me rose to the surface. There was no preparation, no introduction, and no apology for it. The part of me that told the story did not want any rehearsal time and did not need it. For the gifts of the soul—the natural talents, and inborn abilities—come to us fully made.

The word talent has two root meanings; one has to do with natural inclinations, aptitudes, and desires; the other concerns the weighing out of gold or silver or money of some kind. The core of the word talent goes back to a sense of carrying or bearing something that has weight and inherent value. Although many now imagine that talents should be traded for gold or money as quickly as possible, the older sense was that the talent was part of the inner gold that each person must find and learn to bear and carry throughout their life. A talent can be a weight on the soul, especially if it is used improperly, even more so if it isn't used at all.

The talents and gifts set within us can be as a flame that burns a clear way through the confusions of life; but a bright talent can also burn a person out. The inner gifts are divine seeds that can erupt at any time and that can burn with such incandescent heat that the one who bears them can be incinerated by them. Meanwhile, the point of having a talent isn't a matter of measuring the size of it or of comparing it with those who have a similar ability or interest. Our inborn talents and natural gifts are woven within the greater threads of fate and destiny in us. The way that the gifts and natural abilities appear will include a story that foreshadows, prefigures and partially reveals the nature and style of one's soul.

There is always a story that goes with the revelation of a god-given gift and the story that surrounds the gift has significance for the one who bears it. Each talent or ability will manifest distinctly because of the uniqueness of the individual soul. Our innate gifts are set within an inner story that has specific elements of style and a distinct narrative shape. Returning to that story and reviewing it helps in learning the purpose and meaning of one's life as well as the deeper nature of one's gifts. The troubles and desperations of youth typically become the drama through which the inner gifts and hidden gold of the soul first surface and become known.

For me there was a threat of physical harm, a palpable feeling of life and death. The sense and nature of the inner drama appeared both in the threat of harm as well as in the theater setting. Each soul requires an outer drama that in someway reflects its own nature and the style of life it is seeded with. Not every story has such dramatic elements, yet in many ways the question of each person's inner gifts and inherent gold are a matter of life and death to them. What is at stake and must become evident in some way is the true nature of the story seeded within. The shine of a talent or natural gift helps in recognizing the hidden gold, but the details of its appearance reveal something of the inner story that tries to bring it to light.

The events in the theater became my way of further encountering fate and destiny. It was also fate's way of pursuing me and destiny's way of suddenly appearing in the midst of fate's necessary dramas. It was an indelible moment in which the Golden Fleece was near, when the inner gold became available and had to be handled and offered and given away.

For the true nature of the inner gifts only appears when they are given fully and given freely. Each soul is gifted in some way and each grows bigger and deeper when the natural gifts are given away. It doesn't mean that a person can't be compensated for their natural gifts; it does mean that they endanger themselves and others if that becomes the only reason for giving what has been freely given to them.

The thread of each life is suspended between fateful limits woven within us at birth and an inner destiny that tries to manifest and become evident right until the final bow is taken. Although mostly forgotten now and increasingly misunderstood, the inner nature and natural gifts of each person will manifest in some way during youth. How it happens and under what circumstances will indicate critical aspects of the inner shape of the individual soul and the story through which it would grow.

Whatever the story might be, we must act it out and inhabit it fully in order for the shape and meaning to become known even to us. Fateful characteristics shape the plotlines while the threads of destiny pull toward some unseen destination. Natural talents and inner gifts are an essential ingredient of each story and part of the seeds of the soul and the lights of the self. They are the necessary vehicles that carry the defining aspects of fate and the golden promise of a life fulfilling destiny. When seen through the underlying dynamic of each life story, fate and destiny become a living archetype that gives essential shape to the necessary drama of each soul. All our lives we hang by the thread of story woven within us that seeks to reveal who we are at our core and what we came to contribute to life.

THE TABLET OF THE SOUL

Call it a universal myth, call it an open secret, an eternal truth; call it a governing principle, a defining image, an inner code; the sense of each soul bearing a seed-story and carrying it to life appears in cultures throughout the world. The relationship between the human soul and the fruits and leaves, the roots and seeds of mythic trees goes back before time. Set within the seed of the soul is not just a fleeting image or a vague pattern but a life-long story enfolded within and waiting to be cracked open and lived all the way out.

Old myths and stories often revolve around something golden and essential that is missing or lost and must be found for life to have meaning and for nobility to return to the center of communal life. After basic survival, the search for the golden seed of the self was the primary purpose for the individual as well as the true responsibility of the culture. Rather than the issue of which kind of life to choose or the dilemma of what kind of person to become, the true issue was how to give birth to the life-seed that the soul already carries within. The intuitive sense of an inner value and inherent meaning in each life gave people the courage to face the winds of fate and the vision to seek a true destination.

Unfortunately, when one's fate in life is not found and faced and struggled with, a person tends to invent or adopt outer values unsuited to their soul. When a majority of people seek to outflank or cheat the hand that fate has dealt to them, mere cleverness and untutored will power become the dominant cultural values. Secretly, the loss of inner value and individual meaning becomes a depression within the soul and a collective blindness within the culture. The underlying problem is that in refusing fate, we lose our destiny and we fail to find coherence in ourselves and in the world.

To be modern means to live in an un-reconciled world where the pieces rarely fit together and the sense of random acts replaces notions of an inborn purpose. As the modern world view tends toward an "accidental universe" the individual can seem to be the random result of an "accidental birth." If there be any consideration of the soul at all it tends to take the form of a "blank slate" on which society writes its collective story. The old Latin term was the "tabula rasa," the "scraped tablet" ready to be filled in by family values, local rules, and cultural expectations.

In this view, each newborn becomes a "blank slate" unmarked and unmarred by specific characteristics and therefore empty of any inborn knowledge. The soul is pure, if a little vacant and any sense of character or meaning must be gained from experiences of the outer world. This sets up the common belief that one's environment determines who they are and shapes what they might become. There is a seeming freedom in this blank slate or empty shell approach; yet there is also a lack of inherent meaning or innate and soulful purpose in life. A person can "be whatever they want to be," yet may never know if they became who they were intended to be.

Under the rule of tabula rasa, each must "make something of themselves" or run the risk of "being a nobody." On one hand, you might become just about anybody; on the other hand, you might amount to nothing at all. You can be overlooked your entire life and be dismissed as being of no account or you might turn out to be a big shot who calls the shots for others. On one hand, it's all up to you; on the other hand, your environment may have already damaged you and ruined any chance you had of being special or important. Either way, outside forces determine who you are in the world and how you are treated and mistreated.

If the soul is empty both of inherent character and specific purpose, the knowledge and resources needed to "become somebody" and "make something of your life" must be found outside oneself. In order to fulfill our lives the original blank tablet must be informed by ideas, meanings, and purposes gathered from other people and outer institutions. Lacking any genuine inner form, a person must learn to "conform" to the beliefs and systems that prevail. Each must adapt to the circumstances that surround them and adopt an inner character that simply reflects societal "norms" and approved purposes.

Personal success in life comes to depend upon adaptation goals set by others that can be measured in terms of collective values. If the rules are followed and the outer goals are achieved, a person may eventually retire from the struggle to "make something of themselves." Then, they might begin to live the way they truly desire and find some measure of individual fulfillment before they die. In a sense, the inner shape and inherent aims of the soul are somewhat acknowledged, but only as an afterthought to the adaptation to the collective "rat race." Notions of genuine longing and hints of a destiny were there all along, but were repressed in favor of adapting to a "normal life."

Unfortunately, after so much adaptation the original shape and seeding in the soul may be hard to find and harder to live up to. Searching outside for what exists within can be a critical mistake that can lead to a life lived in the wrong direction and for the wrong reasons. A person can wind up alienated from themselves even if they achieve many goals set by others.

It's like the old story of the man who climbed a tall ladder that leaned against a high wall. He pulled himself up step by step and finally reached the very top. When he was able to see from above, he realized that the ladder was leaning against the wrong wall. He had learned to climb, but didn't know what climbing was for. He had reached the top only to find that something essential and life defining had been left far behind. The soul has its own leanings and inner inclinations and the ladder of genuine success must be found where it begins in the grounding of one's own life.

When we find and follow how we are aimed from within, there is a growing down as well as a climbing up. A person becomes more fully incarnated and more truly rooted in life. When following the gradient of the soul the climbing effort itself has value and satisfaction can be found and felt and learned from at each step along the way.

If the soul is already seeded before we are born there can be an instinctive orientation and inherent sense of direction and purpose in one's life. If the tablet of one's being already contains a core pattern and vital shape then answers to life's burning questions can be sought for and found within as well as encountered in the outer world. Answers to the age-old questions: 'Who am I?' and 'For what purpose was I born?' 'What should I do with my life?' can be found inside the questions themselves and inside the one asking, and inside the story already being lived.

When young people are not given a chance to awaken to the story seeded in their souls, something greater than careers and potentials becomes wasted. Something golden and noble becomes lost and more people begin to wander in confusion, seeking in the outside world what has been lost within themselves. Blind greed and rampant egotism begin to substitute for genuine vocations and for being called to find meaningful paths in life. Soon, most believe that getting to the top of any heap will make life meaningful. As the inner character essential to human dignity and nobility becomes increasingly lost, one person seems to be exchangeable with another. How a culture treats and answers the basic questions of human identity determines how it will be remembered.

WHICH ONE AM I?

Clearly, myths of fate and destiny go the other way around. If a person lives out their inner inclinations and follows the inner dream and living story seeded in their soul, they have a chance to arrive at a genuine destination in life. At that point, they will have become the living story embedded in their soul. Having served the inborn spirit of their life and kept their appointments with fate and destiny, they will die empty of disappointments and clear of resentments. They will meet death without the angers and fears common to those who suddenly realize that they lived a life that was shaped and molded by others.

The deeper questions of identity and life purpose have always been there. It's not a new problem, but an old issue that has been exacerbated by the speed and mass confusion of modern societies and the exaggerations of materialism. There's an old story of a simple country fellow who had to go to the big market town for the first time. He had managed to remain all his life in the little village where everyone knew him and where he knew most everyone. Now, something else was demanded of him and he had to step out into the wide world. He had heard travelers tell of the hordes of people and the rush of activities in the market city; he feared that he would become lost amidst so many people.

So, he went to seek advice from a friend who was more experienced than himself. He blurted out his questions along with his fears. "When I go to the city I will have to stay in one of those big inns where all the workers and travelers stay in the same room. I will have to sleep in a room full of strangers. I have never done that before and I am afraid that I will become lost and confused. I will know myself when I lay down to sleep; but amongst all those people, how will I know which one I am when I wake up?"

His friend saw a chance to play a trick on him, as people often do when someone indulges in their innocence or foolishness. The friend advised him to first go to the market and buy a large and colorful watermelon. He instructed him that before going to sleep he must tie the watermelon to his ankle. After that, he should take his rest. The friend went on to explain that in the morning when he woke in the company of strangers, he would be the one with the watermelon tied to his foot.

The foolish fellow thought for a while, then asked: "What if during the dark of night someone unties the watermelon from my foot and ties it onto theirs? How will I know which one I am if the watermelon has been switched?" At that point, his friend was wise enough to become silent on the subject.

It's a simple story of a simple-minded fellow, yet more and more people seem to depend on a watermelon, or a degree, on a certain home address or prestigious title for proof that they are in fact an individual and someone of worth and value. Ironically, more and more people fear becoming victims of "identity theft;" as if the watermelon approach is taking precedence over the sense of a true identity that is seeded in the soul. The statistical view of the world, the massing of people and the obsession with appearances makes the dilemma of the country fellow an increasingly common experience. Modern ideas tend to follow the fears and concerns of the fellow whose identity is but an appendage to his life. Either the presence of a unique soul is considered impossible to prove and therefore not to be believed or else the soul is deemed a blank slate to be conditioned by one's life circumstances.

If our identity has been determined by other people and by forces outside ourselves; then our sense of self will be like a colorful item that we purchase in the world-wide market and tie onto our bodies. If our identity in this world can become nothing but an appendage to be manipulated and adapted to outer circumstances, we are in increasing danger of losing it or having it taken from us. In forgetting how the soul is seeded to begin with we can be in danger of becoming completely lost in this world, both empty within and completely disoriented as well. Without a genuine sense of an inner life and deeper self we become increasingly subject to those who cleverly manipulate the marketplace as well as the elements of politics and even the premises and promises of religion.

Most advertising is based upon the notion that people don't know who they are inside and secretly doubt that they are anything at all. Being more interested in growing adaptable citizens and life-long consumers, modern cultures have a vested interest in people believing that they are but blank slates waiting for society to write upon them and empty shells waiting to be filled with one product or another. Those who don't know who they are tend to consider everything to be for sale or for use in some bizarre experiment that pits humans against nature. The willingness of modern people to experiment with and recklessly alter the seeds of plants seems partly to rise from a lack of understanding of nature and from a misunderstanding of human nature.

A true identity must be grown from within and such a soulful presence and sense of self cannot be purchased at any price. To become ourselves we must ripen from the seeds of self already planted and sown within us. We must grow from the inner roots that secretly connect us to the tree at the center of all life. Only such an inner awakening can gives us a true orientation to life. Turning our attention to the life already seeded within and nourishing it leads to the development of a true identity that cannot be simply misplaced or taken away. What is truly ours cannot be taken from us nor even be given away.

KNOW THYSELF

The advent of youth includes necessary encounters with fate that can serve to awaken the inner character and intended identity of each person. Just as the natural seed must first settle in some ground in order to grow, each child nestles within a certain family and social arrangement. When childhood comes to an end, life becomes more open-ended and a further identity is required as the inner seed tries to break through the earth of its origins in order to rise and stand on its own. Such an awakening inside requires an outside drama that can match the intensity of and style of the individual soul.

In reflecting back on the fateful events in the theater of my youth, I realized that I had gotten myself into the "right trouble." A certain amount of trouble is needed to provide the heat for the inner seeds to germinate and sprout. Young people quickly acquire the habit of getting in trouble, as if the soul knows that something about the drama needed in order to uncover and discover the inner story. The issue in this life is not to avoid trouble, for trouble eventually comes to everyone's door. What may be an overwhelming threat or unbearable pressure for one person will be just the right turmoil and exacting challenge for another. The issue in this life is to get into the "right trouble" and learn from it who we already are inside, how we are seeded and what gifts we have to give.

Most of the cynicism, violence, apathy, and depression that youth suffer can be attributed to not being recognized and seen as the unique individual that they already are inside. Most of the trouble that youth get into secretly seeks to reveal the inner character and natural genius within them. Too often, those dealing with the problems of youth try to apply general rules and abstract systems of morality and belief, while it is the inner uniqueness of each one that is the source of the problems and that can become the natural cure as well.

Coming of age means coming to know something of one's true self and awakening to the way we are each already seeded and aimed at life. What happens during youth marks each of us in some way that remains indelibly tattooed on the walls of our soul. The life and death circumstances that attend the dramas of youth remain in the soul and wait to be re-viewed and opened again. The seeds of our innermost stories surface repeatedly and especially when a life change is required or when life itself is threatened or challenged in fateful ways.

The fateful book of stories that fell into my lap at the onset of youth quickly became the basis for becoming a storyteller. In the sudden grip of both life and death I had to tell a story, I had to become what was seeded within me. In doing that I began the process of coming to know myself. "Know thyself," was the advice carved in stone above the threshold of the famous oracle at Delphi in ancient Greece. Know thyself before trying to simply fit in somewhere. Know thyself before trying to grasp the puzzling messages that life keeps delivering. Know thyself from the inside out. Know the oracular nature of the inner seeded self that holds the tale trying to unfold from within.

Becoming a true individual means learning what is already seeded inside in order to properly relate to all that occurs on the outside. The true individual is not the increasingly isolated self fostered by modern mass societies, but more the awakened self, the inner self in the life-long process of awakening to its own genuine nature.

CHAPTER 3

LIFE SENTENCES

It has often been remarked that the long journey home from war that forms the books of the Odyssey presents a continuing metaphor for the Western World. Odysseus, or Ulysses as he later became known, spent ten years trying to find a way home after being victorious in the Trojan War. Often enough those who lose a war are left to bury the dead, while those who win find themselves far from home in some way. A poet once said that every war has two losers; for war is kind to no one and brutal to most and the effects of it continue to burn within the soul long after the fires have been put out and the bodies buried down.

Ulysses was considered to be wise. He was called "double-minded," meaning one who could see more than one side of a given issue; one who had "second sight" and deeper insights than most. Being double-minded also meant being "wily;" both able to see the tricky ways of others and capable of devising tricks as well. It was Ulysses who invented the famous strategy of the Trojan horse that hid danger inside a shining gift and led to the downfall of Troy and the success of the Greek forces.

Not all of Ulysses tricks worked as well as the Trojan horse. He had at first declined to enter that war, before he wound up in it and found himself struggling so hard to find a way home. He must have seen something of the great troubles that the battles and their aftermath would leave, for he failed to respond to the initial summons to join the "great war." Eventually, Greek officers were sent to his island kingdom to invite him personally and learn why he had not responded to the original request.

When Ulysses saw the warlords coming he began to act strangely and it appeared as if he had lost his mind. The officers found him plowing away at his fields behind a team of oxen. However, they could see that he was sowing salt instead of planting seeds in the earth. Determined to test the apparent insanity of the young ruler of Ithaca, one of them found the infant son of Ulysses and placed him in the furrows before the oncoming plow. When the father quickly drew the oxen back and stopped the plowing in order to avoid crushing his son, they knew that he was sane enough to go to war.

You could say that it was the fate of Ulysses to survive a war that devoured the lives of most of the heroes of Greece. Yet, it was also his fate to suffer great dangers and come near death many times while trying to return from that war. He couldn't find a trick to get out of the war and after going to it, he couldn't find an easy or direct way to return from it. To this day, it remains easier to undertake a war than to recover from it. Soldiers and warriors often survive the war only to succumb to the battle that ensues when trying to arrive home. The case made for undertaking a war and the grand causes that seem to justify it tend to fade over time, while the traumatic effects of a war linger and malinger inside those who survive and suffer through it.

Those who attend a war will tend to carry it, in one form or another, inside them afterward. Perhaps, the real Trojan horse is war itself which can appear so noble and shining and even glorious, yet can eat away at a person and gnaw at a culture from the inside for many years after the battles are over.

Like many others at the time, I was drafted into the army during the ill-fated war in Viet Nam. I received the draft notice when I was twenty years old and at first, declined the invitation. Having followed news reports, I had concluded that the war made little sense. In fact, it wasn't a declared war but more of a military action. I sent a letter back to the draft board arguing that the reasons for fighting weren't clear, nor were the goals defined. I declined the invitation, but offered to consider future requests. In short order, I received a summons to appear before the local draft board for a hearing.

After listening to my arguments the members of the board insisted that I was either an objector on religious grounds or a draft resistor who could be sent to prison. They sent me to a minister who explained the rules for becoming a "conscientious objector." I found myself unable to sign the document that could lead to a deferral. Receiving objector status required that I claim to never have been involved in violence and swear that my appeal was based on my religious training and practice. Since neither was the case, it seemed too devious to make those claims. My objection was deeply personal and looking back upon it, wildly subjective.

I drew up my own document of "conscious objection" and that was summarily rejected. Soon, I received a letter ordering me to appear for induction into military service or else be subject to arrest and a prison sentence. I found myself in a dilemma. My objections were clear, yet they were subjective and personal, not religious and doctrinal. My conscience objected to the war that was not actually a war; yet I felt both cultural and familial pressure to conform to collective expectations and appear for duty.

The "anti-war" movement was just getting started and I had no immediate connection to it. Almost everyone in my family and in my neighborhood was in favor of the war. And, to my surprise and regret, they were uniformly in favor of me joining it. My father and many uncles had answered the call during previous wars and my mother seemed to say that our sons always go when they are called. Yet, I didn't feel called to it at all. I was waiting for a different call, waiting for a more specific "calling." For some, military life and battle can become a true calling; I knew that wasn't the case for me. Yet, I didn't see an honorable way out of it.

For weeks, I wandered the streets of the city turning the issue over and over in my mind. The pressure to accept the demand of the culture, of my immediate community, and my family was evident and palpable. Yet, there was something in me, an instinct or intuition, a foreboding or oracle that pulled me in the exact opposite direction. It wasn't that I wouldn't fight, but that I needed to know more truly what the fight was for. It wasn't simply that

I was afraid to die; I was, but I was equally afraid to die for the wrong reason.

The truth was that I didn't see any Golden Fleece in the adventure, didn't feel that there was nobility or specific honor involved. That's how I felt and there was nothing I could do about that. I didn't want to go to prison, couldn't see a clear reason or meaningful outcome in that direction. So, partially out of fear of being considered a coward, partially out of fear of going to prison, and partially out of family fate, I eventually went into the army. I decided to show up for my induction appointment and let the chips fall where they might. It wasn't the appointment with a greater life that I had harbored since my thirteenth birthday; it was far from that. Yet, in the strange and twisted way of fate and destiny, it did lead to unexpected experiences and a further awakening of the deeper self within me.

SELECTIVE SERVICE

Suffice it to say that I was not a good soldier, although that didn't become clear until a few months in the army had passed. I liked the activities and exercise well enough and enjoyed meeting guys from different backgrounds and ethnicities. I quickly found some good companions and hoped for the best. But, there was a basic problem—I didn't take orders well. I had always been headstrong and willful and inclined to go my own way. Now, people were ordering me all over the place. At a certain point, I couldn't go along with it, couldn't do it, wouldn't do it, and couldn't be made to do it.

I began to be selective about which orders I would accept and comply with. If an order made sense I would likely follow it; however, if I was given an order that was foolish or mean-spirited or clearly ignorant, I would refuse to do it. Such discretion did not sit well with my superiors and I found myself being given one courts-martial after another. I had a new dilemma, for I could not commit to a course of blind obedience. Despite the threat of ongoing punishment, I found that I could not simply follow orders and I could not back down. I realized that I had made a crucial mistake and it would be better for me to leave the service. Of course, my military superiors took a contrary view and simply gave me more orders.

When I continued to refuse to obey I received the first of several company courts-martial decrees. When endless periods of KP, other petty details, and constant threats didn't change my mind, I was given a special court-martial before a panel of officers. A military lawyer was assigned to defend me. He was a recent college graduate like myself. He asked my reasons for disobeying orders; he took notes and arranged for me to use the library to prepare my own defense.

Meanwhile, other officers became curious about my actions and attitudes and also came to interview me. In a kind of reverse psychology, they offered me a place in officer's training school. I explained that I could hardly give orders to others that I was reluctant to follow myself. In turn, I asked them how they could send troops into deadly situations without genuine clarity about immediate dangers and the purpose of the overall mission. They had few ideas for justifying the war. One was the red-lined idea that the enemy was the embodiment of evil. If they weren't stopped over there, they would soon overrun the world and destroy all freedom. I talked with many officers about this reasoning, including several colonels and one general, and none could make the connection between the general fear of an overwhelming enemy and the seeming civil war in Viet Nam.

When I pushed the conversation beyond this sense of a gathering evil out there I encountered the second reason intended to convince me to risk my life and moreover my soul in such an unclear battle: you do what you are ordered to do. The idea of simply killing on orders seemed unreal to me. When I challenged the sanity of that rule, I was informed that I had signed a paper accepting my induction into the army and at that point had given up certain rights and would follow orders no matter what they entailed. I owed that to my country. I felt that I owed more than that and that part of what I owed was being true to myself.

Being young and idealistic, I was outraged by this kind of reasoning and by the notion that it would be better for me to give orders that might cause others to die than to receive such commands. I offered to write out clearly all of my objections to the current and still undeclared war and my reactions to the arguments for fighting in it and sign that. Then, they would have a signed document to offset the first signature and I could go about my business elsewhere. They thought I was joking. I felt that I was responding to their need for written agreements and intentional signatures.

Since my life and sense of self worth were on the line, I was taking everything seriously. Since the lives of so many were in their hands, I assumed that they were doing the same. My mistake, as it turned out. The court-martial never addressed any of the issues that caused me to defy military authority. The night before the court convened, the lieutenant assigned to my defense informed me what the verdict would be and what sentence would follow it. He said that he had just come from the officer's club where it had all been decided over drinks. I made my defense anyway, then learned that I would be sentenced to six months in the stockade. That was the longest sentence such a court could decree at the time. They said they would have given a longer sentence had it been in their power.

From the moment of conviction I began a descent, not just in entering the prison, but a turning inward and cycling down. Of course, I was singled-out for special attention in the prison and subject to an endless series of orders, threats, and humiliating treatments. When I refused all orders I wound up in solitary confinement and stayed there for many months. I had chosen to enter the army rather than go to prison; yet I had wound up in prison anyway. Somehow, the choices for me had narrowed down until something like fate took over.

Although I was already confined and out of contact with everyone except the prison guards, I somehow remained a problem to the military. Officers continued to appear and give me orders as if my refusal to comply threatened everything they believed in. Each officer seemed to think that he had the magic power or unique style that would cause me to obey. As the situation deteriorated and greater punishments loomed, I suddenly decided to fast and refused all food. My idea was to demonstrate that I wasn't present in any normal sense. If I didn't eat I couldn't be considered to be participating in any way. To further make the point, I threw out my uniform and bedding and lived both naked and solitary in my cell.

Strange behavior to be sure, but not completely out of context or out of character as I found out later when I read about Irish political prisoners fasting against British power and dying rather than forsaking their vision of sovereignty and justice. There was something ancestral in my blood that not only could boil hot with a temper, but that also knew old ways of responding to oppression. It turns out that the ancient Irish would fast when faced with a relentless and superior power that they couldn't defeat.

There I was, barely over twenty, alone and isolated, caught up in a cause that gripped me and would not let me go, hard fasting against them in order to make the point clear. Fate places people in unremitting circumstances and forces surprising qualities to the surface. The fellow in the cell next to me went the other way entirely. He swallowed strange objects including some nuts and bolts under the theory that eating hardware would prove him too disturbed to remain in the military. Although the scheme had some Ulysses in it, he was wrong. The guards simply took him to the hospital where they x-rayed him and surgically removed all the nuts and bolts. Later, they returned him to his platoon, sent him off to the battlefield, and charged him for the surgery to boot.

I decided to stick with my plan of refusing to eat until I received a discharge and could return home. I remained alone in my cell day after day, night after night, only leaving for a shower every other day. In the shower I would drink more water than I would wash myself with. I found I could go a long time without food, but not more than two days without water. Eventually, doctors who specialized in the effects of starvation were brought in and they told me that I could die at any time.

Still, I would not eat; somehow I could not eat. Something had been triggered deep inside me and I had found *my* battle. Despite losing well over a third of my body weight and being warned that my organs were failing, I would only agree to eat when I received discharge papers. In a strange way I had found an adventure that took all my energy and all my will and that almost cost my life.

NEVER ALONE

Once again, I was in the circumstances of life and death and in the hands of fate. Many things happened during those months in solitary, but some things became indelibly emblazoned on my mind. I was alone day and night except for the guards occasionally checking on me. I was not allowed reading materials and my pen and papers had been confiscated. I found myself recalling myths and stories and imagining the characters in them. On one level I was simply recalling old stories; yet the characters seemed to be near at times.

I felt nourished somehow by the stories and supported by a sense of being in a mythic condition similar to those in the old tales. Orpheus had entered the underworld and Ulysses went there repeatedly while trying to find his way home. I seemed to have found my way there as well. It wasn't just that I could picture the tales, more that the characters appeared and seemed to have things to say. At first, it was shocking and I feared that I was falling apart, coming unglued because of the isolation and the starvation. Yet, the presence of mythic figures felt reassuring and actually seemed to settle me.

Eventually, I considered that I was either losing my mind or else I was just finding it. Either I was going "round the bend" or I was actually coming around to how my psyche was essentially inclined to be. Since accepting the presence of mythic characters felt more assuring than simply succumbing to despair, I began to welcome them and tried to learn what they wanted me to understand. That shift of attention brought the mythic world closer; it helped to settle and focus my mind and seemed to provoke an even stranger series of events.

By then, everyone at the nearby bases knew the story of the strange kid who had been in solitary for months and had stopped eating and refused to wear a uniform. Although I was not allowed visitors, a veritable parade of officers began to appear at the door of my cell each night. Whether it was a colonel, captain, or lieutenant, they would each enter the cell, call me to attention and give me an order. When I failed to respond, they would sit down and begin to talk. Inevitably, they would confess something that weighed on their heart or soul.

Some spoke of their fear of dying in battle and never seeing their loved ones again and never learning what their life might have been. Some wanted to explain that they were not in favor of the war, but felt they had a duty to perform. Most wanted to unburden themselves of something deeply personal; as if they just needed a place to confess. Having been raised Catholic I understood something of the ritual of confession and I mostly played the role of confessor. I didn't give them absolution for their sins or assign penances, but I listened with all the attention I could muster and offered guidance where I could.

In the course of time, I learned how some beat their wives out of blind frustration and felt terrible for doing it. I heard how others frequented the prostitutes outside the base only to feel anguished about betraying wives and sweethearts back home. Some wanted to tell of an old offense that involved a friend or a family member. Mostly, they didn't want to die without stating how sorry they were for some past transgression or omission. The captain of the prison came frequently, always with a long list of complaints and worries. He was actually afraid that he would wind up in prison for his whole career. I could sympathize and had a similar concern.

Meanwhile, the doctors would wake me in the middle of the night to say that they could barely find my pulse. Inevitably, they would ask if I wanted to die. I would say that I did not; that dying wasn't the point at all. The point was what I was living for. I had become literally caught in between life and death and found that I would accept death rather than lose the life I had inside me. They had great trouble understanding me and I had trouble understanding myself. A course had been set and I no longer had the power to change it. Fate can work like that; a crossroads is reached and a path taken and there can be no turning back. I refused the collective fate of going to war and entered my own personal battle. I can't explain it logically, that's not the point; it never is when it comes to fate or destiny.

STEALING LIFE

I withdrew from life in order to save my sense of life. I refused to eat in order to demonstrate that I wasn't part of the military, not a combatant, not even a member. As time went on, I became increasingly fragile; yet I was under armed guard twenty-four hours each day. The guards were drawn from my own company and most were sympathetic to my situation if not exactly to my cause. We were all draftees and there was some way in which the training itself made it more clear that the war was questionable and had little justification. Also, we were all a little closer to death than before and seeing my condition made that more evident to all of us.

In order to learn my own meaning, I had to face death in my own way. In the long, empty nights I made my peace with death. Eventually though, a point was reached where I had to shift from being willing to die to being willing to live. The point of embracing life can also become a point of no return. There is a dusky area between life and death, a turning point in a penumbral world in which death is welcomed or else life is embraced. For me, a strange turning point came when one of the soldiers who guarded me on a regular basis slipped me a chocolate bar.

I felt a new dilemma take shape within me. On one hand the chocolate represented the sweetness of life; on the other hand eating it would violate my code of not being present and not participating. Technically, it wasn't military food and it was being offered out of genuine concern for my well-being. Yet, eating anything at that point seemed to be giving in or could be seen as giving up. I was on a mission and feared that one bite could change everything and compromise the clarity and ethical purity of my position. On the other hand, not to accept this helping hand could represent a final turn away from life.

I didn't wish to refuse the gift and not acknowledge the generosity behind it or the risk being taken in offering it. So, I accepted the chocolate in its colorful wrapper and told myself that I would decide later whether to eat it or not. Later came quite soon as I found myself thinking of the concealed sweet continually. I had little else to consider except the basic issues of life and death and the subtle exchange between one breath and the next. As I was under guard all the time, the only privacy I had was when I went to the toilet to urinate. One day, I took the chocolate bar with me.

Without a great amount of further consideration and driven by what I now realize was an instinct for self-preservation, I unwrapped the chocolate and quickly ate it. I had been too long without food for it to register fully as a sensual treat. I found it moderately enjoyable and decidedly strange. Happily, it was semi-sweet. I didn't like milk chocolate and much preferred some bitterness with the sweet. As soon as I ate the contraband chocolate I knew that something within me had changed; I decided that I would face life as well as death. I knew from a deep place inside that I wanted to live and that I would even break my own rules to do so. I received a bitter-sweet reprieve from the extremes of my own excesses.

In a strange way, I owe my life to a fellow soldier and a piece of chocolate. Obedience may make for a good soldier; but taking risks for another is the essential glue in the deep bond between warriors. My fight against the military could easily have ended in death had not a fellow soldier taken a risk for my benefit. It wasn't that a little bar of chocolate could suddenly make me healthy or even offset the effects of starvation. Rather, it was like a trick in which a little move toward life seemed to cause life to move toward me. Shortly after that, the military intelligence decided that it would be counter-productive to have a draftee die of starvation while in military prison. Soon, experts who had treated survivors of the Nazi holocaust camps were brought in and they decided to force feed me.

Not long after I secretly swallowed the chocolate, I was subjected to an archaic looking device that would pry my teeth apart in order to allow food to be forced into me with a plunger. Strange to say, the ice cold mixture of liquid nutrients was often flavored with chocolate. Accepting the little bit of sweetness seemed to produce a greater flow of nutrients. In a way, I was saved from dying of starvation against my will. I was nourished back to life by food that was literally forced into me, a chilling assault of nourishment administered with sadistic force.

Ironically, I was being forced to live. Having chosen death more than once, I was being forced to accept life. Except for one thing, I had already chosen life in accepting the chocolate just before food was forced upon me. Seen another way, I stole my life back from my own will, by secretly wishing to live and not die, by accepting a gift from someone ordered to guard me. I was forced back into life on one hand and I stole my way there on the other. If I hadn't already decided to eat something on my own, I think I would have fought to the death against any attempt to force me to live. Accepting the chocolate gift and eating it made the force-feeding redundant and allowed me to accept it as well. Although part of me felt that I had broken my own code and cheated, I also realized that I had stolen my life back from death.

A SECOND BIRTH

Many years later, while studying various rites of initiation in order to understand what could motivate a young person to act the way I did while in prison, I came across the idea that initiates were often required to steal food. In parts of Africa, initiates were required to steal whatever they ate during rites of separation and ordeals. In some tribes, the penalty for stealing was death; as if demonstrating that each must risk death in order to become fully initiated into life.

The norm of the tribe is that you never steal, especially the food of other people. Yet, in order to become fully initiated into this world, everyone must steal their life; steal it from their own culture, from their own family and even from the certainty of their own beliefs and willpower. There is a greater will, a greater need and purpose hidden within each life, and there is an inner law that knows best how each must live and that is worth stealing for; it's worth dying for, and worth living for as well.

Immediately, I understood the dilemma the initiates were put in and the brilliance of its solution. Initiation rites offer a form of rebirth, a second birth that is more conscious and psychological than being a newborn. This second birth must be a conscious choice of life made in the face of a threat of the death of one's spirit and reason for being alive. Thus, rules must be broken and penalties must be risked in order that choosing to fully live becomes a truly conscious act. Although rites of initiation have virtually disappeared from the modern world, the human psyche understands that critical events are required for a young person to consciously inhabit their own life.

Under certain conditions it becomes necessary to violate all the rules, even one's own beliefs in order to truly live and feel the deeper pulse of one's being. After contradicting the beliefs of my family and the rules of the society, I still had to go against my own rules in order to encounter something greater than my little-self. Something within me desired to live no matter what. It may have been the source of my desire to take a dramatic stand against what I considered false demands; yet it would not allow me to throw away the life I had been given.

Each life is subject to a complex and intricate sense of inner justice; that is the real meaning of conscience. Not simply living in accord with moral prescriptions and abstract principles. The natural inner law tends to appear during great dilemmas; if *it* is contradicted, a fate worse than death can occur. Eventually, we must learn the inherent ethics that are inscribed in the soul and must even learn to steal that which was already given to us freely. We have to want to live enough to confound, to convict, to condemn and also to release ourselves. We have to live within the life sentence we receive unwittingly and must one day choose consciously. Fate requires that we accept the way we are woven in this world; in accepting that unique arrangement, a thread of destiny can unwind and open the way before us.

FATEFUL INTERVENTIONS

The whole thing might still have ended badly had it not been for another intervention and a twist of fate. The authorities had decided to move me to a cell block at the back of a hospital that had been built during the construction of the Panama Canal. Hardly anyone knew about those cells and no one had been in them for decades. At first, I assumed that they wanted me closer to medical care; but the guards told me that reporters for magazines like *Time* and *Life* were poking around trying to find the soldier who was starving to death. I never learned how reporters discovered what was happening to me. Since I only spoke with guards and doctors, one of them must have leaked the story.

One day an officer came and offered me discharge papers. All I had to do was sign on the bottom line and I would be on my way home. The idea came as a shock and it was hard for me to believe the offer. I had been threatened many times, had been mistreated in many ways, and roughed up repeatedly. Several times I had been offered an immediate commission as an officer if I would just sign some papers and agree to salute the flag each day. I didn't trust the authorities or even the military doctors to be acting in my best interests. I knew that my health was deteriorating despite the forced feedings, yet I didn't trust any new offers and suspected some kind of Trojan horse intended to cause me to give up my fast and then lose my resolve when the discharge didn't materialize.

When I refused to sign, an entire group of officers gathered to convince me that there was precious little time to do so. The real cause for concern turned out to be that a U.S. senator had sworn to come and see the situation first-hand if I were not released from prison. And, it was not just any senator, but Robert Kennedy himself. He had become a senator for my home state of New York and someone had gotten a message to him telling of my struggle and precarious condition. Apparently, he had called the commanding officer and insisted that I be released or he would come in-person within forty-eight hours.

No one involved wanted Bobby Kennedy poking around in the back rooms and hidden cells of the army. The authorities did not want the situation to become public and turn into a media event. There were already many soldiers interested in how I was faring and whether there was a way out of the forced service. Suddenly, there was a big rush to give me my discharge papers and get me out of Panama as soon as humanly possible.

Eventually, I signed the discharge and was escorted back to the states by two young sergeants returning from the battlefields of Viet Nam. They had earned their stripes in brutal combat and were returning home at the end of their tour. They held me under armed guard and I was handcuffed between them on the flight back. They asked why I was so emaciated and bearded and decidedly strange looking. Although I feared it would make me seem like the enemy to them, I told them how I had refused orders and wound up in solitary confinement. To my great surprise, they both felt that I had been in my own war and they assured me that I had won. Where I expected them to attack me for standing against a war that they had barely survived, they felt we had each entered our own battles and received our own wounds. Where I was confused and still caught in a struggle to survive, they were newly released from the war and wanting me to feel that freedom as well.

It's strange to consider, but those warriors took me to be a brother in arms, or at least one who had fought in his own way. Although they were only ordered to deliver me to the base, they stayed with me throughout my contentious discharge process. They could see that I was fragile and still being threatened by hard line military types. After their official guard duties were complete, they decided to continue as my protectors. They went wherever I went and even gave up some off-duty passes when I got in a little trouble before leaving the base. I never saw them again, but I have never forgotten their instinctive integrity and their care and kindness toward me.

They never explained their feelings, but exhibited for all to see the difference between a soldier and a warrior. There are places that run deep enough that all the conflicts at the surface of life become mute. There are currents of empathy that surpass even the most intense disagreements. There are depths of understanding that open when people get to the very bottom and deep center of themselves. I hope that they found ways to return from the war as they gave me a way to understand my own battle.

Within a week I was back in New York City. I was home again, but was not at home at all. I had gained my freedom yet had no way of understanding what had happened. The stroke of fate that caused my release remained a mystery to me and I struggled to understand what had caused me to act in such an extreme way. There was a tangle of threads that I couldn't simply unravel at the time. Later, I related it to fate because the circumstances were fateful, because both life and death were involved, and because common notions of free will and choice don't carry enough gravitas for an understanding of the situation.

Shortly after my military experiences the authorities established a lottery to decide who would have to go to war. The idea of a lottery begins in the stories of the Sisters of Fate. *Lachesis* is one of the fateful sisters whose name means "disposer by lot or dispenser of lots." The draft lottery was a way of putting everything back in the hands of fate. The time of one's birth became a true moment of fate for many young men and for their families. Despite modern arguments for free will and the gilded ideas of fighting for freedom, individual lives would be put at risk on the basis of fate.

Some received the dark fate of dying in distant lands; others survived the battles only to leave parts of themselves on the battlefield; and everyone involved still carries the war with them as part of their extended fate and lot in life. For certain events in life continue to live inside where they either become a deep source of meaning or a profound and suppurating wound. A slender thread of destiny would seem to be the fine filament that makes the difference between unending trauma and a further initiation into one's life.

Many years later, I learned a compelling detail that amplifies the mysterious ways of fate and destiny. After the assassination of his brother John, Bobby Kennedy fell into despair and couldn't find a way out of the depths of darkness that followed upon the tragic loss. His Catholic faith in a good god was shaken and in the ensuing months, he was devoured by grief. He barely ate and friends remarked that he seemed to shrink, his clothes no longer fitting as he became wasted and gaunt.

Jackie Kennedy, the widow of the fallen president, suggested that Robert read Edith Hamilton's works on the Greek myths and ancient tragic plays. He did exactly that, apparently annotating certain parts and memorized many passages. The ancient tales and poetry provided him with comfort, and helped to support him in the great devastation he felt in his heart. He would carry the ancient texts with him when he traveled and wore out their covers. Biographers say that he discovered the ancient notions of fate and hubris and that he studied and considered them for years.

It seems that he was reading Hamilton's writings on the ancient myths and philosophies while I was recalling them from memory in my solitary cell. A weird thread of fate caused him to have immediate sympathy for a young man he knew nothing of except that he was in prison and was likely to die of starvation unless someone intervened and altered the situation. It was as if something of the hand of fate that caused the Greek myths to fall into my lap when I was but thirteen, caused him to call for my release from prison some eight years later. Some might call such strange things accidental or an odd coincidence; but I was learning to see the hand of fate in the course of life and also learning to perceive a thread of destiny as well.

THE OLD THIEF

One of the things a person can learn while in a prison is that everyone is doing time; everyone has their own life-sentence to deal with. Inside a prison a person can often learn what most imprisons their natural spirit for life. It seems that anything can become a prison if it begins to fetter and restrict the soul. School can often feel like a prison and many jobs have an incarcerating effect. Marriage, which can be such a delight, can also become as a prison and a even spiritual path can lead to a deep isolation. An illness can wreck the body and trap one's soul and the loss of a loved one can leave one enshrouded for a long time.

Most people wind up doing "hard time" of one sort or another and the soul is always on the verge of some greater awareness or some deeper trouble as we are eternally unable to simply "live and let live." The strictures of time continually rub against the infinite, intricate patterns of the soul, troubling life toward its awkward and necessary revelations. Everyone gets trapped within their own dilemmas and everyone gets caught, eventually. The holy man is caught making love to the wrong person. The pillars of moral society indulge in greed or gambling, in secret hoarding, or compulsive eating. The holy mother mistreats animals and the peaceful saint secretly slaughters thousands in his mind. No one in this life can exist without some kind of shadow and some fateful dilemma. Eventually, the question becomes whether or not we find some element of destiny inside the fateful situations that entrap and imprison us.

There's an old tale of a thief who came to be imprisoned in a dark cell that seemed to offer no way of escape. He had been a thief for most of his life and everyone knew that he practiced stealth. Yet, he was good enough at the secrets and tricks of the trade that he had never been caught or charged with a crime. He knew a great deal about secrets and hidden things because he spent so much time sifting through the possessions of others. I'm not recommending stealing as an occupation as much as considering the secrecy and solitary skills involved in doing it. And, the capacity for observation required if one were to become good at it.

Didn't Prometheus steal fire in order for humankind to be able to cook food? Wasn't Ulysses using stealth when giving the gift of the Trojan horse? Didn't Jesus hang with thieves in the end? He made a distinction between the two kinds of thief. One was but a common crook who took from others to satisfy personal greed; but, the other was capable of a great awakening and wound up going to heaven.

There's a way in which all good counselors are thieves in the sense that they steal into the minds and hearts of others; they pick amidst the feelings and memories that shape the inner lives of those who trust them. Academics of course are great thieves; most only make their way by taking a thought from someone who had more ideas than themselves. Then, they either disguise the stolen thought as their own or use it to attack those who think another way. Some even steal unripe ideas from their students in order to ripen them in their own garden until they can bring them out to the marketplace.

Artists are the greatest thieves of all. For all art involves some stealing and a good artist will be the first to admit that. One artist will steal from another and all art has been borrowed from the sacred sources of inspiration. Lesser artists work mostly at disguising what they have stolen or borrowed, while the great artists recreate and improve upon the captured image or idea. Call it imitation or education, a willingness to steal is required for many an occupation.

The old thief was an artist in his own way, having learned the trade at first out of need, but having elevated the work to a level of art. Like many an artist before him, lifting things without being noticed soon came to him naturally. At times, his practice might be petty and inconsequential; at other times, it involved things more sublime than obvious. People considered him something of an artist because everyone knew that he stole things, but he had never been caught red-handed.

At least, not until the day he was in the local marketplace and decided to steal some herbs in the bright daylight. Perhaps, someone was ill and needed a potion; perhaps he was simply taken by the smell of flowers or the shape of roots. Perhaps, it was simply an accident, a moment of weakness or else it was a moment of fate. At any rate, the thief was spotted taking the herbs and caught in the act.

The authorities lost no time in taking him before the most severe judge in the realm. The judge promptly demanded a heavy fine which the old thief was unable to pay. They happily converted the fine into a lengthy jail sentence and the old thief was led away without recourse. He was taken to an old prison and down into the deepest cells of the place. Throughout the descent, he observed everything carefully looking for any means of escape. However, he could find no crack in the defenses of the place. By the time he had been placed in a dark cell, he had begun to give up any hope of an escape from the depths of the stone prison.

He began to spend his time in deep reflection, recalling all that he had seen and all that he had learned of life. After some time had passed, he called out to the guard and insisted that he be brought before the king of the realm. When the guard laughed and called him a lunatic, the old thief explained that he had a gift of extraordinary value, suited to royalty and only fit for a king to receive. The guard was impressed with the seriousness of the demand, but didn't know what to do about it. Eventually, he told the warden what the old thief was claiming. That noble character quickly imagined how he would be rewarded for bringing such a valuable gift to the king.

The next morning the old thief was taken from the depths of the prison to make an appearance at the heart of the royal court. There sat the king on a large throne and all around him were the members of the cabinet and the elite of the realm. The king was used to receiving gifts and had come to expect valuable things to be handed to him. In this case, he asked what treasure such a lowly thief might have that could be fit for a king. He asked for the item to be handed over as he had important affairs of state to attend to.

The old thief explained that he came to present a rare and valuable gift. He slipped his hand into his old cloak and carefully withdrew a small box, then handed it to the king. The ruler quickly opened the box and looking inside, suddenly flushed with rage. He yelled at the thief demanding an explanation for why in expecting a great gift he found that he was holding nothing but an ordinary plum pit.

The thief agreed that it was a plum pit, but insisted that it was by no means an ordinary seed. He explained that whoever planted the seed would reap a golden reward; for once planted the pit would become a sapling that would rapidly rise in the form of a tree that would then branch before their eyes and blossom in no time, and bear golden fruit even as they watched. That was the nature and the value of the little seed he offered freely as a gift to the king.

The king thought for a moment, then asked why if the seed was so magical, had he not planted it himself and avoided the life of a thief? The prisoner explained that whoever planted the pit had to have a clear conscious and a soul unblemished by the misuse of power and authority. If someone had stolen or taken the land or the goods of others the seed would not sprout at all, but would simply be inert. Since he was known to be a thief, he knew that the magical seed would not sprout for him. However, he was certain that the king, who must have a clear conscience and an honest soul, could plant it and immediately receive the golden reward.

The king became quiet again. After thinking over various shady dealings and some downright cruel events, the king realized that he would be exposed before all if he attempted to plant the magical seed. Stating out loud that he had never possessed a green thumb, he passed the pit to the queen. After a brief reflection, the queen passed the thing to the secretary of state, who passed it along to the secretary of defense, who gave it to the leading general, who sent it on to the treasurer, who offered it to the head of the prisons, who simply stood in a deep confused silence. Other leaders politely and promptly declined and a number of wealthy patrons simply shook their heads and turned away.

The old thief spoke again, this time saying that it was clear that each and all of them were guilty of treacheries and violations that they did not wish to be revealed. He pointed out that everyone knew that they misused their power and authority, yet never went to jail or paid for their crimes. He searched their faces as he spoke and declared that he had been sentenced to years of isolation and dark confinement simply for stealing some herbs; while they held themselves above the laws they claimed to enforce.

At that point the king felt that things had gone far enough. He called all the officials together for a consultation. After discussing the situation, the king announced that all present would contribute in order to pay the fine placed upon the thief and that he would be absolved and released presently. Then the king gave the box with the little seed back to the old thief. He stated that everyone present had been educated on that day, further promising that they would remember the lesson and be more just and more forgiving in the future. When the king asked if in fact the plum pit could produce golden fruit instantly, the old thief simply slipped it back into his cloak as he turned and walked off, a free man again.

ALL ON TRIAL

The trick employed by the old thief was more than simple sleight of hand. It was genuine magic, in the sense that magic means to change one thing into another. The thief managed to be released from his sentence while putting all the authorities in a prison of their own thought for a time. It was a bit of alchemy that changed the entire realm, at least for a moment, as greed and injustice gave way to a deeper understanding that temporarily opened the doors of forgiveness.

For one moment, everyone regardless of social stature and authority had to imagine a small but magical seed that could produce a sudden tree and burst forth with golden fruit. Each had to imagine the tree and golden fruit in their own way, for that's how imagination works. At the same time, each had to recognize a shadow within themselves that grew as quickly as the tree. Each had their own version of a golden fruit or seed and each had some darkness within them. The presence of a gold producing seed brought with it a recollection of wrongdoings and abuses of authority. For such actions also produce a kind of fruit, the kind that is darker and can leave a poison taste within.

In surrendering to the period of descent and dwelling in the depths, the old thief had found the roots of imagination that alone can undo the locks of self-imprisonment and that can surprisingly help restore the deeper foundations of the realm. Dishonesty has to begin somewhere before it comes to rule the day. "Better an unjust government than corrupt people," a poet said when considering where the roots of dishonesty might come from.

Once the old thief realized the nature of his own divine seed, he had the key to unlocking many doors. Once he accepted the fate that had befallen him, he was near the source of his release. The key turned out to be residing in the darkness within him. Having faced his inner situation fully, he became able to face anyone and anything. In reaching the seed and core of his own life, the thief became able to unlock the door of his own prison and at least momentarily open the minds and even the hearts of those in power.

The story doesn't describe the details of what he found within; rather it offers a symbol that allows each person to consider the golden seed of their own self. The plum tree has exceptional blossoms that appear before the more familiar aspects of Spring become visible. In Asia, the plum is connected to the sense of an eternal youth and the capacity of life to renew itself especially from winter's dark and desolate depths. The plum has come to symbolize the radical root of new life arising from the depths and also appearing the living seed of destiny that cracks open the hard ground and helps one survive trials and tribulations.

INNER AUTHORTY

Having found the gold hidden within the darkness, the old thief was able to turn the common world upside-down. For it is most common in this world for people to rise to the top who have not done the work of inner transformation. Being unaware of the true nature of the self and the gold hidden within, most assume that power resides in outer wealth and dominant strength. Since such outer powers always fail when faced with the deep wounds of life and pale when compared to the genuine nobility of the soul, most of those in power take to cheating and manipulating others in order to retain their power.

In the absence of a genuine authority that rises from the deep roots of being, those who hold power tend to abuse it, leaving many to think that all power is damaging and that all authority is abusive. In order to shift the typically unjust situation in the outer world, the old thief must become an authority unto himself. He must draw upon a greater source of authority than common law or elitist rules. He must be connected to an authentic authority that transcends common institutions as well as common law.

Authority is a big word that often troubles people, especially in the form of "the authorities." Yet, the roots of authority go back to words like author, augment and authentic. Genuine authority involves authoring things, being creative and original when faced with difficulties. The trouble with most authorities is that they substitute rules and use force when being truly creative would serve a greater purpose. It turns out that there is a form of "authentic authority" that is rooted, not in the daily world, but in something ancient, original, and creative.

When a person finds the root of their deeper self, they become "authentic," both original and essential. *Authenticity* involves acting from one's deepest essence, so that the uniqueness of the person becomes more awakened and involved in life. In being authentic a person acts not as a copy but as an original with first-hand knowledge and inherent creative force. In becoming authentically oneself, a person becomes capable of originality and becomes able to author aspects of their own life.

As fate would have it, that which is authentic in a person exists deep within; it is hidden, even buried like gold that must be mined in the dark depths of the earth. In order to reach the inner gold some descent into the depths of life is required. Since such descents are painful and forbidding, most people avoid them at any cost. Since such descents are necessary for true growth, life provides them in the form of fateful events. Everyone carries a golden seed in the depths of their soul, but each must also inhabit and come to know their own darkness in order to find where the inner gold has been sown and how it is to be given.

CHAPTER 4

WHAT NOT TO FORGET

An old idea suggests that a wise person finds in the depths of themselves a pattern into which everything they know fits and into which all that they don't know might fit. In other words, the inner "uniqueness" of a person contains the exact knowledge needed for life and also forms a container into which all kinds of knowledge can be placed and held. Wisdom begins with a radical self-knowledge before it becomes wise enough to be helpful and useful to others.

In traditional cultures, young people would be taken aside and introduced to their inner-selves through rites and rituals. Initiatory rites would serve young folks as occasions for self-revelation as well as opportunities to absorb wisdom from their elders. Meanwhile, the elders could observe the uniqueness of each young person and consider which life path they were intended to follow. Often, the exchange between youth and elders included a conversation about death. After all, a kind of death was required in order that the young people might end the period of childhood, while the elders were facing a more literal form of death. The youth had to let the ways of childhood die in order to grow a bigger life and the elders had to grow deeper as the end of their lives approached.

Modern mass cultures tend to overlook the uniqueness of the individual soul while also avoiding the presence and meaning of death. Whereas traditional cultures would introduce the presence of death at the onset of adult life, modern societies put off questions of death until the very end. Even then, many refuse to admit the inevitability of death or the possibility that their death could be meaningful. Modern cultures are forgetful when it comes to the unique nature of each person and disoriented when it comes to the end of life. And, increasingly modern people tend to forget who they are in the later stages of their lives.

It's not just that people go to great extremes to prolong life at any cost, but also that most have an extreme fear of death and many try to deny it altogether. Many die without dignity because death has lost its dignified place in life's mortal drama. Death is only admitted when the bodily functions fail and there is finally no alternative left but to give up on life. Having lost its connection to fate and its secret ties to destiny, death has become nothing but a failure of life. Unfortunately, when death is diminished, life loses some of its natural dignity.

Mortality is the necessary agreement for entering the road of life to begin with and all life eventually returns to the eternal night from which it arose. An exaggerated fear of death can only lead to a growing fear of life, because life includes death. Death is not the simple opposite and mortal enemy of life; rather it is the opposite of birth, and a full life includes more than one brush with death. Those who avoid death at any cost will likely fail to live life fully. In the end, the issue isn't that life fails and death claims us, more often the issue is a failure to face one's fate and live one's life the way it was intended.

An old proverb suggests: "You don't know who a person is until their last breath has gone out." In that sense, the last breath can be a revelation as much as a failure, a meaningful statement as much as a dead end. Death is the necessary punctuation for the sentence of each life. Our life includes our death and our death raises questions and sometimes offers answers about our life. Each individual life is a specific question being asked of the world and the answer is not complete until the end of the road is reached. At the end, as in the beginning, it is a question of both life and death; for the last breath brings round the original question of one's life on earth.

It's like the story of the old rabbi who lay upon his deathbed as the final hour drew near. His name was Zushya and he had lived a long enough life. He was a holy man who had studied scholarly texts and taught others for many years. He had become widely known and greatly respected. More than that, he was revered and loved by his students for his honesty and for his wit.

Now that his time had come, his faithful students gathered around to share in his final moments. With characteristic honesty, the old teacher told his students the truth of his situation. He explained that with the hour of death approaching he feared having to face God. "I am afraid," he said, "of God's final justice. I fear that I will be punished in the world to come."

The students were shocked; how could such a thing be possible? Their teacher was an exceptional religious leader who had taught them generously and guided them wisely. Now, the students began to reassure the teacher: "Rabbi you are a pure and righteous man. You have shown the leadership of Abraham, the courage of Jacob, the vision of Moses, and the moral fortitude of the greatest prophets. What do you have to fear in facing God?"

With his final breath Zushya replied to his students, "I am not afraid that God will ask me, "Zushya why were you not more like Abraham? Why were you not more like Moses? I can answer honestly that I did not have the god-given abilities of Abraham or the talents of Moses. But, if God asks me, "Zushya why were you not more like Zushya? For that I have no answer at all!" In so saying, Zushya passed into the world that waits beyond this one.

Death, they used to say, is a great teacher and often a great teacher will use their own death as a final lesson on life. The final exam turns out to have but a single question and it involves the specifics of life rather than some generalities of religion or philosophy. People go about asking: What is the meaning of life? In believing there is some general answer they miss the fine point. Since each life is specific and cannot help but be so, a better question would be: What is the meaning in my life?

In facing the end openly, it became clear to the old teacher what the divine was interested in all along. While you had the chance to live, did you become your true self? Having received the gift of life, did you learn the nature of your gifts and the purpose of them? Have you lived the life that was given to you or substituted some general model or abstract ideal? If each has but the one life to live, then there will be but one thing in question when the time for living comes to an end.

Although the teacher is a rabbi, the issue does not concern doctrines or dogmas. Rather than religious beliefs or general moralities, the divine has something specific in mind.

The same question suits everyone; it fits all shapes and sizes, yet at the same time distinguishes amongst them. All meet a common fate, saint or sinner, rabbi or banker, rich or poor. Yet, each must answer specifically and each answer is measured against the gift of life that was given to them to begin with.

When it comes to the question of whether or not you have become yourself, there is no way to cheat; there can be no excuses, no real complaints, and no big reprieves. There is no higher authority to call upon; for the final exam is not about things outside oneself. Those who believe that all the answers are "out there somewhere" are in for a shock when the final question asks who they are within themselves. The answer to the question of life was hidden inside the questioner all along.

The qualifications for entering the after-life do not derive so much from following rules and obeying commandments. We qualify for the next world by living uniquely and creatively in this one. When someone's life becomes meaningful to them their death will have some meaning for others. The old teacher made his death meaningful and memorable by stating the case for the uniqueness of each life.

The saints and prophets, the great philosophers and wise teachers may be proper models for finding the paths of discovery, but each life must eventually become a revelation of itself. Simply imitating a Moses or a Jesus, an Abraham or a Mohammed doesn't satisfy the question that the divine has for each soul. Living by religious rules and precepts may open a path of learning, but in the end no outer model can lead us all the way to becoming who we are at the core of ourselves.

For this conversation *god* is simply the shortest way to refer to the divine. When the created meets the creator something exact must be considered; something particular must be examined. The divine turns out to be most interested in the unique life of the individual soul. That's what was meant by the old idea that "inside people is where god learns." It's not a religious idea, more of a spiritual insight. When a unique life becomes fully lived everyone involved learns something and it becomes clear that god was involved all along.

The point seems all the more profound as the teacher had lived a religious life. The students may have expected a display of piety or the reassurance of a man of faith meeting his maker; but the holy man proved to be a genuine teacher right to the end. Zushya had the gift for teaching and was still using it in the last moment. He turned the attention of the students not to some divinity outside themselves, but toward the seeds of the divine within them.

Seen this way, the final judgment will not pivot upon doctrines or dogmas; for there is no theory or system that can substitute for a life unlived, for a story undeveloped, for a fate not faced, for a destiny not embraced. That's the final lesson, the last word, and essential wisdom that the good rabbi was honest enough to communicate with his final breath.

THE QUESTION OF ONE'S LIFE

Life is full of questions and beset with all kinds of problems, but in the end, each soul has the "Zushya problem." Each must answer for the life actually lived. Better to begin the consideration of the divine question sooner rather than later. Better to enter the question of one's life while still alive rather than be in fear of a final judgment. If there is a unique seed in one's life, it would be best to uncover it while there is still time to learn from it and live by its guidance.

One of the open secrets of life on earth is that the answer to life's burning question has been inscribed in one's soul to begin with. The soul is a kind of ancient library that holds the exact knowledge we seek and need most. Life is a pilgrimage intended to arrive at the center of the pilgrim's soul. From that vantage point, the issue is not whether we managed to choose the right god or the only way to live righteously; such fearful notions fail to recognize the inborn intimacy each soul already has with the divine.

Moses began being Moses when he was placed in a basket and given to the river of life. Later, he knew how to part the waters and lead others from bondage to safety. The waters held both his fate and his destiny; the knowledge he needed was within him even when he was abandoned. The basket served as the particulars of his fate from which his destiny slowly unfolded. Didn't Noah become awash with dreams before he could receive divine instructions on how to fashion ships and survive floods? Each became a prophet in their own way and each is remembered for the way they became themselves.

The great religions help to recall specific ways to serve the divine, yet what truly serves the divine is specific in each person. Buddha had to find a way to go between the two great religions of his time because he could not go along with either of them. In following the thread of his own life he passed through the eye of the needle and a "third way" was found. Those who are remembered and revered had to first remember and come to revere something seeded inside themselves. The rabbi honored the old prophets best not simply by trying to be like them, but by becoming more like himself.

Those who learn to paint like Da Vinci imitate a master; yet as long as their own inner mastery remains unknown, they are impostors. They may grow by following the brushstrokes of an original, yet only become themselves by grasping their own originality. The great teachers and artists can indicate genuine paths to follow, yet following them can only take us so far. In order to truly emulate a saint or a teacher those who follow must eventually take their own lead and make their own footprints.

We may enter paths where others have found meaning and even transcended; that's a worthy way to begin a quest. But, in order to answer the question of our own lives we must risk taking our own steps. The only genuine safety in this world comes from risking oneself completely in order to become oneself more fully.

THE UNIQUENESS OF LIFE

The most revered figures throughout the traditions of the world became memorable because they were uniquely themselves. Their behavior was uncommon, exceptional in some way, even radical. Whether a spiritual teacher or an artist, a healer or a leader; they are remembered because they managed to manifest the uniqueness within them.

Each had to awaken to a vision already in them in order that the tale of their life could become instructive to others.

Rabbi Zushya may be remembered for many valuable qualities, yet the tale of facing god's question has carried his name throughout the world. Because the drama at the end of life is universal, because the divine is involved, and because the rabbi pointed to the uniqueness of each life, the tale speaks to everyone. Being a true teacher, Zushya revealed an essential truth about life at the moment of his death. His death became a gift of life for others. It is especially a gift for those who take hold of the lesson that the divine is most interested in the self revelation of each soul. Those who claim a great interest in godly things often forget that the divine is most interested in the spark of the eternal already placed within each soul.

Meanwhile, a person doesn't have to believe in god or subscribe to a particular creed in order to intuit the question waiting at the end of life's road. Some say the final encounter involves a meeting with the deep self that was dwelling within us all along. Call it the inner spirit, the great soul or deep self, the inner genius or divine twin. It has many names but each refers to the older, wiser self that waits to be discovered throughout our lives.

The wise old woman or wise old man that dwells in the soul already knows the way our lives are aimed and styled and inclined to go. The older, wiser parts of the soul try to catch up to us at each critical juncture in our lives. Each critical turning point has a little death in it and a chance to deepen and become wiser about the life we have been given. Each person seeks a particular kind of wisdom, the kind already seeded within them.

Wisdom, like love, like life, depends upon the specifics of the person and of the situation they are in. What is wise on one occasion can be foolish on another. Whether the occasion involves a little death or a great awakening, the wisest thing is to become oneself. Life and death both conspire to uncover the essence of the living soul.

WEIRD AND WISE

In living fully and dying meaningfully, Zushya played the role of a genuine elder. With his final breath he continued to teach; he used his last words to open wider the hearts and minds of his students. Teaching was his gift, a part of his fate and part of his destiny as well. As an aspect of fate, our inner gifts incline us in certain directions and shape us in distinct ways. As an aspect of destiny, our gifts can carry us beyond normal limits and to higher levels of awareness.

At the end, the living spirit of one's life is supposed to shine through the tatters of the body's mortal cloak. The gold of the self is supposed to become more visible despite and because the body begins to fall apart. The inner knowledge is supposed to shine through and become more available as the elder becomes a kind of "living library." Traditionally, elders were valuable resources and depositories of knowledge that could provoke wisdom in others.

Zushya was at the end of the line, yet he was teaching at a high level. Perhaps he was fearful at the end; perhaps he was using the fears of his students to point to the importance of being fully alive before the end comes. They may have come to mourn his fate, but he turned their attention to their own destinies. Death is the shared fate for all who live, yet the issue at the moment of death remains the uniqueness of the individual self.

One thing the elders are supposed to be wise about is death. As an old African proverb states: The elders are wise because they know more dead people. Elders can be wiser about life because they have spent more time considering death. Knowing something about death deepens one's understanding of the gift of life. That's the old idea in which growing older also means growing deeper, incarnating further, and thus becoming wiser.

In old traditions those who acted as elders were considered to have one foot in daily life and the other foot in the otherworld. Elders acted as a bridge between the visible world and the unseen realms of spirit and soul. A person in touch with the otherworld stands out because something normally invisible can be seen through them. The old word for having a foot in each world is *weird*. The original sense of *weird* involved both fate and destiny. Becoming weird enough to be wise requires that a person learn to accommodate the strange way they are shaped within and aimed at the world.

An old idea suggests that those seeking for an elder should look for someone weird enough to be wise. For just as there can be no general wisdom, there are no "normal" elders. Normal bespeaks the "norms" that society uses to regulate people, whereas an awakened destiny always involves connections to the weird and the warp of life. In Norse mythology, as in Shakespeare, the Fates appear as the Weird Sisters who hold time and the timeless together.

Those who would become truly wise must become weird enough to be in touch with timeless things and abnormal enough to follow the guidance of the unseen. Elders are supposed to be weird, not simply "weirdos," but strange and unusual in meaningful ways. Elders are supposed to be more in touch with the otherworld, but not out of touch with the struggles in this world. Elders have one foot firmly in the ground of survival and another in the realm of great imagination. This double-minded stance serves to help the living community and even helps the species survive.

A genuine elder stands at least partially outside the social order and outside the lines of civil authority. The authority of a true elder is of a different order. The elders are not the keepers of "law and order" for they serve a higher purpose as well as a deeper order. Elders have inner authority developed by becoming the authors of their own lives and the bearers of a living destiny. Elders learn to dwell where they are most deeply connected to the vitality of life and the deepest places of connection are always avenues to the divine.

The weirdness of the elders involves roots that reach back to the origins of life and branches that stretch toward a vision of the future. The elders lead by remembering farther back than others as well as by seeing more clearly ahead. Thus, they are less likely to be strictly political leaders and more likely to be cultural and spiritual guides. The elders serve as "seers" who can see behind and beyond the politics of the day and perceive the needs of the future.

The wisdom of the elders connects survival with creation so that sustainability depends upon true creativity. Elders command genuine respect because they remember the essentials of survival as well as the arts of creation. Elders become "agents of the weird" and thereby able to bring the wisdom of the eternal to both the need for survival and the necessity to sustain the great imagination that allows culture to continually renew and revitalize itself.

In becoming weird and wise the elders become more able to stand where this world and the otherworld meet, where the temporary and the eternal converse and exchange. Thus, traditional elders become dream interpreters and keepers of life enhancing visions. They become natural healers because they have seen the wounds of life; they have learned how things fall apart and how they might come back together. Having survived their own troubles the elders are not shocked or overwhelmed by the mistakes and dilemmas of others. When more people become wise and weird, it becomes more likely that we might find solutions for the great dilemmas that plague both nature and culture.

OLDERS NOT ELDERS

Although an infant becomes a child simply by aging, a person cannot become an elder by simply becoming older. Elders fall into the category of things that are made, not born. Becoming an elder is not a "natural occurrence;" the qualities needed don't simply develop from physical changes brought on by aging. Rather, there is something meta-physical involved; something philosophical and spiritual that is required. Old age alone doesn't make the elder.

The passing of time makes everyone older, but not necessarily wiser. Many actually become more infantile and childish in old age. An extended old age can easily lead to a return of infantile attitudes and exaggerations of the ego-drive. A person either wises up to who they are at their core or else slips into narrow patterns of ego-centricity. Either a person develops a greater vision as they mature or they simply lose sight of who they were intended to be.

Increasingly, modern societies become populated with older folks who become more disoriented as time goes on. Due to better diets, "medical advances," and "technological improvements" many people live to a "ripe old age." Yet few seem to ripen into elders able to harvest knowledge from life experience and pass it along as genuine wisdom. Simplistic ideas of progress seem to diminish the true value of older people even while adding years to their lives. Instead of helping to answer essential questions about life and death, those who live longer often seem to forget more about both. The end of life seems to be becoming less revelatory and more disorienting, less meaningful and more and more meaningless.

In traditional societies the old people became the guardians of the mysteries and keepers of the higher laws of life. Having grown both older and wiser they knew best what needed to be preserved and remembered for life to be balanced and noble and meaningful. Either those "old enough to know better" became actual depositories of wisdom for the next generation or everyone suffered a kind of degeneration.

Experience alone cannot add up to genuine wisdom. Wisdom combines life experience with insight into oneself and into the world. Those who would become elder and wiser learn to extract living knowledge from the specific dramas and struggles, the tragedies and comedies they experience in life. Wisdom requires a sense of story, a feeling for where things are headed, a narrative intelligence for what is important and enduring and what is strictly temporary and mostly distracting.

The elders carry a greater vision of life because they develop insight into their own lives. They faced up to whatever fate had in store for them and found threads of destiny amidst the illusions and delusions of life. This shifts a person from holding a closed ego to a having a greater circumference that can connect the troubles of this world with the wisdom of the otherworld. Genuine wisdom relaxes hostility, settles common fears, and makes an inner balance more possible.

The elders are not supposed to be simply "out of it" or be out of touch with the hard times being faced by younger folks. Inside the elder the eternal youth remains awake to its life vision. Inside the youth an old sage is beginning to stir and seek for knowledge. Awakened elders are necessary if youth are to awaken to the inner dream of their lives.

Yet, in the current collective drama of the world, something strange has developed when it comes to the issues of becoming older and growing wiser. Although many people live longer, fewer seem to be the wiser for it. There seems to be a loss of memory and a lack of wisdom exactly where one might expect to find it. There seems to be a great forgetting where one might hope for a deep recollection of what is most important.

It's not just that people try to appear younger than their years and seem willing to trade the possibilities of wisdom for the appearance of youth. It's not only that people exploit the present in ways that damage the future for others, but also that those we expect to remember what life is all about increasingly forget who they are and have been. Modern societies seem to produce "olders" who forget instead of elders who remember what is most important about life and about death.

An increasing number of people arrive at the final moment having forgotten who they are. Some mutual forgetting is going on in which those who should help recall what is most important about life now tend to forget the meaning of their own lives. Something has happened that makes the end of life full of forgetting instead of a place where the essentials of existence are recollected and preserved.

What is the point of living longer if it doesn't mean becoming wiser and being more able to serve something beyond one's little-self? Youth may often be "wasted on the young," but now old age seems to be increasingly wasted on the elders. When those who are "old enough to know better" forget what it is all about, then older is not wiser and aging is being wasted on the aged.

The olders are elders "in absentia;" not just absent minded, but increasingly lost on the roads of life. It isn't simply a matter of disorientation, but a collective vacating of the later stages of life. Instead of elders sustaining imagination and wisdom in the world, there are hordes of "olders" who might just forget who they are and where they came from at any moment. Instead of having answers to the essential questions of life, the olders become a growing question mark themselves.

People "retire" as if there were no later stage of life to bring their full attention to. Many wander golf courses while keeping track of their "handicaps," as if willing to exchange a common handicap for a genuine purpose. Others can recount a lengthy list of their growing ailments and complicated drug treatments, while forgetting what meaning their life might entail. Some go on "permanent vacation" as if to vacate all premises before disappearing altogether. Modern culture seems to encourage older folks to remain in the cocoon of egotism with notions of simple retirement or fantasies of being forever entertained.

A GREAT FORGETTING, A LOSS OF WISDOM

Some great confusion has fallen like a shadow across the world, a mass forgetting in which the sense of meaning waiting to be discovered right under the surface of events has been obscured in favor of a compiling of information and a recitation of facts that only become forgotten. This is a time of great forgetting; especially forgetting that life is full of mysteries trying to be revealed.

"Knowledge makes a person older," they used to say and the opposite was implied as well, so that growing older should make a person more knowledgeable. Yet, it has become more common now to associate aging with forgetting. When there is no genuine growth in "growing older," aging becomes all about loss. The longer people live the more of life they seem to lose.

Some forgetfulness is natural just as eyesight begins to weaken over time. Losing all sense of who and what we are and what story we have been living involves a different order of forgetting. The first kind of forgetting misplaces things in the moment causing short-term losses; the deeper forgetting creates an absence that leaves holes in reality and makes life an unfinished story. This great forgetting has tragic results for individuals and for their families; but there is also a collective symptom involved.

Think of Zushya again. His fear wasn't that he would forget who he was; he feared that he hadn't become what he was meant to be. There is a difference between simply dropping some details and becoming lost altogether. The end is anticlimactic for those who lose the thread of their story before hand. What can god ask of a person who no longer knows who they are?

The story of human life seems to be fraying at the ends. It's not just the details of the story, but the meaning woven within it that seems in danger of being completely forgotten. If the end of life becomes less meaningful, the rest of life becomes more meaningless.

There are medical questions and biological mysteries involved; but there is a mythological ailment, a sense that more and more people are falling out of the story of life even before the end is in sight. There is a lack of wisdom and a loss of knowing elders who can recall essential things in midst of the great crises troubling both nature and culture. When those expected to remember what is most important forget almost everything, then everyone loses something. A collective forgetting in the latter ages of life drains something from all the stages of life.

Can the increasing loss of memory be a collective symptom trying to call attention back to deeper issues and greater meaning than the simple length of people's lives? Is it possible that life itself is trying to provoke an effort at recalling the deep memories and imagination that form the true inheritance of human kind? Does the problem of memory loss begin with many people forgetting that they have come to life with an inner story already seeded within them? The disease of forgetting that plagues modern people seems related to the lack of living with a conscious purpose early on.

Life depends upon the particularities and specifics of the individual soul and only there do we find real facts in the making. The loss of memory that increasingly characterizes the end of life may begin with a failure to awaken to the purpose and meaning of individual life to begin with. Under the common notions of the soul as a blank slate and the freedom to "be anything I want to be" people may be giving up and losing touch with the genuine threads of fate and destiny that make it possible to become who they are meant to be.

The increasing disorientation in modern culture makes it more difficult for individuals to find a genuine orientation in the course of their lives. Amidst notions of an "accidental universe," people come to feel accidental and lacking in genuine purpose. The lack of coherence and orientation on the outside makes the inborn seeds of self and inherent sense of direction more critical than ever. Amidst the flood of changes, the mass confusions, and the great forgetting already underway, the inner poise of the soul is essential for shaping a genuine life.

ALEITHIA: WHAT NOT TO FORGET

The ancient Greek word for truth was *aleithia* which translates as "not to forget." To be true to oneself means not to forget the nature of the life-seed planted in one's soul to begin with. Truly becoming oneself means to bring to fruition the life already seeded within. What does a person gain who learns many things but fails to know who they are at their core? When so many forget to live the life of the soul the truth will be in short supply.

The evening of one's life is intended for deep reflection not for blind regression. In the second half of life reflection is intended to replace simple reaction as the soul tries to slow down and deepen and return to its original dream of life. The later stages of life are not intended to be an appendage or an afterthought, but a chance to reveal more of life's inherent meaning before entering the afterlife. Unless this second and inward adventure develops, the outer arc of life expansion continues blindly and the inborn purpose of the individual life disappears in a fog of memory loss.

The issue at the end of life is not so much the horror of death as the tragedy of not having lived the life one was given. At the end of life our own soul must question and consider what we did with the thread of destiny we were given at the beginning. At the end of our life the gods who spoke the inspired words of fate into us review and judge what we did with that divine breath of life. At the end we become responsible, not so much for the lives of others as for our own. We become responsible for how close we came to intuiting and living out the life breathed into us at the beginning.

In so much as we become ourselves we can be said to have lived meaningfully. Only if we live meaningfully can our death also be meaningful in some way. In the end, it becomes clear that the primary task we have is to find and fulfill the shape seeded in the soul before birth broke the spell of eternity and dropped us onto the road of life and death. To conform to that shape which can only be found by shedding all other shapes, that is the "natural law" and inner gradient of our own nature which requires that we at times go against nature and against the narrowness of culture.

An old Native American teaching suggests that the elders made the most critical decisions for the tribe based upon effects that would appear seven generations down the line. The elders were seen as those with the longest vision and most able to remember things of great importance. For no one can see very far ahead who is not well anchored in the deep past. Memory is a river that flows in both directions at once; seeing what lies ahead requires remembering what went before. In losing deep memories we lose the past and the future as well as our footing in the present.

In order to see far into the future a person must stand firmly in their own life. True insights develop from finding the deeper currents that run within one's own story. The wisdom of nature seems to invest in the creation of elders by diminishing simple sight in favor of a greater and more enduring vision of life. People may have to lose some sight in order to develop long-term visions that help to connect the past to the future.

In order to see generations down the line a person must be somewhat free of the ego's typical entrapment in immediate needs and self-serving designs. Aging may lead to "coming apart at the seams;" yet falling apart can also lead to revelations of what held us together all along. Amidst the collapse of their bodies the elders stand for all that is enduring and weird and eternal in life. An old idea has it that symptoms are purpose seen from the other end of life. The symptoms of forgetfulness can be seen as attempts of the psyche to call attention to the importance of remembering. Especially remembering what is most important in the life of each person.

THE WELL OF MEMORY

Remember old Odin who gave up an eye in order to better see into things hidden below the surface of life? Odin had a great desire for wisdom; he had a dream of becoming wise and knowing. When he learned that the giant Mimir kept a deep well where all wisdom originated, he went in search of the waters of ancient knowledge.

It's helpful to know that *Mimir* means "memory" and that the deep well of knowledge was also known as the Well of Remembrance. Mimir's Well represents the living waters of life wherein the ever-flowing ancient memories continually rise to the surface in order to keep the past and the future connected. The well was situated at the roots of the World Tree that stands at the center of life. So, Odin went seeking the Well of Memory and found the center of life. He encountered the old giant and asked for a draught of the mead of wisdom. Of course, it turned out that there was a price to pay, no free lunch in this world and no wisdom for free either.

The price for a taste of wisdom was the sacrifice of an eye. Becoming wise means seeing things differently; it means not seeing in the usual ways in order to see what is unusual and extraordinary. In order to develop insights and see issues more deeply Odin had to sacrifice an eye that saw in the normal way. Anyone who would become a true seer must also become a little blind. Gaining such great vision and insight requires a sacrifice at the ordinary level of life.

Odin sacrificed common sight to gain uncommon wisdom and he did so at the well of memory. Thus, memory is essentially related to wisdom and wisdom resides where memories run deep and the ancient sources of life can be tapped. Those who would truly know something and become wise in this world must sacrifice something to the otherworld. Old age can be seen as a sacrifice that nature makes in order that wisdom might become possible and available before death arrives.

Failing eyesight is bound to dim the outer world with all its passing glories. Yet, in losing sight of common things the vision of an uncommon knowledge might grow more fully. Many immediate things may fade in order that enduring things might clarify. True learning involves a great act of remembering and short-term memory loss may be a little sacrifice intended to open the mind to a recollection of what is most important about both life and death.

The elders are supposed to forget some things in order that they might better remember the most important things. The later stages of life are supposed to revolve around the resilient tree and deep well where life ever renews as ancient memories become the source of life's future dream. Those who live to a ripe old age can lose their sight and forget themselves or else remember in deeper ways and serve as seers that can point the way for others. Those who would be wise in that way must seek and find the center of their lives and once there learn to drink from the deep well of imagination and memory.

The last stages of life either move toward a cloud of forgetting or toward a dusky light in which a person comes to see the reflections of meaning and purpose in their own life. If a person does not come to know themselves in some depth, they come to the end full of fears and angers, they arrive at the final moment unresolved, having forgotten who they were to begin with.

The point of aging is to slow downward, to descend further into the life intended by the soul. The point in aging is to fully incarnate the dream that brought each soul to life to begin with. In consciously slowing down something ancient and meaningful may finally catch up to one's life. In turning consciously within, a person may more readily find what they were longing for and looking for all along.

The presence of attention in an aged person attests to something eternal amidst the time-bound, something enduring within the temporary conditions. Sustained attention, generous intention and wit in an elder are perhaps the greatest evidence of something eternal seeded in human life. The continuity of consciousness amidst a collapsing body speaks of an invisible, underlying continuity in all of life. Thus, the elder becomes the physical embodiment of the eternal, both a dying life and a living shrine. It's not a new idea, but one known in every culture before modern times began to forget the presence of eternal things.

Being in touch with ancient things means being both old and young at the same time. The ancient and knowing part of the soul is the seat of the "beginner's mind" as well as the dwelling of the wise old soul within us. Those who are willing to become truly old also become young again as the dream of life continually returns to them. In being nearest to the door of death, the elders can see back along the course of life and identify what is essential and what is not. In becoming wise old souls, the elders more firmly know and more clearly hold the inner sense of meaning and purpose that first surfaced during their youth.

The genuine elder becomes a complex living symbol; on one side evidence of the inevitable decay of life; on the other side an example of the inner gold of the deep self shining through the tatters of one's life. When a person learns to become who they already are at their core they find a way to live with themselves even in dark times. They become valuable and effective within the terms of their own fate, within the alignment of their own destiny. They leave footprints that others can follow at least part of the way. They mark the road of life with signs that remind everyone that there are ways the soul would follow no matter the condition of the world.

The idea isn't simply to age well, but to become ancient in ways that can draw upon the archetypal knowledge that sustained the ancestors and that can assist the future. If those growing older become more like elders, the roots of deep imagination may be found again. If life becomes more attuned to the promptings and yearnings of the inner life, culture may become less random and accidental and become again more purposeful and meaningful, less filled with fear and more imbued with beauty.

CHAPTER 5

OUR LOT IN LIFE

There's an old tale that tells of a great jar with bits of wood in it. The pieces of wood are taken from the Tree of Life and each bit has an essential word written upon it. Before a child is born the jar is shaken and the first chip that falls out becomes the "lot in life" for that soul. *Lot* is an old word meaning a "chip of wood." In a sense, we are each a chip off the same old universal block and each a living word taken from the Tree of Life that stands at the center of the cosmos. Our fate falls to us by virtue of a mythic lottery and our lot in life secretly connects us back to the tree at the center which is also called the Tree of Destiny.

As an element of fate our allotment is just a small share in the great game of life; yet it is also our human lot to be inscribed with a divine word. At some essential level we are each a word in the great alphabet and living language of eternity. "In the beginning was the word" and each birth repeats the original act of creation as the paradox of life on earth makes us both limited and divine at the same time. Our life potential is inextricably woven to our limitations, just as our fate holds and hides hints of a destiny that secretly ties us back to the unseen.

We are human by lot and divine by origin; limited by fate, yet driven by destiny, each person a living puzzle as well as a divine experiment. The divine pattern within gives us our essential chance at life as well as the specific inner language and poetics of our soul. In the midst of the confusion and uncertainty of the world around us, the divine pattern is the underlying source of unity within us. Should we learn to express the divine word within us our destiny becomes pronounced and we become agents of the ongoing creation of the world.

Finding the inner unity of the soul requires that we first accept our lot in life, not in some fatalistic way, but in a conscious recognition of the necessity of it. For whatever comes to life must pass through the womb of necessity. Our fate includes the bit and bite of necessity that places us in time as well as the timeless song in the soul that keeps us longing for the eternal. If we don't live out the portion of eternity given to us, no one will ever live it. For each soul is unique, each life a project conceived by the divine, and each a chance that life itself is taking.

Life is the original game of chance, the ancient lottery, and in the end the "only game in town." Since no one can "have it all," each must begin with their specific share in the grand lottery of life. Our fate is "what we bring to the table," the hand that we were dealt when we first entered the game. Coming to life is a big gamble, one our souls have an essential stake in, for there are risks our souls would take even where others might play it safe. The divine word that gives us our first chance at life also provides us with any second chances we might receive.

In the end, and when all the "chips are down," the only safety in life involves taking the right risk and risking the life story already set within the soul. We either play the hand dealt to us at the beginning or run the risk of not really living the life we were given. If we refuse our fate, we lose our true sense of destiny. As long as we follow the threads of fate and destiny woven into our soul, we always have a chance.

THE SISTERS OF FATE

When considered as a group the Fates have the title *Moira* meaning "allotment or share;" for they share out the elements that make each life specific and uniquely woven within. *Moira* refers to the lot given at the beginning, but it also shares roots with *mors*, an old word for death that gives us our sense of "mortality." In that sense, the Fates are the arbiters of our chance at life and they are the harbingers of death; they are part of the "immortals" and they also represent mortality.

The Sisters of Fate are part of the essential mystery of life, primordial members of the universal mythic family who layer the world with secrets and lay each thing in its place and lace it through with light and dark. They spin the subtle threads of existence and weave the lasting patterns of life and set the endless web in motion. In Greek myth, the Fates were considered to be first-born, the primal daughters of life birthed from the eternal darkness of Night and the elemental presence of Necessity. Of necessity, they sit at the intersection where the threads of the eternal become woven with the limitations of time. They touch each thing created and incarnated into this world where necessity rules and even the gods must at times obey. In mythic terms, the presence of fate is as necessary as the night for the world to exist.

The Sisters of Fate represent the feminine touch that weaves the subtle designs and patterns set within each soul. The gods may pronounce their words upon us, but the Fates do the handiwork of connecting the divine threads to the earthly fabric of life. They handle the fine filaments of fate and destiny and weave the warp and weft that sets each living soul into the web of the world. As master spinners they know how to weave a good tale with secrets waiting to be discovered and fateful events that cannot be avoided. They know that in a good story, the essential aspects of the tale are present at the beginning and that the end is implied as well.

Being first-born, the Fates attend each subsequent birth and give each newborn its particular share of life. Lachesis is the sister who presides over the process of dispensing the lots. She is also the one who sets the divine word within the soul and pulls from it the subtle and surprising thread of one's destiny. For the Fates are weavers extraordinaire as well as divine storytellers. They set the plot of each life in play and bring it all to a conclusion at a time that they choose and that we must obey. They spin the inner stories that tie us to the web and pull us onto the stage of life in order that we may take part in the divine drama and play a role in how it continues.

They dress our souls in the threads of fate and destiny as we are secretly costumed for our roles in life's drama from before the moment of our birth. They measure out the thread of each life, and twine it to the living drama of existence. Clotho is the sister who fixes the pattern and fashions the texture within each soul. We derive the word *cloth* from her name as well as *clothes* and a wide patchwork of words related to spinning and weaving. It is Clotho who gives the unique "twist of fate" that makes each person an "original," never to be repeated no matter how many souls are born.

Of the three sisters, Atropos was considered to be the oldest. Being oldest makes her the first one born, yet much of her work has to do with how things end. She was said to fix the end and cut the life thread with her shears when the time comes. Atropos is the hard sister in life who fixes the pattern in the depths of each soul making the inclinations and purpose of one's life irreversible. *Atropos* also means "inflexible" and "she who cannot be turned." She represents all that is "hard wired" in us, the intractable qualities and inevitable characteristics that can't be denied.

Also called "the inevitable," from her name we derive "atrophe," the sense that things diminish and wear down and wither away. Being involved with endings, Atropos specializes in "hindsight." Often fate's inevitability appears only in review, as looking back we can see what was bound to happen all along. The third sister stands at the end of life's road, but is also present whenever we encounter the specific limitations and dramatic twists of fate that wind us close to our soul's intended destination.

MIDWIVES OF THE SOUL

The Sisters of Fate are the original midwives, for they touch each soul when it is mid-way between the divine realm and the manifest world. They hold the soul again when its earthly tale has come to an end and it is time to return to the place of origins. The old practices of midwives derived from the sisters of the soul, for midwives used to attend to wakes and funerals as well as to births. They would wash each newborn and wrap it in swaddling cloth and they would also anoint the newly deceased with oil and wrap them in mournful shrouds.

As handmaidens of the critical times of birth and death, midwives worked close to the mysteries of life and were considered to have the sense of "second sight." Modern people may have ultrasounds that expose the aspects of the fetus before it is born, but midwives were keen observers and subtle seers that could often see what others failed to notice. They were "diviners" who could catch glimpses of divine elements that appear at the critical moments of life. When assisting at births they would watch for signs and symbols that could indicate the nature of the soul being born and the way it was aimed at the world. Midwives were the earthly representatives of the Sisters of Fate and were often the first to notice the inner nature of the children coming to life with their allotted patterns, their innate gifts, and their woven destinies.

An old Mayan tale tells of a time when midwives could see with second sight and attended carefully to each new soul coming into the world. That was before the disasters that made it so difficult for people to perceive the gifts that each child brings. They say the trouble began in a simple village where a certain woman entered her time of labor and called for the midwife to come. Shortly after the midwife arrived, the crowning moment occurred and soon the newborn could be seen for the first time. The midwife observed that it was a boy, but she could also see that the child came bearing gifts.

The little fellow had a green cloak on his back and he held a small bowl filled with water in his hand. In the intensity and excitement of the birth no one else noticed the child's gifts. The mother was too exhausted from laboring and the infant was too new and helpless to know anything of the gifts he carried. The midwife took the cloak and the bowl from the infant and hid them away.

After seven days, the midwife arranged the traditional ceremony for welcoming the newborn and giving thanks that both the mother and child were healthy. Everyone came to celebrate the birth and make a proper welcome for the new one in the world. The baby was washed and cleansed and was given a name that carried many meanings. He was called Poder which meant gift, for every child is a gift to this world. Poder also meant power and ability and fate and fortune as well. Some said it meant luck and they repeated the name as if to instill good fortune in the child.

After completing the welcoming ceremony, the midwife took the child's gifts and carried them out into the mountains beyond the village. She gave the gifts to certain people out in the hills and they hid them away carefully. No one told the family of the gifts the child brought with him and nothing of it was mentioned to Poder.

After being welcomed into this world and being nursed, the boy took to life and grew rapidly. He did all the things that a child was expected to do and had his share of the good and bad experiences that shape childhood. Eventually, Poder reached the period when childhood comes to a close and something else must begin. In becoming a youth, Poder began to ask the questions that young people often ask. He wondered why he was here and whether he had something to give to this world. When he was unable to come to a meaningful conclusion on his own, he sought out the midwife whom everyone considered to be a wise person.

When he found the wise woman he asked her if there was a purpose for his life. He asked if he had a gift to give to this world and if the world had something to give to him. The midwife answered indirectly. She said that everyone comes to this world with gifts intended to be given. She explained that each child was welcomed by everyone because most understood that they would be the beneficiaries when the child became able to give forth what they brought to this world. In the meantime, she said that it was time for him to leave his childhood behind. It was time for him to make a journey to the holy hills and seek the answers for himself.

Poder wasted no time. He went to his parents and told them that he would be leaving in order to search for knowledge. His mother gave him food for the journey and a blessing for the road and Poder left the village and left behind everything he knew. With nothing but a little food and some water he began to wander in the holy hills. After a time the food was consumed and all he carried were his questions about himself and the nature of this world.

After wandering about, Poder came upon some people keeping vigils and doing ceremonies in the hills. They welcomed him warmly and asked why he walked the hills alone. Poder explained that he was searching for answers and that he desired to know if he had something to give to the world and if the world had something to give to him. The people answered that both things were true and that each person was intended to be part of a vital exchange that sustained the world. After sharing food with the youth, they fetched the green cloak and the earthen bowl full of water that formed his birthright. They handed the items to Poder and explained that he had been born with those exact gifts and that the time had come for him to learn the purpose of them.

Poder was introduced to a person who had similar abilities in order to receive training in how to handle and protect his gifts. That's when he learned that those who were born with a green cloak and bowl of water were intended to become rainmakers. Since that area was hot most of the time and dry most of the year a talent for bringing rain could be lifesaving for everyone. Poder paid close attention and soon became able to roll up into the clouds and loosen the rain waters that they held. He learned how to handle his gifts and when to use them and he became ready to give something to the world.

When he returned to the village, Poder was in possession of his natural gifts and he began to serve the people by bringing rain down so they could grow corn and beans and enough squash to sustain life. When he wasn't using his gifts, Poder kept them hidden. Nevertheless, people recognized that he was gifted and that he used his talents to sustain the lives of everyone in the village. Poder became recognized as being gifted and soon became a favorite son of the people.

Then, it happened that there was a youth in the village who had no idea of his god-given gifts. For some reasons no one else knew the nature of that boy's inner inheritance either. As a result, that fellow felt that he had no power of his own and no luck that he could draw upon. No one seemed to know how to help him, so he became interested in Poder who everyone else had an interest in. He began to follow Poder around in order to learn where he kept his gifts and how he was able to accomplish the rainmaking.

One day, when Poder was occupied elsewhere, the other fellow found the cloak and the bowl and took them from the hiding place. He began to imitate the motions that he had seen Poder use to roll up into the clouds. Soon, he was able to roll up and land in some dark clouds that were laying low over the land. Once up there the fellow began to experiment with Poder's gifts. Soon enough, the clouds began to rumble and rain started to fall down upon the world. However, the one who stole the gifts had no real knowledge of how to use them and what began as a shower soon became a downpour.

The imitator had no notion of how to stop the rain once it began and the downpour swelled into a great storm. The winds gathered and torrential rains began to pound down on the village and pelt the crops below. It became clear to those being rained upon that all their plantings were being washed away and that the entire village might be lost in the ensuing flood. No one knew what to do and no one had the power to stop the flood that the thief had let lose on the world.

People say that the flood would have continued with no end had god not become angry at the misuse of the god-given powers. They say that it was god who finally stopped the rain and sent the false rainmaker back down to earth. After the deluge Poder was able to reclaim his gifts and the people were eventually able to restore the village and plant new crops when the land dried out.

However, after those events they say that no one, not even the midwives were able to see the gifts that children bring to this world when they are born. Furthermore, they say that we are the descendents of those folks and that is why most people now don't know what their natural gifts and powers might be. Everyone remains gifted in some way, for that is a necessity for human life and even the anger of god can't take that away. Meanwhile, the gifts of many people remain hidden. Many live without finding their luck and learning how they are fated to be and where their destiny might lead. To this day people wander about and often become lost because they fail to learn what it is that they have to give to this world and what the world has to give to them.

SECOND BIRTH, SECOND SIGHT

It's a cautionary tale, the kind of folklore used to explain the mess that the world can fall into. It also reminds everyone that coming of age involves a search for self knowledge that can affect one's whole life and the lives of others. Poder stands for the luck and power, the fate and fortune that each person carries whether they know it or not. For no child comes to this world empty handed or with a completely clean slate. What was given before birth tries to be found again when childhood is over and the time has come to claim one's natural birthright. Those who fail to find and claim their natural gifts run the risk of not living out their true purpose and thereby darkening the fate of the world and adding to the storms of life.

The story of Poder is a birth story, but also a second birth or re-birth story. It is the basic human story of losing and finding one's inner gifts and true orientation to the world. It is an initiation tale and a myth of how community grows greater or suffers more deeply depending on the knowledge and use of the natural gifts of its members. Poder's birth is exemplary, an example to learn from, a prototype for seeing the underlying issues and deeper questions of all who are born. Each child born is another Poder; everyone arrives already gifted and fated to wonder what they might have to give and receive in this world.

Everyone has their own "poder complex," their inner mixture of powers, gifts and fortune; the fate of the world can turn according to the way such inner qualities are used. The great flood of destruction was precipitated by the misuse of natural gifts by someone who lacked a proper welcome to this world. If people don't find and learn to use their innate gifts and powers, those who have no idea how to handle power will rise to the top. It happens all the time as those who don't know their inner value or true purpose become hungry for power of any kind. At the same time, others who don't understand what they came here to give will willingly give their power over to those who can't help but misuse it. When things turn upside down and power is in the wrong hands, all kinds of exploitation results and even the basic elements of life become endangered.

Culture means to cultivate, both to grow crops that sustain life and to develop the inner resources and natural talents of each person. Life is not neutral or tame and each has the ability to become a boon or a bane to the rest of the human village. The difference turns on whether people feel welcome in this world and whether they find ways to use their gifts and make a meaningful way in life. When a culture forgets this, it will fail to welcome the newborns, it will neglect its own youth, and its old people will cling to lives not fully lived. Deficient of meaningful signs and symbols, lacking portents of purpose and destiny, people can become reduced to vagrant consumers of a world in which they have nothing essential to give or to learn.

The birth of each infant is a rebirth of meaning in the world. Signs and symbols, auguries and fates attend every birth and are part of each birth-rite. Once upon a time, midwives and others studied the moment of birth looking for signs not just of life, but also seeking for indications of where that child might go in life. That was before the flood tide of facts and figures obscured the second sight needed to see the more subtle aspects of this world. Now, the mystery of new life with its threads of fate and hints of destiny becomes reduced to statistical measurements. The "vital signs" no longer include glimpses of the vital symbols that are the inner inheritance of each child. Birth has become more literal, life has become more linear, and death has become mostly a dead end.

Meanwhile, each child arrives as a little epiphany accompanied by symbols and imbued with hidden gifts and unseen potentials. *Infant* comes from the Latin "non-fans" meaning "not speaking." The infant cannot speak for itself or of itself, but can only cry out with the sound of life caught between the teeth of time and the song of eternity. Midwives used to represent the communal interest in the inner value of each newborn. For each child is a gift to their community as well as a descendant of their birth family. The inherent gifts of each person are intended to be given to the human community and a second birth is required for the inner value and life direction to become fully conscious.

Throughout youth the hidden signs try to appear again as part of the psychological birth intended to deliver the shape and meaning of one's inner life. The inevitable troubles of youth are a kind of second labor of life intended to lead to a revelation of the inner nature and innate gifts of the soul. The infant that was unable to speak for itself becomes driven to learn the inner language and speech of its own soul. Each child may be a gift to its people, but each can become a burden to the community until their inner abilities are found and used. Young people need hints of their inherent orientation to life or they can become rebellious in the wrong direction or else passive consumers at the table of life.

Imagining each child as gifted doesn't simply solve the problems of identity and self worth that develop in youth. In many ways, it creates a bigger problem as it shifts the welcoming of youth to a deeper level of engagement. Like Poder, the soul of each person expects to have a revelatory appointment with their own gifted nature and an encounter that confirms and anoints their purpose in the world. The second birth is the second chance for a community to welcome fully and properly bless the child who came to them bearing gifts. Youth need an education of the spirit, not simply the kind of general instruction given to children still unable to speak for themselves.

All the potentials of each life return again and try to surface at the crossroads between childhood and adult life. The questions that Poder asks continue to echo in the soul of each person: Do I have something to give to this world and does the world have something to give to me? Each person is a question being asked of the world, each a unique version of Poder. Each is marked from birth, not necessarily with an original sin, more likely with original gifts and an imbedded sense of purpose. Some kind of offense or sin against nature does occur when people are not welcomed as gift-givers and not assisted in the necessary search to reclaim their own birthright.

We are born within a meaning that we live an entire life to learn and some aspect of that meaning must become revealed during youth. At each critical turn and at each new stage of life the essential questions and fateful issues try to arrest our attention and return us to the search for our inner inheritance. If the soul's critical appointments remain unfulfilled we can become ill-fated and deeply disappointed with life itself. Life can seem a wasteland of accidental hills and empty valleys; instead of the dance of life, we can find ourselves simply passing the time and wasting away in the village of the un-awakened.

THE HOLY HILLS

The powers and abilities that enter the world with each child may be increasingly hidden from the eyes of people, but even god couldn't remove the natural gifts altogether. It may be our mutual lot in life to be born at a difficult time and in an era when many essential things are forgotten. However, it remains the nature of humans to be imbued with a pattern that can make meaning and value from the events of both the inner life and the outer world. Forgotten knowledge can never be completely lost and what we so desperately need waits to be found again in the holy hills that wait beyond the busy streets and rushing highways of the modern world.

In order to find genuine answers to essential questions, Poder had to leave the village of daily life and wander in the holy hills. The hills are holy because gifts can be reclaimed there and because people dwelling there understand the nature and purpose of god-given talents and can give training in how to handle them. The holy hills appear wherever people recall the deeper purpose of learning, they are the site for the second birth and the true ground of a "higher education."

The holy hills appear whenever people receive a proper welcome in this world and become able to give their natural gifts. The gifts we have been given are intended to be given to others and others must also help us recognize and understand what we carry within. In the holy hills that extend beyond what most call the "real world," people can receive the gifts that are theirs to begin with and learn how to use their talents and enter fully the ongoing creation and great dance of life.

Although we are each born with a divine message etched within us, we must search far and wide to decipher the meaning that we carry. We can't fully claim our god-given talents and abilities until others recognize the divine word within us and help to reveal it. We each have our in-born gifts, but they must also be given to us; we carry them from birth, but must find others able to help us reclaim our true birthright. That which is naturally ours to have must become consciously ours to give, otherwise we are but uneasy guests on the dark face of the earth.

Meanwhile, the paths to discovering the inner gifts become more difficult to find. Wide roads and broad highways run in all directions while the pathways for inner awakening become more obscure. In the rush to "get somewhere in life" more and more people wind up disoriented and unwelcome in the world. From the view of natural talents and inner purpose, from the angle of fate and destiny, the world seems to be turned backward and upside down. Despite the ancient instinct to become one who gives as well as receives from life, most people now identify as consumers.

The trouble with consuming is that in the end people can't get enough of what they don't really want. The trouble with a "consumer society" is that it eventually consumes itself. In becoming aware of one's natural gifts the need to give something to the world becomes stronger than the hunger to consume it. Giving from the inherent gifts leads to receiving a blessing from the world. Such a genuine exchange nourishes both the individual and their community at the same time as it employs others to become proper mentors and elders. In assisting young women and men to grasp their natural gifts, older folks retouch their own potentials and reactivate their own gifts and purposes in life.

Typically, someone other than the physical parents must perceive and nurture the hidden nature and genuine core of a young person. Those who assist at the second birth become the metaphysical parents who take responsibility for protecting and guiding the life-spirit awakening in each young person. The true teachers and genuine guides in our lives are those who can see the gifts we bring and help us learn how to handle them and give them freely. Whoever does that, man or woman, younger or older, becomes a midwife to our souls.

Whoever takes a genuine interest in the lives of others can help their inner "Poder" to awaken. My aunt did that for me even though she thought she had given me the wrong book. The inner gifts and natural inclinations are trying to become conscious to us; when someone takes an interest and offers a helping hand, even mistakes can help us awaken. My aunt asked what I was most interested in at the time, but my soul was already asking the "Poder question:" What do I have to give to the world and what does the world have to give to me? For a moment, my aunt and I met in the holy hills as the hand of fate turned a seeming mistake into a gift that spoke to the signs and symbols trying to become conscious in me.

The holy hills can suddenly appear where fate and destiny conspire to reveal who we are and what we must become to make a genuine path through this world. The moments in which we first encounter elements of our fate and destiny can be small, yet can also be momentous as they give momentum to the life-spirit trying to grow within us. Each person must have at least one "Poder moment" in which their inner gifts and natural inheritance can be seen. The occasions when we stand near the complex of our birthright mark us in some way that cannot be erased, but can be seen in reviewing our life and in reflecting upon our youth.

Each already carries within them what most needs to be awakened and recognized and what most needs to be blessed. Before taking up the paths of responsibility, young people need a "walkabout" in the holy hills that can lead them to a discovery of what they already carry within them. A general education, whether it be in the "finest schools" or the "school of hard knocks" prepares a person for getting along on the surface of life. A genuine education involves a true awakening to one's purpose in life as well as a recollection and confirmation of one's god-given gifts.

People complain that young people think that "the world owes them something" and actually, it does. The world owes young people genuine opportunities to find what gifts and abilities they carry within and what story they came here to live out. When the second birth expected by the soul doesn't occur or else happens in a haphazard manner people can be disoriented throughout their lives. Feeling existentially unwelcome and unblessed, young people can easily become overwhelmed and lost in the floods of change and in the storms of life.

The "generation gap" exists so that genuine education might develop and creatively connect everyone to the hidden threads of being. Mentors and elders are those who have awakened to their own inner gifts and life callings. In learning to live with genuine purpose they develop second sight and become able to perceive the gifted nature and natural inclinations of other people. In perceiving the god-given gifts of the youth they become midwives of the soul and "god-parents" in the original sense. The idea of god-parents derives from the intuition that someone needs to protect the gifts of young people and help them reclaim what is essential for fulfilling their lives.

Until, modern times when it became mostly a civic task, education was considered a sacred work. It was sacred because it involved the indwelling spirit in the student and because it required an awakened spirit in the teachers. Spirit to spirit, genius to genius, soul to soul go the true lessons that help young people become themselves. Ultimately, each person holds the key to the story trying to be lived from within, but first someone else must help unlock the mystery of one's life. There is a second level of midwifery that is needed for a person's fate to be opened up so that a glimpse of a true destiny can occur.

Genuine teachers represent the inner qualities lived out, the potentials actualized, the purpose of the soul being truly embodied. Remember old Zushya? He was trying to remind everyone that the question asked at the end of life develops from the questions that form in the soul during youth. In seeking to learn what we have to give to the world we move closer to finding a genuine way to be blessed by it. Finding genuine answers to the questions that burn within leads to becoming the person we were secretly intended to be when we first received our lot in life and the divine word written upon it.

When the true birthright has not been found or been confirmed, young people can feel inclined to throw their own life away or even wreck the lives of others. The young thief in the tale of Poder had not been welcomed properly. He had no sense of his true nature and no knowledge of his inner name. He had no wise midwife to turn to and no blessing for his journey on the roads of life. He did not hear the promise of a genuine calling in life and did not trust that there were answers within him. Unlike the old thief in the tale of the golden pit, he had no sense of what he carried inside the cloak of his life. When he grew old enough to have an effect on the world he caused a furious storm by trying to handle powers not tuned to his own nature.

Empty of some intended meaning life can become the mere surviving of circumstances rather than an adventure of self discovery. Being unanchored in the world many drown in the common details of life, overwhelmed and swept away on the tides of chance. We arrive at a place where most adults, lacking a blessing for their own inner life and purpose, become powerless to bless the lives of the next generation. Instead of a village waiting to receive the innate gifts of its children, youth become a burden, an increasing cost in a world where everything has a price. Feeling fundamentally empty and bereft of inner meaning, people accept the role of simply consuming the world, as if the hunger of infancy is extended to the entire course of life.

The exaggeration of the importance of choice in consumer societies is a weak sister when compared to the old idea of a vocation that truly calls to the indwelling spirit in one's soul. In the long run, the point is more to be chosen than to simply learn to choose from a menu of options. In being chosen and in responding to a genuine call a person becomes more capable of meaningful choices. Once they know that they have something specific to give to others, they become more able to choose wisely amongst what the world offers to them.

Once awakened to their inner life young people are naturally altruistic. They need to give of themselves in order to have a genuine sense of being meaningful and in order to find a way of feeling welcome in the world. At later stages of life people need to give back from what they have learned, as that which is given to us must in turn be given to others. Giving from one's gifted areas helps to reveal genuine elements of one's destiny and helps to sustain the vitality in one's life. Each person either contributes to the great gift-giving at the center of life's continuous exchange or else steals from the dance of life. Truly participating requires that we find and learn to give what we have already been gifted with.

THE SECOND HAND OF FATE

It may be our shared fate to live at a time of great storms and sea changes that affect both nature and culture. The presence of the holy hills of learning and the paths of genuine discovery may be obscured by the flooding changes that threaten to overwhelm everyone. The ocean of facts and figures and the speed of mass communication may seem to drown out the importance of individual life. Yet it is only in the deep recesses of the individual soul that the true meanings and genuine purposes of life continue to be born.

We are in the "hands of fate" from the very beginning and our own hands bear a unique imprint that will never be repeated exactly. Fate is written on our hands with compelling lines and distinct fingerprints that mark us as already scripted in mysterious ways. We are touched by fate and leave our own imprints on everything we touch. We begin life with the "hand that fate has dealt to us;" yet, fate always has another hand to play and destiny is the second hand of fate. Our fate is more an oracle set within us than an outcome determined for us. When we accept that which limits and restricts our lives from within we become more available to fate's second hand and the hidden threads of purpose and meaning imprinted at the core of our lives.

Both our fate and our destiny travel with us throughout life, they are the "familiars" of our lives that limit us with one hand and open us to great possibilities with the other. Fate becomes the specific tangle of life issues to which we must surrender if we wish to find a pathway to our intended destination. Fate inscribes a territory that we are bound to enter and destiny can be the only way out of the area we are fated to experience.

Acceptance of fate is only in the moment as happens when Poder accepts that something essential for his life is missing and must be found. A similar shift from restricting fate to awakening destiny occurs when the old thief accepts that there can be no simple escape from his prison cell. In surrendering to the circumstances of his fate he finds the golden seed that opens the prison gates for him and even opens the minds of those who close the gates on others. The gift being sought and the seed needed for growth were inside all along, but could only be grasped when the fateful limitations were accepted.

Our fate restricts us so that our destiny can find us, so that we can find again the gifts we came to give to the world and receive the blessing the world would give to us. Destiny hides within the unique twist of fate that makes each soul original and capable of contributing to the ongoing drama of creation and the imagination needed to "transform a world of fear into a world of beauty."

II

The Dream of Life

"We are wrapped around a mystery to which we were drawn before we were born."

CHAPTER 6

THE TWO AGREEMENTS

Soul is everywhere, but hard to see. It is an essential part of each living thing, but has no substance of its own. The soul is an indwelling, animating, and connecting force without which we cannot live. Yet, it cannot be seen directly or be proven to exist. By its nature the soul is "there-not-there;" we can feel its subtle presence and we can anguish in its absence; but we cannot pin it down or hold it firm. The soul is a betwixt and between thing; neither physical nor spiritual, but something that participates in both realms. The soul is another kind of body, a subtle body that partakes of both spirituality and physicality.

As the third element in the trinity of existence, soul fills the space between spirit and matter, it grounds the spirit while it animating the body and helping to refine the senses. Soul keeps spirit and matter related by opening an in-between realm of imagination, passion, and deep reflection, that is not simply physical or material on the one hand, nor completely spiritual and abstract on the other. The soul can grow and more soul can be made; but it cannot be hoarded or be fixed in a certain place.

It used to be said that soul is the beginning of all motion and the source of all changes. As it moves between one thing and another, between the individual and the sensate world, between one heart and another, between the immediate and the divine; soul is the connecting agent of existence. By its nature soul is the mutable, multiple, changeable aspect of both the world and individual life. As the animating force of natural life, soul was termed to be "anima mundi"—the living, breathing soul of the world. Aboriginal people called it "yorro, yorro"—everything in the world having soul, standing up and speaking to you.

Soul is the essential inter-mediary and subtle go-between that connects unlike things; it holds the physical in touch with the divine and the immediate contemporary with the eternal. As natural intermediary and go-between, the soul is the magical third; it is the narrative force that keeps the story going; it knows how things are secretly connected and that the third time is a charm. Soul is the connecting principle of life, the "both-and" factor, the unifying third between any opposing forces.

When we lose our way in this world it is the soul's way of being in touch with the world that has been lost. We are most lost and truly abandoned when we have lost touch with our own soul, with our own inward style and way of being in the world. Soul is the missing ingredient when things fall apart, just as it was the animating force that first brought us to life.

Old ways of viewing human life involved a unity of three instead of the polarity of two that develops between the spiritual and the physical. The three can be termed body, soul, and mind; or body, soul, and spirit. Body and spirit will one day separate as the body returns to the earth and the spirit departs to the unseen realm; meanwhile it is the intimacy of the soul that holds them near each other. When the old imagination and three-fold way of seeing collapses into a bi-furcated world view, we are left with the famous mind-body split and the blind limitations of either-or thinking.

The soulless split between mind and body generates a gap between culture and nature; as culture becomes more ideological and nature becomes but matter to be manipulated and exploited. When life becomes more polarized than it need be and things become more divided than they should be, it is the way of the soul that is missing and needed to heal the divisions and make things whole again. Soul involves the genuine cultivation of ideas and the living imagination that produces art and culture; but soul also relates to the essence of nature and to natural ways of changing and growing.

Soul is the arbiter of our incarnation and the source of our deep connection with certain places. Any intrigue with place is also an intrigue with soul. For our soul instinctively knows where and how we should sink our feet into the mud of creation and grow our roots down. Spirit may seek peak experiences and the heavenly heights; but soul would have us incarnate fully and would help us to grow deep roots that allow the spirit of our life to branch out.

Soul knows which "walk of life" the soles of our feet are attuned to; just as it knows which rhythms and tunes can keep our heart beating and singing and remaining open to the world. Soul is the secret within culture and the dream within the heart of nature. Wherever nature and culture meet, soul is present and it is the missing element where and when culture and nature collide.

Soul adds "psychic reality" to common experience; it is the psychic go-between that carries messages between this world and the otherworld, between the literal world and the spiritual realm beyond it all. The soul is all-embracing, not seduced by either-or thinking, by us-and-them divisions, or by the pretensions of subject-object dichotomies. Soul is the "missing third" that presents the mysterious, hidden aspect of any situation. Soul is the light hidden inside the dark as well as the shading that gives beauty its shape. It is the inner quintessence that holds things together within us and holds us within the world.

Without our soul and the inner pattern that animates it, we are no one at all. In so much as we are truly individual from others, in so far as we come to know ourselves and live uniquely, we are en-souled. When soul becomes diminished in us we become as an empty shell regardless of our physical attributes or our lofty station in life. The soul keeps body and mind, pulse and spirit connected and we are most connected, body and soul, when we live close to the innate pattern set within our souls to begin with.

Soul has hidden gold, and inner vision, and a light that rises from the deep. The inner light of the soul is not a reflection of the outer world; for the soul flickers with an inward light, a candle that burns with emotional heat and that also knows ecstatic flames. Soul is the secret connection, the hidden glue of the world; it is the erotic factor inside each life and within the blessed intimacy of all things.

ORIGINS OF THE SOUL

Ancient Greek philosophers imagined the soul to be a butterfly or "night moth" that underwent continuous transformations, or else a beautiful and mysterious woman. The old Greek word for butterfly was *psyche* and that was also the name of the soulful woman in the myth of Eros and Psyche. As the psychological factor soul can be called *psyche*, as the inner animating life force it is called *anima*. As a deeply related and essentially connected aspect of life soul has a feminine quality that keeps us in touch with our deepest feelings and would have us ready for continuous transformations.

In contrast to the tendency of spirit to unify under a single idea or singular image of the divine, the soul thrives on diversity and multiplicity. In many ancient traditions a person was considered to have more than one soul. Besides the immediacy of the "body soul," there could be a second soul that maintains a secret relationship with particular aspects of nature. A specific bird or type of tree would be a living symbol of the individual soul and could provide a personal way to connect to the soul of nature. This "second soul" could also be imaged as a flame on a candle that can illuminate the darkness and light the way for the one who both carries it and is carried by it.

Tribal philosophies often connect the living soul to breath as well as to the subtle presence of dreams. Thus, fainting can be imagined as a momentary loss of soul, a slipping out of soul's conscious connections to this world. Dreaming involves adventures that the second soul undertakes while the body soul sleeps its sleep. The dreaming soul participates in another kind of consciousness, the kind of mystery born of darkness and the night, the kind that is necessary if a person would truly awaken. Our soul can't help but be mysterious and mythic, multiple, and mystical as well, for we are threaded through with dreams each night just as we exchange each breath with the trees of nature.

There are many tales of the origins and nature of the human soul. Myths in South America describe the soul as being capable of returning to the center of the cosmos from which it originally arose. When the body falls into sleep each night, the soul is said to travel all the way to the original source of life. As cosmic go-between the soul keeps each person secretly connected to the origins of life. Having arrived at the center, the soul receives a dream message to carry back to the dreamer.

Thus, the soul carries intimate messages between the center of the cosmos and the center of each person's life. Because each soul is unique, the dreams take the form of images and language that the dreamer might recognize and decipher. By attending to the dream messages each person can learn more of their current psychic condition as well as their intended purpose in life. The soul becomes the carrier of the dream of one's life, the keeper of one's innermost imagination and the renewing force of one's being.

In imagining cosmic origins of the soul, Siberian tribes describe a cosmic tree of life with roots that descend deep into the underworld and great branches that stretch across the upper regions of the sky. The living tree of existence forms the axis of the world as well as the root and stem from which all life grows. Human souls are said to dwell on this origin tree and perch upon the sky branches before they come to the earth to be born. The unborn souls wait there in silence, quietly watching like birds until something in the world below intrigues them enough to descend. Pulled by a certain image or pattern in the earthly realm, the bird-soul seeks to incarnate and enters a womb where life is about to be born.

Some say that the soul chooses the parents as if intrigued with a particular set of issues and specific entwining of fate and life circumstances. After birth, the soul continues to reside inside its chosen host as a core pattern and essential imagination, as a life-dream and an innate style, as a way of moving and growing and seeking meaning in this world. The fact that the heart can suddenly flutter, that a person can be deeply moved, and that each one born longs for something greater all serve as evidence of the bird-soul that remains within us, watching for further opportunities to incarnate and spread its wings.

THE DIVINE TWIN

A West African story tells what happens to the soul just before it incarnates and enters the world of bodies moving in time and space. According to that old tale, the soul encounters a spirit as soon as it begins to move toward earthly life. That spirit becomes the divine companion that accompanies the soul on its journey through the realm of incarnate beings. This "divine twin" or "spirit familiar" clarifies the image that first moved the soul and describes the terms through within which this particular life adventure will be shaped.

Compelled by the vision that first drew it and informed by the knowledge just received, the soul enters into a life-long agreement with its spirit companion. At the same time, the divine twin commits to travelling the road of life with the soul in order to protect the understanding they share and shape together. Spirit and soul will soon join the body for the unique adventure of a lifetime.

At this point, the soul has not yet been born, but it has agreed to live a certain kind of life once it arrives on earth. It has made its first deal with the world and confirmed its original agreement for coming to life. This first agreement becomes a kind of "divine contract" that each soul makes before it can enter the body and begin to live on earth. This original agreement and divine arrangement keeps each soul secretly connected to the eternal realm throughout its life. Any originality a person might have derives from the original agreement that the soul makes and any enduring satisfaction a person might find will be a reflection of the soul's first agreement with life.

The human connection to the divine realm exists in the soul as a mystery that seeks its own unfolding, as an inner motion that will secretly pull each person toward occasions of revelation where the dream of life becomes evident to oneself and at times visible to others. The original agreement with life affects a marriage of both worlds as it becomes the nature of the soul to know both realms and feel the longing between them. The most genuinely human moments are moments of the soul, the lived instances and vulnerable occasions when time breaks apart and eternity seems near and the breath of the divine can be felt. In such moments the soul grows deeper and takes further root in this life, even as it recalls again the high branches and lofty presence of the tree of all life.

EMBRACING THE TREE OF LIFE

No sooner has the first agreement been made than the soul is in motion again. Bearing its agreement with the divine and in the close company of its companion and guide, the soul moves toward the womb of life. On the way it comes upon a garden and soon stands before a radiant tree standing at the center of it. The soul cannot help but touch and embrace the tree that seems to stand at the very center of life. The branches seem all-embracing and the soul feels moved to touch the tree the way people instinctively touch certain things, for luck, as a charm, as a knock on wood intended to make something more solid and real.

The tree of life has appeared again, this time standing at the junction where the two worlds meet and diverge. By its very nature the Tree of Life is connected to everything including its own opposite. As the Tree of Unity it is the sustaining and unifying stem of all life; however at the point of departure from the eternal realm, the Tree of Unity becomes the Tree of Forgetfulness.

The soul is ready to depart and as soon as it touches the tree it forgets the essential agreement that has just been made. In order to enter the world of time, the soul must forget the very thing that intrigued it and the original agreement it has made. Only after touching the radiant tree and forgetting why it was moved to life in the first place, can the soul be born in this world.

This is the original irony and enduring enigma of human existence. Being born on this earth is both a begetting and a forgetting and what becomes forgotten is the very reason why each soul first agreed to enter the body and incarnate. The rest of life will be a drama through which the soul attempts to remember why it came to life in the first place and what it agreed to do with its allotment of time on earth. That's the rule and the original rite of passage as the soul makes its way across the threshold that separates the timeless and the time-bound, the unified and the divided, the eternal and the temporal.

The soul departs from the place of primal unity in order to be born and the divine world becomes a distant memory both left behind and buried within us. Having forgotten why it came to life, the newborn arrives open and impressionable and dependent on those in this world for protection and survival. Throughout its life on earth the soul will long for a divine sense of union and will seek to find it in parents and teachers, in lovers and in soul companions. For it is our human fate to become separated from the eternal and it is our individual destiny to search for the divine connection in the confusion and delight of this world.

Human experience begins in this world, but human memory extends further back and beyond earthly limits. Were that not the case people would be more tame and less full of longings; they would be more easily satisfied and less likely to risk everything on a dream. We are never far from the memory of the first agreement although it often seems the farthest thing from us. Inside each soul the life-seed waits to be watered with attention and the life-dream waits to awaken fully. Regardless of outer appearances and contrary notions, each soul has its inner imagination that tries to return to full awareness through dreams and visions, through sudden insights and strange revelations.

When all else fails, the soul will create impossible dramas and persistent dilemmas in order crack open the shell of the little-self and reveal the living seed and divine contract within it. The soul needs an outer drama that can help awaken and pull into conscious awareness the inner myth and seeded story that it carries within and the original agreement it has made with the divine.

ORIGINAL AGREEMENET VS ORIGINAL SIN

Some define the separation from the divine realm as a fall from grace and even as an "original sin." The ancient tale of the soul and its divine companion presents the "fall" as a descent of the soul and a necessary forgetting rather than a transgression or primal violation. Where some see the commission of a sin of disobedience, others perceive a necessary omission, a loss of memory required of all who would take up life on earth. Rather than a punishment for some original sin, the primary purpose of suffering then becomes the labor pains needed to break open the divine seed and primal agreement set within the soul.

Where some imagine that a reconnection to the divine can only occur after death, the notion of a forgotten agreement places the divine connection as a living potential inside one's own life. The struggle of the soul then revolves around a desire to awaken to one's inner nature rather than a struggle against it. The divine connection depends upon learning who we each already are and have secretly agreed to be. In this approach, one's inner nature is divinely rooted and whatever is "second nature" to us will be our natural, instinctive connection to our first agreement in life.

The underlying unity of life becomes a revelation waiting to be found in the soul. In awakening to the inner dream of life a person becomes a living bridge between the two worlds. There's no proof of this, but in this world whatever is proven one day becomes disproved or disapproved sooner or later. What supports the life of the soul are stories and imaginations and hidden connections that can never be proven and for that reason continue to exist. Each person makes a leap of faith every time they open their eyes. Those who require absolute proofs have not yet awakened to the unique story and inner truth seeded within their own soul. Until some hint of the divine appears within, no outer proof can ever be satisfactory.

SECOND AGREEMENTS

For a short time after birth the human infant remains in secret sublime contact with the otherworld through the open center at the top of the head. The newborn arrives wailing, perhaps longing already for the otherworld, but certainly calling for help in this one. The struggle for nourishment and shelter, care and love begins immediately and a language must be found to express one's needs. In order to have essential needs met, a newborn must learn to smile in ways that parents and family can recognize. "Body language" and bodily needs take precedent as even the inner self must adapt to the immediate situation.

The original agreement of the soul is there, but daily life and common concerns soon close around it. The newborn must become a child of time, a member of a family, a witness to history, and a recipient of a cultural inheritance before the time comes for the first agreement to be recalled. In order to survive, in order to grow and enter the delights and confusions of human emotions and earthly love, the first agreement of the soul must become a secondary issue of life.

In order to participate in the flow of life each person must make a series of agreements that include family and friends as well as society and its institutions. This complex array of "second agreements" is necessary for human life to continue. It involves subtle negotiations with one's mother and finding ways to relate to one's father as each child seeks to secure a place in the family arrangement. Some must agree to be quiet and undemanding while others are expected to speak up and demand what they want, even cry for it. Some will be treated special for being first born; others will be special because they are the last to be conceived. Some will have to steal whatever they need, while others will be given more than they can ever use. Each will negotiate in their own way and in the end each will make a variety of deals in order to fit in, in order to receive some attention and in order to play a part in the drama of existence.

Eventually, the child outgrows its own childhood and new arrangements must be made with parents and with the local community or else they will always be treated as a child. The parents also have a need to renegotiate aspects of their lives when the time comes for their children to be "on their own." At the threshold of adulthood the agreements between parents and child must be renegotiated or both will suffer beyond what is required for life to continue.

After childhood agreements must be found and made with a wider community of friends and teachers as well as colleagues and superiors. Such secondary agreements are necessary and important; they bond us with friends and connect us with associates. Second agreements are the necessary negotiations made between one's soul and the "facts of life," between one's desires and the reality of one's circumstances. They involve the additional negotiations and contracts required at each new stage and critical turning point of life.

Change and the negotiations that it requires are a fact that underlies all the facts of life. Intimacy with family and friends is essential and can be a great solace amidst life's slings and arrows, but even the closest relationships can and must be renegotiated at times. No one can remain as a child and still be true to themselves. No one can be a true friend who fails to recognize how friendship changes and grows and requires different loyalties over time. Since second agreements originate in the realm of time, they tend to be "time sensitive." All human relations need occasional adjustments and need to be renegotiated when critical junctures occur.

At the same time, critical junctions in life become the crucible through which the original agreement tries to reawaken within us. Since the pattern in the soul involves the agreement made before being born it antedates and supersedes all other agreements in our lives. In the long run, and it is the long run that our eternal souls are concerned with, all second agreements become negotiable and "all contracts are made to be broken." The one exception to the rule is the first agreement of one's life, the primary and primordial agreement our souls made before our first breath on earth was taken.

The first agreement of life is indelible in the soul; it is the source of our deepest capacity to change, but *it* is not available for renegotiation. Despite critical and meaningful responsibilities to others, the first agreement is one's primary obligation. It characterizes and contains the original reason for coming to life. Because it involves the divine source of our lives, the first agreement cannot be dismissed or replaced. It may be forgotten, but it can't be rejected or rescinded or traded in for another deal.

THE DOUBLE BIND

The first agreement is the context for the talents and gifts that the soul bears and it is the source of one's later calling in life. Although it is forgotten at birth, remains mostly invisible in childhood, and may be denied throughout one's life, it cannot be removed or erased from the soul. The first agreement is the inner dream, the pattern that brought us to life and the seed of awakening waiting to blossom from within.

Each life has a genuine calling and each calling in life is also a re-calling of the divine agreement made before earthly life began. It is a living echo in the soul that calls us to a greater life than we might otherwise seek. The original agreement with the creative force of life is what drives the soul forward; it feeds ambitions, inspires acts of love as well as occasions of nobility. Once the forgotten agreement of the soul becomes more conscious, it is the deal that breaks all other deals; it is the agreement that must be kept and all other agreements must be renegotiated in order that we keep it. That's the deal; it's the first deal, the primary arrangement and the real deal in this life made of so many deals.

Meanwhile, the tension between the two agreements of the soul places each person in a "double bind." In the sleight of hand enacted by the hand of fate, the first and second agreements are typically at odds with each other. Both involve matters of necessity as each person is bound to the eternal as well as subject to the immediate pressures of time, place and social conditions. Thus, there is an innate tension between the facts of one's life and the destiny the soul longs to find. Each person is a "double being," each a citizen of both worlds; each a descendent of eternity and each a child of time. Being fully human means being double-minded and often means being at odds within oneself.

Each meaningful step we take on the path of life involves some tension between the common world and the life of the soul. That is the basic tension of life as well as the source of vital energy needed for the soul to further incarnate in life. Each soul lives on the verge of remembering the forgotten agreement and original dream that it carries. Each life is ever about to burst into a unique bloom and each is on the verge of forgetting the whole point of existence again. That is the eternal story and daily drama of awakening and falling back to sleep again.

In creating ourselves from the hidden seed within we also play our unique part in the great drama of creation. Each time we remember a piece of why we came to life we pull the seeds of eternity further into the world of time. At critical junctures in life the inner seed tries to sprout, but often our fate must nail us to a cross before we pay proper attention to it. If we try for a bargain or in any way compromise the agreement that the soul requires, we simply double-cross ourselves.

EUDAIMONIA

As guardian angel and natural voice of one's innermost conscience, the divine twin remembers the pattern etched in our souls and continually recalls us to its essential message and aim. *Eudaimonia* was an ancient Greek word for happiness, meaning to satisfy the *daimon* or living spirit that accompanies one's soul throughout life. Being truly happy depends upon being true to and living close to the pattern woven in the soul. For that satisfies the daimon in us and brings some level of spiritual fulfillment.

The daimon is an "intermediary," a betwixt and between figure and go-between that occupies the space between the human soul and the divine. As part of the divine twin it is responsible to the original agreement, as "spirit familiar" it is most familiar with our core pattern and more familiar with our purpose in life than we are. As an inner resident of the soul, the daimon can be seen as another component of the complex arrangement of one's fate and destiny.

Being woven close to the thread of fate and destiny within us, the daimon knows which way we should turn whenever we enter the great crossroads of life. The voice of the daimon can act like a resident oracle speaking from within at crucial moments. We participate in this "daimonic relationship" through our intuitions and hunches, through our guesses and leaps of faith as our "fluid familiars" help us retune to the inner direction of our lives.

Whether we term it a guardian angel or a "little bird that told me," the inner guides tend to move with the subtlety of wings. An idea or image suddenly appears before us; it arises from nowhere or from the realm of in-between things. If we allow it, we leave room for the guiding spirit and can learn the way we are inclined to divine things. Should we hesitate or doubt too much, it is gone. It disappears from us; it slips back into the ether and may not return until like circumstances bring it round again.

The intermediary realm exists at the edges between one thing and another; it involves the extremes as well as the subtleties necessary for both culture and nature to exist. People used to live side by side with the "invisibles" and closer to the "impossibles" until they were driven from sight by the hard reign and cold rule of the subject-object split. In dividing the world into stark opposites and endless defining categories, the subtle realm of things that are neither one thing nor another has been lost. In losing such subtleties we also lose touch with the genuine mysteries and dilemmas of life and our own unique ways of solving them.

The insistence on the subject-object division reduces the subtleties and complexities of life just as it falsely divides literature into fact or fiction. Neither life nor literature can be divided so simply; the separation of fact and fiction is itself as much a fiction as it is a fact. Much of what people fervently believe to be the "absolute truth" one day turns out to be patently false. Much of what might be dismissed as fictional with no "actual basis in fact" turns out to be true. When the in-between things and intermediary factors are dismissed simply because they defy categorization, then the parts fail to add up to the whole. Wholeness includes all the parts, even the invisible aspects and the mysterious elements that defy definition but refuse to be dismissed.

Subject and object are only two parts of a greater mystery, one that can't be reduced to simple opposites or be solved with a single-minded point of view. Whenever things become too far divided and too firmly separated, some of the essential in-between, either-or aspects that give the world coherence are being lost. In losing a felt sense for the unexplainable we lose some of the connecting tissue of life and feel less connected to it as well as more isolated from it.

The intermediaries hold the continuity between nature and culture just as they form the connections between the human and the divine. Without the living sense of the betwixt and between we not only lose touch with our inner sense of fate and destiny, but the human community becomes isolated from the soul of the world.

THE GENIUS OF THE SOUL

The resident spirit of the soul gives each person their unique way of perceiving life. Whether it be called a guardian angel or an inner muse, a divine twin or the genius within us, it represents our own way of seeing the world. Through the presence of the inner genius we are called and recalled to the first agreement of our souls; we are pulled and stretched and driven until we enter and accept the grip of our destiny.

Genius and its older form *genii* refer to the "spirit that is already there;" the inner genius that enters the world with each child born and that tries to present itself repeatedly throughout one's life. The genius of a person is specific, an exact shape and often exacting quality that is native to them. As indigenous inner spirit, the genius is the source of our true identity; however, should it remain unrecognized, it will create great identity problems. The genius within can inspire a person to reach great heights or being rejected can distort whatever they might touch in life.

As resident spirit in the soul the genius combines the inherent gifts and talents with inner inclinations and a style of being that together comprise the fate of a person. Fulfilling an individual destiny involves the revelation of one's genius as well as the development of the character needed to carry it to the world. The inner genius marks not simply the exceptional within the norm, but more importantly the style through which each person can escape the dull trap of normality. For each genius represents its own "norm" and unique ethic, an inner constellation that holds the keys to understanding the meanings and purpose inherent in each life.

Genius is a subjective quality or collection of qualities, the only measure of which can be the life lived through it, lived from it, lived for it. At critical moments, a person must follow the rule that reflects the inner constellation in their soul or they will "miss their star" and "follow the wrong gods home."

The resident spirit of one's life acts as the guardian of one's destiny; it is the inner tutor and intuitive guide that can be cultivated by paying attention to the little voice inside oneself. In crucial moments the inner spirit or muse of the soul will offer its guidance, but we must first learn its language. In tribal lore, the "helping spirits" can be hostile when first encountered. The individual goes through initiatory experiences in order to open the inner life and experience a self-revelation of the inner nature and style of their resident spirit.

Remember the tale of the Spirit in the Bottle? A young student came upon a great tree while looking for signs of rare birds in a deep forest. Hearing a tiny voice coming from the roots of the tree he finds a strange bottle with a genie or spirit inside it. Opening the bottle out of curiosity releases a huge spirit greatly angered by having been bottled up too long. Although the genie could provide exactly what the lad needed and truly wished to have, he would first have to become wise enough to contain it.

The genie was the rare bird of spirit that he was unwittingly searching for. It was his own bottled-up genius that knew how to produce what he most desired. However, he had to trick the spirit back into the bottle and learn how to handle its power before he could derive any benefit from its presence. *Genie* is an old word for genius; it means the "spirit that's there." As in the African tale of the soul's origins, the inner guide and spirit companion is connected to a remarkable tree. The words *tree* and *truth* grow from the same roots and the inner spirit and divine companion would keep us close to the truth and inner beauty of our own lives.

Fairy tales were once called "fated tales;" the word *fate* shares roots with *fairy* and *fee* and other elements that enchant us from within. Many fairy tales deal with conditions caused by fate, the restrictions of birth, spells cast upon people and curses that must be faced and defeated or else life won't progress and love won't prosper. We also live within spells and near wonders like the characters in fairy tales. We know it when as children we desire to hear certain stores over and over again. Folk and fairy tales contain images that relate to issues we are fated to struggle with in our lives. They depict aspects of genius that are necessary for true transformations to occur.

We cannot become who we are at the core of ourself unless the genius in us becomes recognized and released. However, the awakening of one's genius produces the problem of how to handle the inner powers and gifts of the soul. A person can love their genius and be inspired by their inner connection to the divine; yet being divine the inner spirit can place "inhuman" demands upon us. While in the grip of the genius we can experience being released, but can also find ourselves being mercilessly driven.

If we keep the inner spirit bottled up too long it can turn against us and make our lives miserable. If we accept it as we find it and learn to work with it, everything changes. Spells are broken, gifts are found and talents serve their true purpose. In the tale of the Spirit in the Bottle, the student receives great riches from working with the genius, but also becomes a great healer. In other words, he finds his innate gifts and his inner value as well as his true calling in life. The genius can fill us with power and vital energy, yet it is also aimed at a destiny that would also serve the lives of others.

THE PROBLEM OF TUNING IN

What begins with the mystery of fate only finds its conclusion in the release of the spirit that was there all along. We are each and all imbued with a resident spirit and called to a divine connection; that is the source of the longing that plagues and delights the human soul. Responding to the call means tuning into the presence of the spirit companion and finding ways to release its energy and follow our genuine life-calling. The problem isn't a lack of calling, for each of us is called to something meaningful. The typical problem involves learning to listen within and tuning in to what truly calls to us.

Like the genie in the story, the resident spirit of the soul must be won over before it can become helpful to its host. Since the inborn spirit of life tends to be at odds with the ego or "little self," we must loosen our ego attitudes and make room for the greater vision and more subtle scope of our own genius. As protector of and guide for our original agreement, the genius is essentially involved in a person's identity and denial of it can cause an extreme identity crisis.

When the spirit companion is rejected or thoroughly ignored it can change from a beneficial daimon to an inner demon. The angel on one's shoulder can become a "little devil" and many of our inner demons are guiding spirits turned against their hosts as a result of the human host turning away from their genuine orientation in life. The demons that haunt us are the perverse spirits that develop when we turn our backs on our natural inclinations and innate styles. Turned another way, they would protect the core meanings of our lives and guide us toward the paths of understanding.

The resident spirit and divine companion is also the "taskmaster of the soul" that demands that we live our life and not that of another. For the genius of the soul would set us the hardest work among those things not impossible for us for us to accomplish. When it comes to issues of the divine, there can be no neutral condition; either we serve the "higher purpose" seeded within us or else foster a distortion of it that can become demonic. What can bring us to spiritual fulfillment and eudaimonia can also demonize us from within. Eventually, the human host and the "spirit familiar" must become more familiar with each other and the original agreement of the soul can manifest more freely.

The resident spirit is the keeper of the inner pattern and the root of memory in the soul. It remembers what is essential to us and too often forgotten by us. Following the lead of one's inner spirit leads us to the aspects of the divine most in tune with our individual soul. Without being tuned into a genuine calling we are simply blind wanderers on the roads of life. Once we receive a calling that resonates with the pattern woven within us we wander rightly, we find a path and enter a pilgrimage that suits our soul. Such a life-path requires that we risk ourselves in order to find ourselves. The path may lead us far from all that we know, yet it does so to lead us to the dream at the center of our souls.

DUENDE AND THE SOUL CONDITION

The soul carries the original agreement that moved us to life in the first place and the divine companion and inner genius tries repeatedly to remind us of the purpose set within. Each soul arrives with a natural genius intended to fashion something meaningful and beautiful from the raw materials of life. Although the first agreement begins in the otherworld it can only be fulfilled in this one. Throughout life the soul continues to descend and attempts to incarnate more fully on this earth where we walk in the dust of the moment on the soles of our feet.

Soul and *sole* are related words that also have shared roots. *Sole* carries the meaning of "being the only one of its kind" as with an exceptional item or a unique and extraordinary person. And, *sole* can also mean the bottom of one's feet. In order to become a unique and extraordinary person we must "walk our walk" and move the way our soul would have us move. We must find the original speech of the soul and become the vehicle of its true expression.

The Old English word *sawol* speaks with the same soulful tone of the "spiritual and emotional part of a person" that animates their being and resonates with the song of existence. The purpose of life can be seen as an effort to create and make more soul and thereby bring more of the song existence into being. The only way to accomplish such a lofty goal is to draw energy from below as well as from within one's soul and bring it up and out to the light of day. What then appears is the unique way in which each soul sings its inner note and each pair of feet finds its way to the great dance of life.

The sole can be found at the physical foundation of the body just as the soul must become the inner foundation and deep root of our lives. The soul within us is secretly connected to the spirit of the earth itself and the living earth has an interest in the growth of our soul. For it was some aspect of earthly life that first drew our souls down to this world where meaning and beauty must be shaped from the union of matter and spirit.

Duende is an old name for the spirit of the earth that can draw the soul down to the ground of life. Duende is the power that compels us to sing the song of our souls despite and because we are torn apart by living. Duende is the essential power of living, not simply work, not only thought, but a struggle with spirit in the blood. Not a question of simple talent, but the song of genius whispering earth-dark sounds to the mind and to the heart. Spontaneous creation, that's what it is; the unique motions of creation rising from the earth, penetrating the soles of our feet, fructifying our souls, inspiring the mind as well, and releasing the song of the soul.

As the force of duende, the spirit of the earth becomes visible when the flamenco dancers begin to call upon it by stamping the ground with their feet. They begin to draw the deep flame of the earth up to the surface where it enters the soles of their feet and rises through the body stirring all the seeds of knowledge and warming the threads of being. In the throes of the rising spirit the dust of life is cast off as each dancer becomes inspired. Stretched between the height of spirit and the depths of soul, the dancer becomes a unique embodiment of the force of life itself.

Each experience of duende is unique in kind for each occasion draws upon the sole qualities of the dancer. Each dance becomes an exaltation of the soul and a singular example the uniqueness at the core of each human life. Whether it leads the soul to a song or a dance or another form of art, the earth spirit intends to have each person awaken to what is unique within them and thereby contribute to the ongoing creation of life.

In Spain, where they make fine shoes of Spanish leather, they used to say that each moment is unique and placed before us to be uniquely inhabited. In Spain, where they study death in order to learn more about life, they used to say that the only way to be fully alive is to be continually dying. For only in dying again and again, do we truly inhabit our lives and walk this earth with a genuine spirit of nobility and grace.

In Spain, they used to say that each person had to learn the way their soul would walk and become a unique manifestation of life on earth. In Spain, they used to say that there are three kinds of people just as there are three kinds of shoemakers. The first kind makes shoes in order to make a living and they make good shoes and thus can make a way for themselves in the world. The second kind of shoemaker toils on a higher plane. These craftsmen make shoes for the art of it. They make the most beautiful shoes that can possibly be made; knowing all the while that the products of their art will be worn into tatters or simply fall out of fashion.

The third kind of shoemaker works on an altogether different level. That one becomes an indispensable, irreplaceable maker of shoes. That one makes shoes that connect people's feet solidly to the goat's earth, shoes that remind whoever wears them of the dance of life. That one has flamenco and duende in mind while making shoes. That shoemaker remembers the passionate spirit that tries to sing its way into the world through each living soul. That one recalls that each soul walks the road of life and death with its own inborn style.

And, that shoemaker is remembered long after his meeting with death; for he shod people for the love of them, for the love of something divine in them. He shod them religiously, spiritually, devotionally, in the spirit of life being fully lived and in the knowledge of death waiting with its inevitable questions. That shoemaker made life-long shoes and wore them as well. No one can fill the shoes of a person who wears life-long shoes, who finds the true shape of their life and learns how their soul would walk in this world. To fully inhabit the shoes of life means to become unforgettable, to be unique in some way and therefore irreplaceable.

To find the shape of one's own life, to become oneself, to walk in the right shoes, be in the right struggle and love in a way that makes things genuinely fit together... that makes all the difference, even in a dark time when nothing seems to make any difference at all.

It's an old idea and hopelessly out of style; for the style has become cynical and short-sighted and the old ideas only work in the long run and in the deeper motions of the great dance. Most don't know it now, but the human soul is seeded with specific ideas from before birth. The soul has "long thoughts" that it is inclined to think all along life's road. The long thoughts of the soul can keep a person aimed and purposeful throughout their life. For each person enters the world on an essential errand that intends to make their life meaningful and purposeful.

Like life-long shoes, a person can inhabit the images and ideas that first brought them to life. In living fully into the soul's shoes a person becomes uniquely themselves and a light in the dark for others. Those who think and feel the long thoughts of the soul find something to serve in life. They help to reveal the wonder and beauty even amidst the chaos and confusion. They leave imprints and tracks so that others can follow in their footprints until they find their own way of stepping forth and dancing on.

When they die, their life will have been inhabited and their soul will have descended fully. They will have written a story on the skin of the world. Their shoes may finally wear out, but their souls will still be singing.

When they die, people will feel that something meaningful has passed and that they cannot be replaced. For those who live in the way that their soul intended and keep the original agreement that continually brought them to the dance of life become uniquely shaped and solely made. They become one-of-a-kind, the kind of person that everyone can learn something from, the kind of soul that no one can ever replace.

CHAPTER 7

THE FEET OF DREAMS

Each night dreams pound on the roofs of our lives like stars tearing at the darkness within us. They speak a language improvised just for us as they provoke and whisper, warn and even threaten in order to awaken us from the sleep of our common lives. They burn with information about the way our soul would incline us to go. They flicker in the soul's labyrinth and intensify when we approach major turning points. Our dreams are the nightly evidence that we remain part of the great drama and dramatic pageant that the soul requires; for each soul is extravagant when it dreams.

We receive the strangely coded messages intended for us many times; yet most fail to follow where their dreams would lead. Many drown in the commotion of life simply because they refuse to awaken to a dream they carry from birth. Many trade the dream that brought them to life for a life someone else dreams up for them. The dream of the soul will continue to pull at the threads of our lives even if we dismiss it from our daily attention. For we are threaded through with the stuff of dreams; each person a body wrapped around a soul imbued with a dream trying to awaken from within.

Despite the modern dedication to facts and statistics, at our core we still live in the dreamtime of deep imagination. Despite the modern obsession with rationality and narrow logic our nightly dreaming sustains a vital connection to the great mysteries of life. Each life, knowingly or not, participates in the mystery of creation ongoing; each is made of "such stuff as dreams are made of." Call it the dream of one's life, call it the holy thread of dreams; we are not holy or even whole unless somehow in touch with the dream trying to awaken and come to life within us.

The old argument goes back and forth: is a person most awake while walking about or more truly awake while dreaming? Is the true awakening found by simply waking from night's realm of sleep or by waking up to the dream woven within one's life? Blindly going through the paces of life is not the same as having a true calling and finding meaning in this broken world. Increasingly, the world is full of distracting devices that drown out the voice of dreams. What many call their "waking life" can also be seen as sleepwalking.

In dreams, the mystery is alive in us and we are carried by it. As dreamers we walk on all the roads of life and can be any age at all, we appear young again, or older than we ever have been. In dreams we change genders, have careers we are unqualified for, run with horses, have nightmares, fly above our earthly cares and peer down into our daily struggles in the time-bound world. A dream can take almost any shape; yet there is a dream behind the dreams, a dream woven into the cells of our being. That inner dream holds the core pattern and exact message that our lives are intended to deliver to the waking world.

It is a dream that first calls the soul to life and one's "calling" in life can come from a dream or seem like a dream. Those who awaken to a genuine calling stand at the junction of the dream and the waking world. For the dream of our life would connect us more clearly to both worlds and give us better vision in each. Dreams may arrive in the depths of sleep, but they intend to wake one up. Being fully awake means to be able to see and follow the dream of one's life wherever it might lead.

Most people have their hopes and dreams, yet both can fade when the harsh light of reality must be faced. Those who truly awaken find the deep and abiding dream of their life; they find the deeper self within them and put all hope in that. At that point, it's not a matter of a naïve or foolish dream that "might come true" some day, but more the sense of something calling us to an intended destiny. Awakening means stepping out of the daydream offered to us and entering the greater dream that called us here to begin with.

Such a dream comes more than once in lifetime because it is closely woven to one's heart. The delicate, yet permanent threads of fate are dream woven within us and they bear a destiny waiting to be discovered. Each time our heart opens to life the dream within it tries to surface and be known. Following that kind of dream means bowing to some mystery that knows us better than we know ourselves. For the dream in our life calls us to awaken to another life already existing within us. Meanwhile, the life we have is what we risk again and again in order to find the life we came to live. When in touch with the thread of our life-dream we know where we are going, even if we have never been there before.

EISIK'S DREAM

It's like the story of the man who had the same dream three times over. He was an unassuming person who lived simply amidst common people in a village where they had all been born. The dream that came knocking on the roof of his little house seemed so outlandish that he thought it foolish to take it seriously. At first he dismissed the strange voice that called him to change his life completely. Eventually, he left all he knew behind in order to follow wherever that dream might lead. There is no simple measure for the soul inside a person and a big dream can come to anyone.

The shape of such a dream speaks volumes about the soul of the dreamer and can stand in sharp contrast to the life that was chosen or pressed upon one. Eisik, for that was his name, awoke one day from a dream in which a voice spoke clearly and told him to leave all he knew and go out into the wide world. The dream voice instructed him to leave his home and travel to a distant city. Once there, he would find a certain bridge; if he dug at the foot of the bridge he would find a great treasure.

It was a wild dream; it didn't fit with his settled ways and it unsettled him to have such a dream. He had come to expect little from life and he had little trust in the world beyond the village he knew so well. So, the dreamer ignored the dream and refused to listen to the voice calling him to another life. After all, it was just a dream and his life felt real and solid and predictable, even if a little empty. He went about his chores and did his work; he lived the life he already had and said nothing about the strange calling to anyone.

After a time the same dream came again. Just as before, the voice told the dreamer to leave all he knew and gave the same instructions about finding a golden treasure at the distant bridge. Eisik wondered why a dream would come twice with the same strange message. His life seemed squarely at odds with the voice of the dream. Why should it come to him of all people?

Meanwhile, the image of the bridge with a treasure underneath lingered longer in his mind and made him less easy as he went about his familiar tasks. He became unable to dismiss the night message and less able to contain it after it came the second time. One day he couldn't help it, he mentioned the dream to his friends. They dismissed it out of hand and reminded him who he really was and where he belonged. Of course, they thought he belonged where he already was, right where he had been his entire life and right where they all found themselves. Besides, it was just a dream and everyone knew that real life was a different matter and that it mattered more than dreams.

Dreams are a deeply intimate matter and no one else can hear the voice that calls from within our dreams. The calling arrives clothed in mystery because it comes from mystery; it comes to remind us of a mystery we agreed to take part in when we agreed to enter this life. Telling others about it can make things worse; especially if those we tell never listen to the voice calling to them. In that case, they will resent us for reminding them of their unlived dreams.

Some friends will instinctively support the dream in one's life; others envy the dream that calls their friend to a greater adventure. Those who have buried their own dreams cannot afford to invest in the dreams of others. Those who refuse the knowledge of dreams will also dismiss the longings natural to the soul. So, Eisik didn't mention the dream again and nothing more was said of the voice that calls to another life beyond what people commonly admit and allow to be present.

Daily life may be full of charades and cover-ups, but dreamers are naked before the dream which speaks the specific language of their soul. In the realm of sleep our defenses fail and our denials fall flat. In the end, the dreamer cannot hide from the dream planted in the garden of the soul. Something from before birth wants to be remembered and the soul makes subtle moves toward it each night.

HEARING THE CALL

A dream can be a kind of leaven working inside the dough of one's life. Eisik found that he could no longer dismiss the feelings and longings that began to rise within him as a result of his dream. He wasn't a greedy person, but the notion of a treasure waiting to be found stirred something deep within him. Time went steadily by; dreams pounded nightly on the roofs of the village and the night sky swirled with the milk of churning stars. And secretly, Eisik's soul sang of treasures that only he could find.

When the same dream came again Eisik could not ignore the message. By then, the call had managed to reach all parts of the dreamer. The third time is a charm and he could no longer deny that he had been called and had in fact had heard the call. Although facing the unknown was fearful to him, remaining in the blind safety of his existing life began to hold another kind of fear. Eisik worried over leaving everything he had and everyone he knew; yet he feared never knowing if his dream could be true.

Of course, Eisik is anyone of us; ultimately he is every one of us. Each comes to this life secretly tied to a dream trying to awaken from within. The call that awakens gives both a vision worth pursuing and the permission necessary to take up the pursuit. Yet, becoming able to hear the call requires some submission on the part of the little-self which typically harbors our fears and insecurities. The little-self resists our true calling for it fears being overwhelmed or rejected and typically prefers a familiar pain to an unknown joy.

Answering the call to a bigger life involves taking a greater risk and finding a different kind of security. Sometimes, the only security comes from taking the right risk in life; sometimes letting go is the only way to go. The time comes when a greater life calls to us and existing ties must be cut. After all, a human being grows from more than one umbilical. Someone must cut the birth cord or our individual life can't begin; later a person must learn to cut the cords themselves or fail to live independently. Answering the call requires that we turn away from all that we know and from those that think they know us best of all. The time comes when cutting cords and leaving everything behind is the only way to go forward.

One day, with nothing but the clothes on his back and the echo of the dream in his heart, Eisik left his village and all that he knew. He left all that he held dear in life in order to hold his own life more dearly. He put one foot in front of the other and entered the great adventure of his life. Long before he ever reached the bridge described in the dream, Eisik crossed a bridge within himself that shifted his life and opened it to the force of the unseen world.

Eisik set out on the road of dreams and having no other way to travel he walked on the soles of his feet. When the road became long he kept walking and walked right through his shoes. His clothes became worn and covered with the dust of the road. For it is hard to keep up appearances and follow one's dream at the same time. Eisik walked out of one life to find another; he became lost in order to find himself. Eisik joined the long line of dreamers and searchers and seekers that stretches back before time began.

The journey was hard at times and he felt unprepared for such a long endeavor. He began to doubt the validity of the dream's promise as well as his ability to see it through. He was no longer subject to the doubting and disbelieving of those who knew him, but a deep uncertainty of his own began to weigh him down. Far from the sleepy comforts of home, Eisik became enveloped in a cloud of doubt that he had always carried within. At times he feared that others would condemn him for being a fool on a fool's mission. At times he simply feared to take another step.

Troubled with fears and weighted with doubts, he asked himself what many seekers have asked before. What good is a dream that doesn't test the mettle of the dreamer? What good is a path that doesn't carry one to the edge of their capacity and then beyond that place? The dreamer is secure only in the dream; in the waking world everything else becomes less certain. Despite what the "true believers" believe, the greatest prayers are held together with doubt and the greatest maps lead directly into the unknown. Eventually, the dreamer is secure only in the dream as everything else becomes less certain. Eventually, the dream of the soul becomes the only hope; it becomes a prayer and a map as well.

Eisik's clothes became worn and tattered and out of style. It could also be said that he became naked and exposed. For a true calling involves a great exposure before it can become a genuine refuge. A true vocation requires shedding anything that would impede or obscure the call. A true pilgrimage requires letting go of the very things most people try to hold onto. In seeking after what the soul desires we become pilgrims with no home but the path the soul would have us follow.

That's how it went with Eisik; at first he resisted the call, then the calling replaced all that he knew and held to be dear. There was no certainty that he would ever arrive at the goal. He had no guide, no map, and no description other than the dream he carried as it carried him. He joined the old road where dreamers are carried along by visions and bidden on by voices that most people refuse to listen to. He became a pilgrim with nothing to hold at all except the dream of his life and the life he was called to find.

THE JOURNEY OWNS YOU

As the old proverb says, "Before you begin the journey, you own the journey. Once you have begun; the journey owns you." When we risk allowing the journey to "have us," we become lost to our usual selves in order to find our original self again. For there is a deeper self and inner nature that waits to be awakened in each of us. Each moment that the inner journey takes us over is a moment of the soul taking up the true enterprise of our lives. If we follow the intimations of the deep and knowing self we move closer to the dream of our life no matter how we appear to others.

Answering the call gives primacy to unknown places and foreign lands; it requires that we seek farther in the world than we would choose on our own. For lost souls are the only ones who ever get found. As lost creatures we become real creatures again. We rejoin all the other creatures that trust what they can't fully see. We enter our essential creatureliness and learn to sniff at the world again. We try to read the wind and find our way by sensing and intuiting, by imagining and dreaming on. In the soul adventure we become a self unknown, a self unexpected, and in that way find the greater self within us.

A certain kind of courage is required to follow what truly calls to us; why else would so many choose to live within false certainties and pretensions of security? If genuine treasures were easy to find this world would be a different place. If the path of dreams was easy to walk or predictable to follow many more would go that route. The truth is that most prefer the safer paths in life even if they know that their souls are called another way.

The truth is that the treasure we seek involves a mystery that has something of the divine in it. Call it a dream or "the treasure hard to attain;" call it a vocation or the awakening of one's innate genius. Call it what you will, upon hearing the call we must follow or else lose the true thread of our lives. What truly calls to us is beyond what we know or can measure. It uses the language of hidden treasures and distant cities to awaken something sleeping within us. That's the nature of the soul language that knows how we must be drawn out of ourselves in order to truly become ourselves. Once on the way, we must face our fears and withstand our doubts in order to hold onto our dreams.

If the genuine way was simple and straightforward, no vision would be required, no dream would be needed and no one's soul would be truly tested. Everyone would set out and arrive directly; no need to have one's assumptions defeated or illusions shattered. Point A would simply lead to point B and each would arrive just as they were when they departed. That may be the desired effect when making regular travel plans, but it can't be the aim when seeking a greater life. The greater life requires that we shed the false self fashioned for survival and made for simply fitting in.

If we could arrive the same as when we departed, there would be no reason to go. If we could go directly there, there would be no *there* when we arrive there. The only reason for undertaking the soul's adventure is to become completely other than who we have been so far. Until we become lost we have no way of knowing that there might be a true path for us to follow. We must go missing to be found, become lost in the world, washed in the unknown, wrapped in confusion and hidden even from ourselves before we can find what we are truly aimed at. The map of self-discovery leads away from the goal before ever turning to it.

In this life a pious journey is required. It is pious in the sense of a path that brings out our devotion, but also because it cleanses and clarifies our sense of self. The result may be pious, yet the process may look and feel like a stripping down to bare bone. From the common comforts, we must go to the edge of life; from simple self assurance we must go to the extremes of our nature. The inner thread of one's vocation began in the otherworld and it will lead us in that direction again. The importance of others and of *otherness* is part of the revelation our souls have been seeking all along.

People say that what we seek to find in the world already resides in ourselves; but only after reaching some extreme limit or margin of life can we locate it. For what we search for is both part of us and other to us; it is an "other that is also us," an "other self" that is the true self hidden within us. The necessary resources may lie within, yet we must go far out into the world before we learn how to trust what is within us all along. The hardest thing to trust in this world tends to be our own selves. Before we can learn the other within us, we must experience the otherness around us.

THE DIVINE IS CALLING

Each life involves an essential errand; not simply the task of survival, but a life-mission imbedded in the soul from the beginning. Life is an experiment in which we attempt to decipher the errand the gods have sent us on. Any true calling has something of the divine in it and what calls to us is "of the gods." For our dreams and visions are given by the divine and the gods have an interest in the paths we take in this world.

This isn't the pronouncement of a religious doctrine or the issue of believing in god or not. It's a matter of recognizing that something divine is behind the whole thing and hidden within us as well. The point isn't to prove or disprove one god or another; the point is to answer the call and learn where the path might lead. Whatever the divine connection might be, it will appear if the soul follows where it has been called; for the speech of the soul knows how we each are aimed at the divine.

What waits to be found in the stumbling of each life are the divine connections that the soul already carries. Failing to answer the call means living an unexplored life and likely means dying without having fully lived. People say that "many are called but few are chosen." Seen another way; each receives a calling yet most chose not to hear. Most refuse to listen to what calls to them while all along complaining of bad fates, unjust treatment and great disappointments. The real appointment is with one's own destiny and each true destination involves something divine.

What calls to us is greater than our little-self and is mostly at odds with the common beliefs and accepted ways of our daily lives. The problem isn't a lack of calling; the problem is the lack of following what beckons to us far enough to learn its true nature. So much of life becomes arranged to obscure and distract from what called us to come to life in the first place. People easily misplace their deepest longings and tune themselves to someone else's idea of a life. Most people remain unwilling to be extravagant enough to wander where their soul would lead them and simply adapt to an endless series of short-term goals.

Once Eisik accepted the call he joined the ranks of the wanderers and vagrants who follow dreams and visions seeking something beyond the obvious levels of life. Like the seekers of old, Eisik became "god-struck;" not caught up in religious issues, but more responsive to hints of the divine. Eisik was on a divine errand that stirred his doubts and raised his fears in order to clear his soul and open his heart.

We are each Eisik in our own way; each called to an adventure that we cannot control and would best surrender to. We live on the edge of an errand that the divine sent us on and that our dreams try to indicate. Such a soulful errand necessarily involves a long road with twists and turns that can't be anticipated. Many things are lost along the way, especially we must lose any fixed notions about ourselves and about the true nature of this world.

The issue isn't one of having a fixed faith or system of belief, unless those attitudes provide a stepping-off point. There are many ways that can lead to the treasure hard to attain; but no map can truly mark the entire path where our souls would go. Divine errands are intended to change how we see the world altogether and how we see ourselves almost entirely. Too many fixed beliefs, whether they be personal evaluations or religious doctrines, just get in the way. We are called to become ourselves and since each self is unique, the calling comes uniquely to us. In answering the call we learn how we are threaded and where we are aimed. Eventually, we must find our own way and follow our own dream in order to arrive.

WAITING FOR THE CALL

Our souls are secretly tied to stars that even in the midst of the day-blind world proceed and continue unseen upon their endless errands. Inside the soul our god-given gifts, natural talents, and endless imagination wait to awaken and be put to greater use. Not responding to the call that comes to us leaves the soul aching and makes the mind anxious. Failing to heed the call can cause a depression of the spirit; for both spirit and soul are poised to respond and both are expecting the call.

It used to be better known and often stated within earshot of young people, that the first great problem in life is not to have a true calling; not to recognize the distinct pull of a true vocation. The problem is not the lack of a career, but the absence of a genuine vocation capable of provoking one's genius and inspiring one's heart. As it turns out, having a calling isn't simply an option in the plan of life; from the view of the soul, a calling is a great necessity. Until a person hears the call they have no idea where they stand in this world. They may have wealth or status, yet will have nothing genuine to stand upon and nothing truly to offers to others.

The first problem is to not have a calling and therefore to be "on call" for this or that or the other. The lack of a genuine calling is the cause of great anguish and deep disorientation. Life can seem pointless and meaningless unless a divine connection and true vocation can be found. Of course, the second great problem involves hearing the call and answering it. Those who are called often look more lost than those who remain deaf to the whisperings of the soul and the voices of dreams. Those who respond to the call appear as vagrants before they find the extravagant way their soul has been called.

Learning one's true way of fitting into this world often requires becoming unfit for regular duties and common expectations. What truly calls to us would have us go beyond the usual limits. In responding to the call we join the lineage of those who are burning with an inner fire; not simply fired up with the heat of ambition, but awakened to a dream and flame that flickers in one's heart of hearts. A genuine calling further ignites the eternal spark originally carried into life by the soul and nothing can sooth that inner flame except when we fully respond and follow it through the world. Answering such a call requires that we become both less and more than we appear to be.

YOUNGER AND WISER FOR IT

By the time he has worn out the shoes of his former life, Eisik seems to all the world to be a fool. Since the dream that carries him cannot easily be seen, he seems to be more empty and forsaken than others. In many ways it is the fool within us that answers the call and ever remains willing to follow where the dream of life would lead. Doesn't a person have to become more foolish in order to one day become wise?

Remember all those youngest brothers and youngest sisters in fairy tales? The dreamer within us is like them and they are often given to lapses and subject to strange visions. They wander off the beaten paths and listen when animals talk to them. Under the rules of the daily world, that part of us is deemed to be stupid, foolish or mad, too dreamy or spiritual or romantic to be useful. Yet, in the old stories when everyone else becomes stuck or falls under some collective spell, it is the youngest one who stumbles into the solution and finds the path of redemption.

Often, they save everyone else by bringing forth a new imagination or by reviving an old tradition that had been overlooked or discarded. The youngest part of the psyche tends to be in touch with what is being newly imagined as well as what has been too long forgotten. It is the eternal youth within us that responds to the dream no matter what age the dreamer may be. Certain aspects of the soul remain youthful and foolish in just the right way throughout one's life. The youngest part of the psyche is the true dreamer within us and the part of us closest to wising up to the true purpose of our life.

The old stories depict the psychic fact that the youngest and most foolish part of us remains connected with the unseen powers of the soul and the deep seeded dream of our life. The part of us that would follow dreams and trust in soulful visions always appears foolish to those who are wiling to settle for the obvious and deny the true mysteries of life. Meanwhile, the eternal youth within us cannot be normalized or be completely socialized. That part of the psyche remains young and weird and connected to the divine no matter what age a person reaches.

The youngest, most foolhardy and visionary part of us is often held-back because it can't fit into the family plan or the social system. Being too weird or dreamy to be of use, it becomes the forgotten part of us. Yet, it remembers the dream hidden within us and understands how foolishness can lead to genuine wisdom. Whether we heed the call during youth or it finally reaches us later in life, the calling is heard by the eternally young part of our soul.

The eternal youth within us follows dreams and accepts what visions arrive and trusts in unseen forces. It may not provide much help with practical issues, but it has the proper amount of foolish wisdom to know how to ask for help from the otherworld. The youngest sister or brother in the psyche knows how to connect to the dream and how to use it to sustain the entire life project. That part of the soul remains closer to nature and to animals and to life's unfolding mysteries even when the rest of us succumbs to the collective patterns. The youngest part of the self may look particularly foolish to those who would "run the world;" yet it is that internal aspect that knows where to turn when all else fails and the daily world runs out of ideas and inspirations and proper dreams.

The ever young part of us remains foolish in ways that are secretly wise. The calling that calls to us aims at awakening and sustaining the weird and ever youthful part within us. In answering the call we become both younger and older, both more foolish and wiser than we otherwise would be. In order to become wise in that way we must accept and nurture the threads of our own weirdness. That seems foolish to others, especially to those who have forsaken their own dreams. Yet, those who avoid the weird of their own lives turn out to be most foolish in the end. The greatest foolishness of all is to miss the calling in one's life and never know the true nature of the adventure that the soul came to life to live. Walking with the feet of dreams leads to being foolish in the right direction and becoming wise in the end.

THE AWAKENED SELF

The dream of one's life often seems the most extravagant thing one could possibly do and often a dangerous thing to attempt as well. *Extravagant* means to "wander outside or beyond," especially to wander outside the limits and beyond the rules we set for ourselves. For each human life is an experiment on the part of the divine and each soul is an extravagance produced by the greater dream of life.

Each soul is on a life-long pilgrimage and the secret object of every pilgrimage is the center of the pilgrim. The word *pilgrim* means "one who wanders in the fields of strangers." There is the sense of being a stranger, but the word also has root associations with danger. The pilgrim risks dangers and encounters strangers in order to learn strange things, especially about oneself. Besides the risk of getting lost or being injured, there is the problem of never being the same again. When such an awakening occurs, any step in life can become a pilgrimage.

People set off to a famous shrine; they seek to enter a holy place or arrive at a natural wonder. The point seems to be to reach that distant destination and somehow be renewed and confirmed by the experience. Yet, any renewal that happens must happen within the pilgrim and can only happen when the center of the self becomes awakened by the ardor of the effort or by the grace of the unseen. A genuine path must lead us to the center of our own life; for our life is a pilgrimage to find our awakened self. We may set out to reach a shrine or spiritual center, but we only fully arrive when we reach the center of ourselves.

The awakening that turns a journey into a true pilgrimage can occur anywhere along the way, even on the way back from the supposed destination. "Each step is a whole journey" becomes a true statement when the one taking the step is truly awake and not sleepwalking. Any step that leads to the center of the self is a pilgrimage and a full journey; anything that awakens us is a call from the divine whatever shape it may take.

The awakening occurs whenever and wherever the little-self finally surrenders and the original self becomes evoked. Often, the true center of a great adventure does not become realized until well after the event has occurred. For the soul arrives with its own rhythm and in its own time and it is the greater arrival of the soul in our lives that makes us genuine pilgrims and that keeps us on the appointed way.

The story of Eisik speaks to something ancient in our soul; for he is the immigrant of our dreams, the forsaken son and lost daughter secretly residing within each person. We are each his relative, some more distant than others; but each a refugee within ourselves until we find the way already seeded within us. Some dream brought us here and only it knows the way we are supposed to walk in this world.

Walking with Eisik means going against the flow, crossing over where others fear to go and being foolish in the right direction. The treasure hard to attain includes the wisdom hidden in one's life, but can only be found after some foolishness breaks the spell of normality. Just as a lover must enter longing before any embrace can develop; we must feel the emptiness within us or else never find fulfillment. Only after we are worn down and turned back into the essential bones of our life can someone or something appear that can help turn things completely around.

Those who trade their dreams for the safety of a prescribed life make a false and foolish bargain with the world. They live in a sleeping village even as they pursue a busy life. They may have the trappings of outer success, but they fall into the trap of failing to become who they are at their core. They may be clever, yet they cannot become wise. The treasure we desire most hides where we would never choose to go on our own; were that not the case many more would already have set out. Wisdom can only come from a surprising self-revelation and from learning what it is that we truly love. Such a great learning must make us foolish before it can make us wise.

Each night the body sleeps while the soul embraces its dream and prepares for an awakening. It never tires of life's confusing journey because it finds hints of the divine in every event. The soul sits at the intersection of time and timelessness, at the junction of dreams and waking life. Each day it shapes a bridge intended to bring the two worlds closer so that the divine might pour more freely into the mundane; so that the unseen might help us to see. In order to have such a soul vision we must be willing to be foolish for the sake of life's great song. Being foolish for the dream of our own life turns out to be how we help sustain the dream of life itself.

CHAPTER 8

A SACRED AFFLICTION

Eisik had answered the call and had begun walking toward the shrine of his dreams. The journey had taken him beyond everything he knew about the world and about himself. By the time he arrived at the city of his dreams, he had worn out his shoes and had shed several selves. He had become both a shell of his former self and a seed waiting to be cracked open. He passed through the city, blind to its distractions and impervious to its common allures. His mind was set on reaching the bridge and finding the treasure said to be below it.

Just as the dream predicted, he found the bridge that was set at the very center of the city. A bridge is intended to be a crossing place, yet this one could not even be approached. For it led to a great palace and all approaches to it were guarded night and day. Eisik was afraid to go too close and it was clear that any digging was out of the question. He had followed the map of his dreams only to become stuck before he could reach the goal and find the gold.

The dreamer had gone too far to return empty handed. Simply turning back was not an option; but there was no way to go forward either. Eisik had reached the end of his dreams and had no idea what to do or where to turn. He had believed in the dream's promise of treasure and the seeming appointment with his destiny. Now, he felt crushed with disappointment and stuck in a foreign land. Not knowing what else to do, he began to pace back and forth while staring at the bridge that was near, but also far.

The dream that had opened the road before him now broke him down. The treasure was almost in his grasp, yet strangely seemed as far away as when he first heard the voice calling him to it. He became plagued again by doubts and fears. He fell under the spell of his own uncertainties and into the grip of his deepest worries. Back and forth he went, dragged by dreams and doubts; crossing and re-crossing the same ground, unable to fully cross over. Having left everything behind and become but a shell of himself, Eisik could no longer hide his core condition. His troubles were laid bare; his wounds lay open for all to see. Eisik became stuck in his tracks and helpless to proceed.

No further dream or vision came to him and nothing stopped the growing sense that he had made some great mistake. He had followed his calling faithfully and held the distant goal before him. Now that the goal and gold were near, his faith was crumbling and his heart breaking at the possibility that it was all a foolish dream that could never fully cross into reality. Something within him collapsed and all he could do was blindly wear a rut in the ground before the bridge. Something else would be needed to tip the scales of life in favor of the dream and some sacrifice might be required before any treasure could be revealed.

Of course, this is an old scene repeated in many stories as most treasures are found amidst obstacles and dangerous circumstances. Before reaching the gold, whatever guards the treasure must be faced and something that blocks the seeker must removed. Think of all the tales of treasures guarded by fearful dragons or serpents. People fear snakes; it's an instinct to fear something that moves without any legs and sheds its outer appearance only to reveal another already woven inside.

The snake that causes primal fears in us turns out to be part of the treasure hard to attain. It is there to remind us that obtaining the gold requires that we face our innermost fears and shed something old and worn within us as well. In order to qualify for handling the treasure, we must become like the snake: willing to shed old selves and able to grow a new skin. Bringing a dream to life means changing everything and change is most often accompanied by fear and resistance. Living a dream requires the courage to cross where others fear to go.

The dream that calls to us is also a bridge between worlds; uniting the inner realm with the outer world can't be easy or more would do it. Some danger must be faced or the dream of life can't become real. At first the notion of finding a great treasure seemed a "bridge too far;" later the struggle becomes finding a bridge to the depths of the self. Eventually, it becomes clear that the bridge represents a turn to the inner life and a willingness to face those depths. At the base of the soul-bridge is the treasure hard to attain; yet the depths of one's soul must first be plumbed if the gold would be found.

This bridge motif is no accident and the place of crossing over is always distant because of the distance that exists within us. Bridges are compelling because they stretch between opposing sides and offer a way to span the abyss that keeps appearing in life. If everything were unified there would be no need for bridges and no deep divisions inside each life. A bridge stands for all that is separated and divided and opposed in us and in the world around us. And, a bridge reminds that some essential union is trying to be forged.

Without a bridge opposing sides might run parallel forever and the opposites might never meet. Lovers love a bridge for the way it suggests the mystery and tension of attraction and teaches how longing works. Each must cross a great space to find the other, while the act of crossing over generates the heat needed for union. A bridge can make more evident the presence of separation and the expansive longing in the heart. Yet a bridge also serves as a reminder of the abyss that must be crossed each time life needs to be renewed.

There are old myths in both the East and the West about a bridge as sharp as the edge of a sword that must be crossed if one would reach the far shore and opposite world where eternity waits. The soul remembers those things so that a bridge in this world acts as a reminder of connections to the otherworld. Secretly, everyone knows that in the end we must cross from one world to the other. That's one reason why many people think of death when crossing over a bridge, even if on a simple, everyday errand. A bridge simply makes that great journey of life and death more obvious.

Meanwhile, each person who approaches their genuine destiny also becomes a living bridge that joins this world to the otherworld and secretly sustains the union between them. Doing so requires crossing an inner abyss, for each person carries their own emptiness and fear of falling into the void wherever they go. Remember the worries and hesitations that Eisik had when he first heard the call? Those symptoms were indications of a greater fear and a deeper divide within him. Each person has their deep fears and inner demons and being near the gold tends to activate them all.

The greatest issues and deepest wounds of the soul settle serpent-like exactly in the area where the treasure being sought resides. The magnetism of hidden gold both pulls us closer to it and pushes us away. We become more doubtful, more fearful, more enraged or dissociated each time we approach the longings of our soul and the center of our lives. Each step of self-fulfillment requires some self-exposure and some self-evaluation. Some emptiness must be bridged and some healing is required if we are to reach the treasure hard to attain.

A SACRED AFFLICTION

At the level of the soul each person is gifted, but each is also wounded in some way. In the proximity of the treasure we seek, our persistent wounds will become activated and often become exposed for all to see. Everyone has a wounded side, a weak wing or a withered limb. Approaching the hidden gold will bring out each seeker's fears and reveal their specific way of limping in life. If our wounds weren't intimately bound up with our gifts, everyone would commit to the inner life more quickly and treasures would be popping up all over.

The soul carries and at critical times exhibits an inner defect, a sacred affliction that makes us truly human and full inhabitants of this world. For everything here is a little wounded, a little broken or cracked. Ancient artists often placed a defect in their best work in order to honor the necessary imperfections of life on earth. They left an area unglazed or a small crack uncovered and the imperfections in the earthenware made each piece unique, one of a kind, never to be repeated. Don't stories say that humans are also made from the mud of the earth, from the clay of creation? Life on earth includes being afflicted in specific ways and being broken open so that the inner dream can shine through the cracks of our being.

Although many people "strive to be perfect" those who become wise know that perfection is a kind of death and that our weird imperfections actually keep us alive. Being whole means becoming able to live consciously with our imperfections, for they too are ours to bear. No one is born perfect and we each carry an inner limp from before we learn to walk. We are most whole when we are healing ourselves-- not just "walking our walk," but also limping our limp.

Don't be confused about this; whoever appears perfect now will one day be seen to be hiding a great defect. Better to learn to carry the defects along with the gifts. Better to have a little crack that allows others in and lets the inner light of being shine out on occasion. Once we are far enough along the road of dreams it becomes more difficult to hide our defects and keep up appearances; not only that, but we learn better how appearances are often misleading.

It's like the man who desired to be seen as holy by others. Each time he went to the temple to pray, he removed his shoes with great care. He made a ceremony of his approach and entrance so as to be viewed as pious by others. Yet, his desire went in the wrong direction; he forgot that the divine already knows our defects. A temple is intended to remind us of the divine presence in this world and removing our shoes is symbolic of the total nakedness required when approaching the unseen. Seeing it as an opportunity to improve our status with others shows the blindness that surrounds a true vision.

Somehow, closeness to the source of life both draws us near and causes our pretensions and illusions to push us away. The pretender to piety sought to be seen with common eyes; but the true seeker must become blind to outer appearances in order to be devoted to unseen things. True holiness often appears near the holes in life, where the tatters and rends allow the afflictions to be healed as well as the inner spirit to shine forth.

A WEIRD FOOT

Eisik's clothes were in tatters. He no longer had functional footgear and he was wearing a rut in the ground near the bridge at the center. He was wearing his doubts on the outside and deepening the hole he was already in. He looked strange and foolish, yet it was an honest anguish that pulled him in two directions at once and left him at his wit's end. And, we are each Eisik, each on the edge of a dream-laden journey and each secretly limping no matter how we present ourselves to the world around us.

Being human we must walk on two feet and live in two worlds. One foot is an adaptive appendage that allows us to fit into society and meet the requirements of daily life. That foot feels for solid ground and can serve the ego's need for recognition and a sense of accomplishment. Once it finds a way to establish itself in the world it can provide a sense of stability.

This ego-foot helps us adapt to the circumstances we face; with it we step up to life, face the usual challenges and fulfill common expectations. Typically, the ego foot leads the way; we use it whenever we put "our best foot forward." Yet it also holds us in our ego-stance and will tend to block any emotional growth or genuine spiritual learning. It's important to have an ego-self and a "leg to stand on" in this world; yet that kind of stability is always one-sided and eventually leads to too many fixed positions and hardened attitudes.

Meanwhile, there is another foot, a kind of "otherly foot" that often lags a bit behind. This ill-adaptive foot drags a little and continually fails to adapt to common life. The malingering foot carries our limp and holds us back, but it also remembers essential things that we keep forgetting and leaving behind when we rush ahead. The weird foot is always a bit dreamy; it can be a sleepy appendage, a lazy bone not completely shaped for this world. Call it the soul foot, for it moves the way the soul moves; it wanders off and slips into shadows. It goes where it shouldn't; it prefers the roundabout to the shortcut, and it knows where the wounds are and where the fears fear to go.

We may put our most adapted foot forward when practicality is called for; but when it comes to our actual calling in life, it is our mythic and dream-bound limb that knows the way we must go. Call it a spiritual foot or a pilgrim foot; either way it's weird and *weird* means to have one foot in the otherworld. Our un-adapted foot has its own rhythms and its own reasons; it's a foot of longing that remains clumsy with unrealized potentials even when we appear accomplished to others.

Typically, it becomes covered up and disguised so others can't see it; yet it has its own ways of slowing us down and even stopping us cold. If we ignore this symptom-bearing limb or hide it too thoroughly, it can cause an illness or an accident that stops us completely in our tracks.

In the common light of day and on our normal rounds, our limp can be covered up. On the path of our dreams and in pursuit of a genuine purpose, our limping becomes more pronounced. All true paths include dark stretches that expose the afflictions within us, but also make their healing possible. Limping our limp means accepting how we stumble inside our lives. When seen from the other end of life, our affliction is a sacred wound secretly connected to the hidden gold.

A SECOND CALLING

Eisik was afflicted with great doubt and a hesitation that had long kept him from the dream of his life. Now, that he drew near the treasure of his dreams, the old affliction of self-doubt and the inner scourge of worthlessness had returned and with a vengeance. He was deepening the rut that had held him back for most of his life. Although he didn't know it and could not see it, he was in the breakdown that so often precedes a breakthrough.

Eisik became thoroughly stuck and there was nothing he could do but limp his limp and face whatever shadows he had in his life. To the guards at the bridge he looked quite strange and foolish to boot as he continued to cross back and forth and deepen the hole he was already in. After a time the captain of the guard approached the rut where Eisik paced and spoke to him. "We have observed you pacing back and forth day after day. You look and deeply troubled. Friend, are you alright?"

Eisik told the truth for it was all he had left in him. He described the voice in the dream and explained how he had followed the instructions that led him to the center of the city and to the bridge that stood before them. He confessed that he was supposed to dig at the base of the bridge where a golden treasure could be found. He expressed how he wanted to do just that, but feared that he would be harmed or imprisoned by the guards. At the same time, he found that he could not turn away and would not give up his dream.

To the regimented attention of the captain of the guard the dreamer looked foolish and lost. To the doubting soul of the dreamer the captain seemed an emissary of defeat. Both are near a treasure, yet neither knows exactly what to do. As so often happens in stories and in life, a third thing is needed to shift the tension between them and change the situation.

The captain spoke again, "My friend, you are old enough to know better than to believe in dreams. Everyone knows that dreams are not real and that they can have no bearing on life in the real world." He went on forcefully, "Why I myself had a dream last night. In my dream a voice said that a man named Eisik should look behind the loose bricks of the hearth in his own hut. There, he would find a quantity of gold. You see how foolish such dreams can be. There is no treasure to be found in going that way."

For his part, Eisik said not a word. He only bowed deeply and thanked the captain for his timely speech. He turned quietly, left the bridge he sought for so long, and began walking again. Without even looking behind, Eisik began the long trek that led back along the way he had come. At the bridge of dreams he became instructed by the dream of someone who didn't even believe in dreams. The maker of dreams is speaking through believers and unbelievers alike.

Anyone overhearing the conversation between the captain and the dreamer would conclude that the pilgrim had come a great distance on a fool's errand. Then, it would appear as if the wanderer recovered himself. He bows as if awakening from foolish visions and unrealistic hopes. He gives up his strange back and forth behavior. The firm correction of the captain seems to clear things up, straighten him out, and send him on his way.

Inside it's very different. Eisik is being called again and the second calling comes through the dream of one who rejects dreams. Now, dreams are talking to dreams. In the strange logic of the otherworld, the one who risked everything to follow a dream learns from someone who neither believes in dreams nor listens to the language of the soul. The message that reveals the truth comes from one who does not understand the nature or the meaning of the message he conveys.

The captain reports the night message as empty rhetoric, as complete and utter nonsense, as further proof of the foolishness of following visions and dreams. But, there is a method in this madness as those listening with inner ears can hear the words within the words. They discern the message trying to come through even if the messenger understands nothing of it. When the treasure is near and the heart finally opens, anything can happen and usually does.

The captain says one thing, while Eisik, cracked open by his long pilgrimage, hears the deeper language. Eisik has made the effort and has suffered the pain; he has surrendered to the unseen and brought himself to the point of no return. When things are truly ready to turn around even the naysayers begin to help out. The one who rejects all knowledge of the otherworld becomes the one who delivers messages from it.

Imagine the quiet delight inside Eisik when he learns the secret from one who guards this world against messages from the other one. While dismissing the dreamer and his dreams the captain actually pushes him deeper within and closer to the genuine goal. While being called a fool the seeker receives the exact knowledge needed to continue on the path of awakening. The joke reveals that even those opposed to the unseen must do its bidding when the time for a genuine transformation has come.

A DEEPER MESSAGE

Something wise is being demonstrated here; for a person doesn't have to go the entire way alone. At some point along the way the otherworld begins to move toward the seeker. When that happens, helpers appear in unlikely forms. Eisik followed his dream as far as he could go along the path that called to him. When he could go no further, the next dream came looking for him.

The turning point didn't come from digging at the base of the bridge; rather things turned around when the seeker dug deep inside and came out with the truth. He bared his soul and faced his fears. At that point, help can come from any direction and seemingly discouraging news can open the way. At the bridge where things cross between one world and the other, anything can become a source of knowledge. When the two worlds are being bridged anyone nearby can be drawn into the exchange that secretly encourages the pious journey of life.

Sometimes it's a foolish thing to offer the truth, sometimes more foolish to withhold it. At certain moments, telling the truth is necessary; at critical times the inner confusion and pain must be spoken out for things to become clear. That's part of being foolish in the right direction and part of becoming wise as well. This kind of foolishness works its wisdom inside a situation. When it comes to the underlying affliction, logic is of little help; when the inner truth is at stake the heart better knows what to do.

Imagine another dreamer who is afraid to speak the truth to the captain of the guard. He fears being punished or rejected or thinks the guards will take the treasure for themselves. These things are subtle; everything can change with just the slightest false note. If the seeker holds back the painful, foolish truth, the captain will fail to recall his dream. For he guards against the night visions and would have others reject them as well. He can easily forget that he was dreaming of hearths and gold and a man named Eisik.

Instead of everything turning around, the dreamer might simply be turned away as something gets in the way of the transformation trying to occur. Either the inner situation didn't become conscious enough or the affliction of the soul remained covered up. Even on a proper path there are no guarantees that the message intended for us will actually reach us. If the seeker holds something back or becomes enveloped in fear additional struggles will be required before the information needed can get all the way through.

Meanwhile, to one who is awakening fully, everything becomes a wake-up call. This kind of self-awakening changes everything; it opens the gates of understanding so that anyone might deliver the next message. The turning point has arrived and anything or anyone can become a source of deliverance.

A bridge has already been crossed; an inner treasure has been found and form no longer matters. A great turn around is underway and the seeker can accept the whole truth even if it involves a complete reversal of direction.

At a certain point, everything points in the same direction. In the proximity of genuine knowledge mysteries become revealed and in mysterious ways. The real Way is like that; help from an enemy, truth from those who believe nothing, release provided by those guarding the prison. The captain believes that he is bringing a foolish man to his senses; meanwhile the pilgrim has received another revelation, one that turns things inside out and aims him at his own hearth or heart.

The real treasure of life, the one difficult to find and hard to attain, is never far from us. That's an unwritten rule on this earth. What we desperately desire and need most is buried in the recesses of our innermost being all along. That is the "open secret" found in many traditions and told in many ways. Yet it remains a kind of secret because trusting in oneself remains one of the hardest things to do in life.

The bridge between worlds is subtle and delicate and those who dream are always less certain than those who keep a distance from their inner life. The captain of the guard stands for all the dull ideas that guard against the possibility of genuinely waking up to the unique nature of one's life. He represents the certainty of the un-awakened that willingly reinforces the restrictions of collective life. He believes what he is told by those above his station and he wants you to believe the same way. He wears the uniform that represents a uniformity of ideas as well as conformity to whatever the ruling "isms" might be.

A tremendous collective effort is made everyday to ensure that the limited perspective and common beliefs that sustain the obvious world remain firmly in place. Despite the wild dance of dreams invisibly spanning the arc of each night and the pulse of imagination inside every soul, the daily routine requires that the false certainties and ruling orders be guarded zealously.

The irony of looking but not seeing is epitomized by the captain who guards the bridge. He, too, is near the place of understanding and the site of treasure, yet his beliefs make any subtle presence invisible to him. Those who have no hint of the gift of life will often turn others away from searching for it. Being unaware of the treasures hidden within, they try to prove that none exist at all. Knowing nothing of the true situation, they speak with great authority of what is real and what is not. They consider themselves to be "realists," yet they know nothing of the Real that waits to be discovered under the skin of common "reality."

A DIVINE ERRAND

The roads of life are cluttered with signs set to convince us to become someone else, rather than strive to become as we are inside. The great scams of life and our own fearful schemes serve to distract us from the pain and beauty of learning to be who we already are at the core of our souls. People talk of being realistic, of paying attention to the "real world," all the while missing any connection to the reality of the deeper self and the wisdom that resides within it.

Meanwhile, many others make the opposite mistake and reject this world in hopes of finding a better place in the otherworld. The bridge of life stretches between this world and the otherworld and we have two feet and are required to find a way to live in both. If we fail to become established in this world we can lose our footing and slip into obscurity before learning what our soul desires most. If we fail to awaken to the calling of the divine we can become mired in the mud of mundane errands and dutiful tasks.

PLACES OF AWAKENING

We live within a paradox, within the restrictions of a fate that can trap us in a familiar place and a longing for the eternal that won't leave us alone. We go back and forth on the bridge of life collecting knowledge first from one side and then from the other. At times we must follow our dreams and undertake the errands of the divine; at other times we must incarnate more fully and play a role in the earthly drama. We serve both worlds and in moments of awakening become the living bridge that holds them together.

It's like the old story of the seeker who became an accomplished ascetic and spent all his time doing spiritual practices in the mountains. He avoided all the temptations of life and left the conflicts and confusions of the common world far behind. He practiced austerities from dawn until night. He meditated and fasted and abstained to remove the stain of this world from his soul, but also to draw down the attention of the great god Vishnu. For it was Vishnu who first dreamed the cosmic dream and Vishnu whose holy breath sustains the world as well as all the dreams within it.

Narada, for that was the name of the serious seeker, sought a victory over the illusions and disillusionments of life on earth. In order to transcend the entrapments of the common world he left everything behind, he emptied his life and sought refuge in the hills. Through severe practices, he became a bare flame burning naked in the empty heights of the holy mountains. Eventually, Vishnu noticed the "tapas" or holy heat emanating from the spot where the holy man executed his strivings. The gods have great interest in the striving of human souls, especially when someone begins to burn with serious spiritual heat.

So, the great deity of dreams decided to visit the seeker and grant him a boon as a way of recognizing the effort that he was putting forth. Having dreamed the entire world into existence, Vishnu could appear in any form he wished. At times he appeared as a wise sage or else as a poor beggar. The divine often appears in a form that the one receiving the visitation can learn the most from. A powerful ruler might have to bend down to see god, while a poor soul might have to look up in a new way. Vishnu came before Narada in a resplendent and dignified form, but with a little desire... as we shall see.

After commending the saint for his efforts, the god offered to fulfill any wish that the holy man might have. After all, even the gods like to play god. Narada knew that each god had particular powers. He knew that the deity was the original dreamer in the life of the world and that if anyone could fulfill dreams, it was Vishnu.

When offered the fulfillment of a wish, the saint did not hesitate. He knew exactly what he desired and what he most desired was to comprehend the power or "maya" of Vishnu. He desired to understand the magical power behind all of creation and all the illusions of this world. For *maya* means both matter and magic, both energy and illusion; both the stuff of and the play of existence. Like many before him, Narada wanted to know what the god of creation knew; he wanted to understand the power and genius behind all the manifestations of the world.

Vishnu was not exactly pleased by this request. He gently suggested that the holy man try another wish. But, Narada was single-minded on the subject and would not budge. Vishnu had offered to grant a wish and the holy man had responded with his request. An offer had been made and had been accepted; an agreement had been reached and even the gods are subject to certain agreements. The deal was done and there was nothing else for it; so Vishnu beckoned to Narada to follow him.

The saint and the god began to walk along together. After a time, they entered a deserted path and walked under the intensity of the blazing sun. Vishnu suddenly announced that he was thirsty. He asked Narada if he would be kind enough to go on ahead where there seemed to be a village and bring back a drink of water to cool the thirst. The saint was familiar with service and self-sacrifice and he knew that an errand from god was not something to deny. So, he hastened off to the village and went directly to the door of the first house he found.

Narada also felt a great thirst as he knocked on the simple door. He was in a heightened state of devotion due to his errand of seeking water for the divine. As the door swung open before him, a graceful young woman appeared. She greeted him kindly and welcomed him inside. As he stepped across the threshold he gazed upon the beauty of the woman standing silently before him. In the light of all that was happening, she seemed to be the most beautiful person he had ever laid his eyes upon.

As he drank in her beauty, Narada neglected to ask for the drink of water. He simply followed her into the coolness of the house. Once inside, he was graciously received by the young woman's parents who treated him as an honored guest. They made him comfortable, brought him sweet drinks and made friendly conversation. Time began to pass as they all enjoyed the presence of each other. Soon enough, in the cordialness of that house and amidst the exchange of glances with the young woman, Narada simply forgot that he was on an errand from god.

After a time, and how else could it be, Narada and the young woman were married. The saint soon learned the joys of marriage as well as the hardships of a peasant's life. With one thing after another, a dozen years passed somehow. Narada found himself with three children and many responsibilities. When the old parents passed on, Narada and his wife inherited the farm and worked hard to preserve the land and sustain the family.

One year, they were assaulted by a great flood as torrential rains poured unceasingly from the sky. On a harsh, storm driven night, their herds were drowned in the flooding waters and the house itself began to wash away. Water rushed everywhere and solidity nowhere to be found. Narada took the hand of his wife and those of his older children. He placed the youngest child on his shoulder and struggled to lead them all through the raging waters to dry land and safety.

In the midst of the deluge the burden became too great. Narada could not hold them all together against the flood and the youngest child slipped into the rushing waters. Letting go of the others, Narada tried desperately to save the little one. As the torrent swept the child away, he saw his wife and the other children disappearing in the opposite direction. Torn and pulled in two directions at once and caught in the dark turbulence, Narada began to fall and soon couldn't rise again. He fell into unconsciousness and became as inert as a piece of wood.

His body drifted along on the current until he was cast headfirst upon a great rock. The hard knock caused him to suddenly awaken. As he recovered consciousness, he remembered the flood and the loss of his wife and family. Then, all the sorrows of the world came rushing at him and he began to lament his losses and cry out in pain. In the midst of his wailing anguish he heard a familiar voice speaking to him: "Where have you been my child and where is the water you were bringing for me? I have been waiting here for more than half an hour."

Narada turned toward the voice and saw the vision of Vishnu again. Suddenly, they were standing next to each other on the deserted path. All around them the earth stretched dry and cracked and parched by the blazing sun. There was no flood, no torrent, no river and no great rock; there was no water to be seen anywhere.

"Now do you understand the secret of my power and the maya of this world?" asked Vishnu. The god of the dream of creation had granted the request of the holy man and the great seeker received a taste of the divine power. He received the gift that he desired most and found himself waking up between one world and the other.

THE QUESTION BEING ASKED OF US

Do you understand now, the story asks of us. Is it all a dream and nothing but an illusion? Was the lifetime in the village real? Did the god truly come near? In the midst of many other agreements, both sweet involvements and heavy responsibilities, did we forget some divine errand we were on? Or, in longing for the otherworld have we lost all connection to the world around us?

Our love of life takes us in two directions; we burn with holy longings and thirst for earthly delights. We stand at one threshold and then at the other; we live in both worlds and must learn to serve them both. We undertake an errand for the divine only to find ourselves back in the common village of life. The door before us opens, we step through it, and everything changes. We are swept up in the dance of life; we enter it fully and lose ourselves in it; we give ourselves to it, become part of it all, and it is solid and real and meaningful.

Then, the hard times come and the floods of change and loss ensue. All the solidity of daily life slips away and the reality of it all rattles before us. Things we once held dear begin to drift apart and fall from our hands. That which was so real and so beautifully and damningly immediate becomes remote and we wake up in our essential aloneness. We find ourselves amongst the rocks and in the hard places and all that we had gained seems lost. Surprisingly however, we are close to the divine again. When we have lost all that we loved and worked for, we are near the errand of the soul again. When we wail at all our losses and decry the pain of life, we are secretly near the place of awakening.

We are on an errand for the divine all along, even when we knock on doors and forget why we were knocking. We climb the ladders we find before us without considering which wall they lean against. We sit with the neighbors and dream of distant treasures. We fall in love with the beauty of this world and with the souls of others we meet in it. We participate in the magic and maya that keeps one realm in touch with the other. We walk on both paths and cross the bridge between the worlds many times over.

The point here isn't to dismiss the allure of love or the importance of children and family life. Love has its own kind of power and maya and it involves an essential part of each person's fate. Love also has a part to play in the destiny of every soul. Remember the old saying: Without love, the work cannot progress. The point isn't to dismiss the beauty and delight or the suffering and heartache of this world. Wasn't it the god of creation who sent the seeker to the threshold where he found beauty and discovered ways of being and loving and serving the desires of this world?

The door of life is there to be opened and entered. Like Narada, we enter the next village or the next stage of our lives and forget why we came to life to begin with. There's no help for it and no simple escape from it. Isn't that part of what Vishnu was revealing to the saint? It was precisely while he was on a direct mission from god that he fell in love with beauty, with life in the world, with children and with becoming a contributing member of the human community. The conversation with the divine leads the soul of the seeker to an immersion in the dramas and delights of life on earth.

The moment of waking up comes after some life experience, not from completely avoiding it. Narada awakens in the midst of the human dilemma, between the proverbial rock and a hard place. He awakens amidst the drama that requires that we live and love and lose and suffer in the "real world." And, in awakening, recalls that he has forgotten his agreement with the divine. On one hand we must know what it means to be alive in the human drama that alternates between love and loss. On the other hand there is a longing to know the divine and serve something that transcends all of that.

Narada is another form of Eisik, for both are seekers and servants of the divine and each became lost while on an important errand. Whereas Eisik finds an awakening when he fears that all has been lost, Narada must lose it all before he awakens. Both inhabit the village of life and each finds a way to awaken further when the time comes. Narada is the saint who remembers the divine errand and also the sinner who forgets everything but the immediate demands of life. He lost his wife and his children; he lost the whole farm and almost lost himself in the tumultuous waters of life. He is the saintly sinner and the lost seeker and the suffering pilgrim in this dream of life that can become one thing and then another.

Despite all our good intentions and caring dedication, one day we lose what we love, we lose those we love. We fail our families at some point and whatever we achieve in life can only be a temporary gain. Whole empires have already disappeared and armies have faded into the dust. Everything that arises in the great drama of life must one day disappear as if it were all an illusion; there's truth in that. Yet again, the world around us is and will continue to be the Grand Illusion. Call it illusion or call it reality, life is the dream that must be.

At the same time, there is another level where a conversation with the divine becomes possible. For it is the divine that dreams up the world and sets each threshold before us. And, it is the divine that waits for us to awaken and recall our soulful errand again no matter what roads we have been on or what floods and losses we have suffered. What seems like a lifetime to us is but a short time where the divine is concerned. When it comes to the divine errand anytime could be the right time to awaken.

Meanwhile, most awakenings do come as a shock. Whether it be the loss of everything we thought was ours, or a message that says the time has come to turn everything around. One way or another, a deeper calling begins and a voice gently asks: Do you understand now?

The saint asked for knowledge equal to what the gods know. The deity answered by sending him back to the door of life's entanglements and illusions. The answer indicates the necessity of both worlds; for both errands are part of the magic and power and maya of creation. Only after entering the door of life fully and experiencing both the reality and the illusory nature of this world can the saint fully awaken to the conversation with the divine.

The two worlds are close to each other and a person can cross from one to the other in a single step. That kind of crossing over can happen at any moment and can be precipitated by seeing beauty, by receiving a message or by waking up with a dream. It can come through a sudden shock or a hard knock; but can also be found through spiritual devotion and practice. In this world each wake up call is an opportunity to turn back to the conversation with the divine.

The continuous illusion of this world is right next to the divine source that creates and sustains it; two different orders of being, yet both flow from the same source. Life is the necessary illusion from which we drink as well as the circumstantial waters in which we drown again and again. That is the truth as well as the illusion of it. We are each on a mysterious errand and the great beauty of this world requires that we both forget and at times remember it.

We are each a certain question being asked of god and asked of life. Only over time can we learn how to wake up and dry out and take our rightful place in the divine conversation. Just like Eisik, we are closer to an awakening and to a turning point whenever we reach the end of our rope and feel that we have lost everything again. Then, we either fall apart or else we find the thread of destiny that pulls everything together and opens the path before us again.

CHAPTER 9

THE ARC OF RETURN

What is truly ours returns to us when we become ready to return to it. Having received the critical message from an unexpected source, Eisik turned himself around. His calling called him back and the long pilgrimage reversed. He retraced the steps he had taken while first following his dream and saw that nothing at all was wasted; for the soul doesn't waste anything. There's no proof offered for that, it's just a sign posted on the path of return where everything encountered is tinged with revelation. By the time he reached the village again, Eisik had gathered the pieces of himself and gleaned a greater understanding of his fate in life.

The second calling involves a spiritual pivot that leads to the deeper road within the seeker. There was a time for travelling out, but now the time for digging in had arrived. The seeker was finally ready for the treasure that was there all along. Just as the dream of the captain described, there were loose bricks at the back of the hearth and loosening them further allowed the hidden gold to shine forth. Eisik found the treasure hard to attain behind the wall of his own hearth. The gold he sought at the distant bridge was nearby all along and waiting for him to turn to it.

It is far easier to believe that the treasure we seek must be found in some foreign place than to understand that the gold was near all along. It's useful to notice how close *hearth* is to *heart*. Remove a single, almost silent letter and a fireplace becomes an inner organ. Remove the first letter and the place of the fire becomes *earth*. Here on earth a fire burns at the very center and an inner flame burns at the heart center of each earthling. Loosening the bricks around the hearth serves as a reminder for the need to loosen the stones around one's heart. Doing that reveals the inner gold of the "heart within the heart."

Many old stories say that we seek for what is within us all along. That's the message trying to get through, but it only arrives once we have exhausted all other avenues. That which was there all along cannot be revealed until we experience the extremes of our own lives. At the far end of our waking and walking, of our worrying and working, we begin to turn back to our original self. On the arc of return we also turn within and find what has carried us all along.

The second calling involves an inward, downward shift that leads to the inner arc of life and to the deep and knowing self within oneself. It involves a reorientation to the original imagination and living dream that first brought us to life; for that is the treasure hard to attain and the gold hidden in the recesses of one's heart.

Someone says: "This is an outrage; why weren't we told about this at the beginning? We could have stayed home and saved all the trouble and travel, all the trials and tribulations." Not true. It is necessary to go all the way to the end of our dreams in order to learn where the dreaming comes from. We carry what we seek, but it takes a lot of bumping and scraping, losing and loosening to reveal it. Just like saintly Narada, we must knock on some doors and receive a few hard knocks ourselves before we become loosened enough to find what is hidden within us.

On the journey to the center of the self there can be no shortcuts. The seeker had to go far into the world in order to learn how to look closer within. The one who follows dreams and visions to begin with must later seek where the dreams come from. In turning back we learn to see with different eyes and know ourself in a new way. In turning within we learn to see where we truly come from, a place that was hidden from us until we cast our dreams upon the world and saw enough of the road of life.

The arc of return has its own rewards as we view the course of our life the other way around. The returning path includes a life re-view and a chance to re-collect oneself from the road of lived experience. We step deeper into the same prints and find patterns that were there all along but hard to perceive the first time out. When we arrive at the center of the self all the detours, strange side-trips, and reversals turn out to be necessary for us to find the way.

BE HERE NOW

The real journey aims at what already exists inside, yet it can only arrive at the source by first leading away from it. If it were simply a matter of searching within, many might find their way more quickly. However, in order to "be here now" it turns out that a person must be everywhere else first. The answer is within, but the call comes from somewhere beyond. It seems ironic, but the dream that calls us to a greater life both leads and misleads the dreamer. Going out and coming back are both required; for there are two worlds involved and two arcs of life that call to each of us.

If the way was simple and straightforward, no dream or art or true practice would be needed. Everyone would set out and arrive directly at the soul's destination. Yet, the path to the center requires several kinds of surrender; we must stretch and change and suffer great doubts. It takes a certain amount of courage and even some heart-break to learn what one's heart already knows. It takes enough experience of being lost to know how to find one's way; thus the dream of life both leads and misleads us.

Those who state that the present is all that counts are telling the truth; but they didn't start there. They are telling the story of arrival while others are just departing. For one who is about to go on a long journey, it is not that helpful to know that the treasure is within. They might conclude that there is no reason to enter the greater world and thereby miss the exact adventure their soul requires. People keep making the mistake of thinking that their life isn't seeded a certain way or that the experience of others can relieve them of the requirement for entering the world fully.

A genuine seed was planted in the garden of the soul and it intends to grow. Each seed is unique and derived from a divine source; but the seed of self must be cracked open and must take its nourishment from the common world. Even monks who practice the denial of all desires must beg sustenance from those who live more fully in the sensual world. If only one world was involved people wouldn't be so divided within. Exchanging with the outer world is a requirement even when it is the inner life being grown.

Some branching out is necessary before blossoming can truly begin. Some ripening is required even if the fruit is near all along. A person can only be where they truly are and most can only arrive at the present by examining and understanding the past as well as exploring what lies before them. Any time the answer seems too simple and undemanding, it usually is.

There are the subtleties and surprises on any path and only after traveling far can the seeker hear and understand the words behind the words. Only after being driven by the unseen can we begin to see into our own confusion; only then can the messages about the inner life begin to make true sense. It is the willingness to surrender that allows the pilgrimage to the self to begin and the willingness to sacrifice and be vulnerable that allows the treasure to be reached.

The genuine individual only develops from repeated tempering in the fires of uncertainty and even in the flames of inner conflict. A person must break several inner spells and awaken more than once in order to find their true way. The distance to the center is short; yet, the road that leads us there is much longer. Those who take shortcuts at the beginning will find themselves going the long way round later on. Gold is found in dark and forbidding places and usually after a great amount of searching and surveying the territory. If this were a simple matter, people would find gold easily and value it less.

HEART TALK

The great adventures as well as the deeper reflections of life both aim at the revelation of the deeper self within. A true education serves to break the fetters on the soul and crack the shell of the self and reveal the heart within it. A hearth is the figurative center of a house just as the heart can be seen as the center of a person. Heart and hearth both grow from the deeply rooted verb *ker* meaning "to singe, to burn, to glow." From the heat of a fire that burns, to a light that glows and illuminates the way, that is the progression of heart-learning. From the burning questions and searing emotions to the clear light of one's spirit, that's how the forging of the inner gold proceeds. In such a progression the anguished and longing heart becomes the focal point of the work before it can be the golden place that makes illumination possible.

Eisik was a friendly fellow and a good soul, but something essential to life had been walled over or blocked with stone. Some old heartbreak had become walled in; some deep longing had been walled off. Something hard in the heart of the seeker had to be loosened up in order for the inner way to be found. Loosening the walls around the heart brings up many fears; it feels like dying or being torn apart. Most prefer digging for treasure on foreign soil or behind other walls. Beyond our fears of the world around us, there waits the greater fear of encountering our own self.

WHAT THE HEART LOVES

An old proverb states that "what the heart loves is the cure." The heart already knows what it loves most and knows how it is intended to make love in this world. Meanwhile, there is an old struggle between fear and love; for one would separate where the other would unify. Fear and love are opposing energies, yet are often found together. Love, like life, can not be tame. Each approach to what the heart truly loves is likely to raise some level of fear.

The deepest fears often form at an early and vulnerable age when the heart is naturally open and unprotected. Each child is golden in its own way and ready to shine. An infant or a child will offer love freely and expects to receive the same in return. When that clear love is rejected or is met with fear and anger the heart begins to close around itself. The gold of the self is there, but it becomes surrounded by fear and guarded by subtle walls. When the time comes for the heart to open fully again, the old fears will awaken and the inner walls will tighten up.

Life is the ailment and that which the heart loves most is the only remedy for it. The road of longing and self-discovery is intended to re-open the heart and reveal the gold within it. The path of discovery will inevitably raise the exact fears that hold the heart captive. Although fear can become terrifying and paralyzing, what we most fear is where we must go. "Fear is the guide for the true direction of the heart," they used to say when considering the courage required to become oneself. What we love is the cure and what we fear will guide us in making the remedy.

There's an old tale of a young woman who feared that she would never truly know love. The one person to whom she had given her heart had become distant from her and she became afraid that she would never love again. Her fear set her on a journey to find a cure for love. Eventually, she found an old sage who said that a remedy for love could be concocted. The sage offered to fashion an appropriate potion if she would gather and contribute just one ingredient herself. Of course, she quickly agreed and asked what ingredient she needed to acquire.

She was shocked and even offended when the sage asked for a whisker from the head of a living tiger. She asked if all the other ingredients were as dangerous to gather as a tiger's whisker. The sage asked if she truly desired a cure for the love problem or not. What could she say? What could she do? She had asked if there was a cure and could hardly refuse when a solution was being offered. She would now have to face her fears if she would find a way to love again.

She set out looking for love and found herself searching for tigers. As fate would have it, she learned of a path that led into the hills where a great tiger was said to live in a deep cave. Not knowing how else to approach the beast, she began carrying a bowl of food up the mountain path each evening. Each time she would go as far as her fear would allow; then she would leave the bowl of food on the path and descend to safety. Every time she returned to the path she would find another empty bowl. She would step past that marker and enter further into her fear before leaving another bowl.

One night, in the light of the moon, she ascended the path in her accustomed way. Just as she stepped past another empty bowl, she saw the great tiger coming toward her. She stopped cold in her tracks and placed her bowl on the ground before her. Despite overwhelming fear, she spoke to the tiger as it bent its great head to the bowl and began eating. She apologized for what she was about to do, took a deep breath, and plucked a long whisker that stuck out from the corner of the tiger's mouth. As she leapt back in full fear, the tiger pretended not to notice.

Holding the key ingredient in her hand she couldn't resist dancing with joy and lifting the whisker up to the moonlight as she descended back down the path. She carried the precious ingredient to the old sage who held it up in the light of a fire in order to determine if it was in fact a whisker from the head of a living tiger. Satisfied that it was indeed the ingredient that had been requested, the sage let it drop into the fire where it was instantly consumed by flames and turned to ash.

The young woman was outraged and demanded an explanation. The sage asked how she had accomplished the task of facing the tiger. With intense emotion, she described how she carried bowls of food into the darkness of each night while stepping further and further into her fears. The sage then asked if such a practice worked when approaching a man-eating tiger could it not be used to reach the human heart. After some reflection, the young woman began to see how in facing her fears she had found the way to open her own heart.

In seeking for the tiger's whisker she had faced her deepest fears and found her own courage. That was the missing ingredient; it was the only ingredient that was needed. She had the necessary longing for love and she admitted her fears when she sought for a cure. Courage is another *heart* word that refers to the core of one's deepest feelings and innermost thoughts. For the heart harbors thoughts and dreams as well as feelings and emotions. It takes courage to open the heart, to face our fears and learn what cures can be found within.

The heart is a vital organ, but also a great territory. The heart is where true imagination resides and when it opens we find that there are mountains and caves within us. There are tigers and sages as well; and the woman of the soul walks there. She's looking for love and she knows that the cure only comes after the deepest fears have been faced.

The old sage and the young woman are two parts of the wise and loving heart that holds the inner gold. But, the heart also harbors a tiger that needs to be nourished and fed or else it might attack the one who carries it. Everyone has a fierce issue that will devour them unless they learn to face it and make peace with it. The tiger has the missing ingredient and is willing to help, but can only be approached after the little-self relinquishes its fears and controlling attitudes.

What we love is much bigger than anything the little-self understands. The ego-self formed around the earliest fears we felt and it continues to feel the way it did when we were small and helpless. Later, we must move past such fears in order to find the greater self within us. Remember Eisik pacing before the bridge; he was close to the gold, but something was still closed in him. It was no accident that there were guards involved in the pivotal events. He had made the effort and gone the distance, but another opening was needed. He needed something from the hard-hearted captain just as the young woman needed an encounter with a dangerous tiger.

The deeper self is capable of great love, through it we come to understand our pain and learn to love ourselves. Eisik had to release the fears and worries that kept him in a rut. He had to become open when he felt that all the paths had closed before him. He had to forgive his own strange behavior, just as the young woman had to be patient and loving toward her process while she faced her deepest fears. Later, she did not need the whisker because she had tamed the tiger of her fears and found her own brilliance.

We can draw great courage from the depths of our heart, but tend to draw it only when we are driven by fear or by despair or by loneliness. Remember the old thief trapped in his dark dungeon. He had the golden seed all along, but only found it after he faced a period of great loneliness and deep despair. Then, he became a tiger of truth-telling and others had to face their fears and dark thoughts. He became free as a result of his dark period, just as the young woman found her freedom and joy after bravely facing night after night of fear.

The heart can be a heated place where passions and fears run rampant, yet it can be a tender spot that knows how to touch and be touched. When necessary we can each get to the "heart of the matter" and find what truly matters to us. On the way there, we will encounter old fears and infantile attitudes. It helps to know that the inner gold is nearby, that there is a resident sage in the heart, and that the tiger within is inclined to help.

Typically, gold is found in dark places and must be mined and purified in order to shine and become useful. As such it symbolizes something rare and valuable hidden within the darker issues of each soul. The inner gold must be mined from the dark matter or "prima materia" of one's life. Thus, stories use images of digging in the earth and loosening the stones around the heart.

What tries to awaken in us and come to life through us is much greater than the little-self we mostly identify with. There is an authentic interior that waits to be discovered; it can burn with creative heat, yet also can be gentle and loving to others. This inner hearth-heart is the place where the flame of life burns within the soul. The "gold of the self" is a sustaining inner sun that burns like the fire at the core of the earth. The inner fire of gold secretly sustains all our growth and it aims to shine through us into the world.

HABITS OF THE HEART

Meanwhile, the walls around the heart are kept in place by habits hard-held by the little-self. If the greater self within would be found and the inner gold would be released, the core issues must be faced and loosened up. Such breakthroughs usually require a practice that fits the problem and can move the heart as well as focus the mind. There are many kinds of obstacles that can block the heart and keep it from opening. Often, a guide or teacher must be found before the right practice can be applied.

It's like the seeker who found a teacher and asked for a practice that would help open his life to wisdom. After observing the fellow, the teacher advised him to begin giving money to anyone who insulted him. His practice would become being ready and willing to pay for insults and he would have to do it for a period of three years. What could he do? He had asked for direction and he had reached a point in life where something had to change. Either he would surrender and pay the price for waking up or else remain as he had been.

The fellow decided to make the agreement and accept the strange practice. And, he did what was asked of him. Each time someone insulted him, he responded by handing them money and paying them for the offence. Since he was somewhat of an abrasive person, he had ample opportunities to attend to his new practice.

After three years were up, the student returned to the teacher and reported on his odd success. He had managed to give away a good deal of what he possessed and distributed it primarily to those who gave him insults. The teacher applauded him and concluded that he was now ready to learn wisdom. He told the fellow to undertake a journey to visit a certain city. The disciple lost no time in going and enjoyed the trip in the knowledge that he had already paid his dues.

As he approached the gates of the great city he saw a man sitting near the entrance as both holy ones and beggars are inclined to do. Although the man appeared to be a holy person, he loudly hurled insults at everyone who came or went. The funny thing was that there was an uncanny accuracy in each insult, a kind of a reverse greeting that most found difficult to simply shrug off. The disciple was treated no differently and when his turn came the insult landed firmly. The difference was that the disciple burst out laughing and seemed to find great joy where others felt offended and abused.

"Why do you laugh when I accurately insult you," asked the gate guardian. "Because," answered the disciple, "for three years I have been paying for this kind of thing in hopes of finding wisdom and now you give it to me for free."

"Enter the city then," said the gate keeper, "it is all yours."

The fellow entered and he enjoyed the place because he had found a place in himself that needed to open and become clear. The story doesn't explain it, but all indications are that the fellow had trouble dealing with insults. Of course, that is often the case with those who readily insult others. Once he had to pay for insults his attention became focused on his own condition. By the time he reached the city, he was like Eisik at the bridge; he was ready for a breakthrough and in the kind of openness that moves a person closer to their heart and to the joy hidden within it.

Each person has a complex of issues that surround the heart of hearts and for each a practice is needed to approach the problem and loosen the defenses. There's no telling what might open a particular heart and reveal the gold hidden within it; but there is always some accuracy inside the circumstances that keep us stuck.

The young woman who feared that she wouldn't find love was secretly a great lover. Her fear was close to the love in her heart. She had to become as a tiger in order to grasp her own loving nature. In stepping through her fears she moved closer to the love-tiger within. When she drew close to the core of her fear the tiger came to her. When she grasped the thing she most desired, the fearful beast pretended not to notice. Just so, the otherworld moves closer whenever we face the tigers of our innermost fears.

The man who paid for insults had an unconscious way of insulting his own heart. For what we do to others we tend to do more so to ourselves. With his insults he made others pay for his own discomfort and lack of acceptance. Only after he learned the true cost of insults and offensive behavior could he learn to laugh at himself. His joy was hidden behind his insulting behavior. Once he broke through the walls around his heart, he became able to enter the great city of life open-heartedly. Whether it be fear or anger or arrogance that blocks the hearth of the heart, there will be great joy when the stones loosen and the gold becomes revealed.

THE TRUE JERUSALEM

"I give you a golden thread," said the poet, "only roll it into a ball and it will lead you to the hole in Jerusalem's wall." The hole is not an actual crack in the walls of the Jerusalem found on maps. The golden city of Jerusalem did not simply reside on earth; rather it descended to earth whenever and wherever someone broke through the walls that kept the heart closed. The true Jerusalem refers to the "city of god" or the "city of peace," the Jerusalem of the heart.

The original Jerusalem was the city of art and beauty, the inspired design for all great cities because the pattern for it came from the divine. The true

Jerusalem appeared when the heart fully opened and any place you happened to be became "heaven on earth." Before it became a place of great conflict and endless insults, Jerusalem existed in the imagination of the heart and only appeared when the heart fully opened. *Paradise* was another name for the walled garden where beauty and peace could reign. Behind the walls of Jerusalem could be found the garden of the heart and behind the walls of every heart can be found the true Jerusalem.

The golden thread appears as the holy thread of dreams, as the essential thread of art and as the secret thread of destiny that unwinds from the strange twists of fate that bring a person to the holy gates. The golden filament is also the inner gradient and intended direction that can lead a person through all the inner conflicts and dilemmas and guide them to the soul's destination and their heart's desire. That thread is hard to see and easy to lose touch with; yet while a person holds it they cannot become lost; or if lost will be found to be stumbling in the right direction.

For Eisik it was thread of dreams that led him all the way out and finally back to the ground of his soul and on to the heart behind his hearth. Eisik first found his gold when he listened to his dreams. Everyone receives at least one experience of the gold buried in their heart; but most everyone has to go a great distance and pay a price to find it again.

Each person has "golden moments," but they are often misunderstood and easily lost in the confusion of life and in the distraction of daily errands. Every young woman feels she is golden at some moment; each young man feels brilliant in some way. Even a depression is evidence of something shining and bright that has disappeared from sight. For the inner gold cannot remain completely hidden; being an essential part of one's life, it must become revealed, at least for a moment, or the soul will rot from within and wither away.

Revelation of the inner golden self is an essential step for the unfolding of the true course of one's life. For some, the first occasion of making love brings a stunning realization that a golden self exists and can awaken to a loving touch. Loving and gold go well together as so many lovers' gifts to each other can attest to this day. Gold has qualities of endurance and malleability and people seek for the same thing when it comes to love. Gold represents lustrous beauty unearthed, precious gifts revealed, and symbolizes fidelity to what is loved above all else.

We are each golden the first time we truly make love because we each make love to the world in our own way. What a person truly loves is golden for them and we love those who in some way help us to find and better understand the hidden gold within ourselves. Teachers can be like that even if they require us to pay for what most people choose to avoid. Payment up front can make revelations along the way less painful and costly.

Meanwhile, some people find the sense of gold within them the first time they climb a tree and see an entire forest laid out before them and feel the breathing presence of the divine in this world. Nature can pull the gold in the veins of the heart into sudden awareness and trees can appear as a green fire and spiritual presence. Others will find their gold-connection the first time they speak spontaneously as words seem to flow forth and tumble out from a shining river at the back of their throat. For them, language is a stream flecked with golden nuggets that reflect an inner sun that can warm them and hold them near the unique flow and rhythm of the self within the self.

Some find a golden connection the first time they touch a musical instrument. Their fingers already seem to know where the golden tones can be found and how to draw them out. The chords they shape resonate in tune with invisible cords already strung within them. Yet others awaken to a golden realm the first time they commit their entire body to dance. Some inner knowing and essential exuberance awakens in them when they hear and feel the call of life's essential rhythms. They feel drawn beyond themselves, pulled on by invisible threads and secret sinews that cause them to leap. Leaving all else behind, they become the dance and in doing so enter into the depths of themselves shining forth.

INNER ALCHEMY

Just as the heart is more than a physical organ, gold is more than a valuable metal. The "real gold" can only be found in one's own heart. The inner gold is what we each bring to the dance of life as each god-given talent is a conduit through which the inner gold can flow out into the world. Some brilliant ore exists within us, already fully formed and waiting to be revealed, to be confirmed and polished up.

The golden aspects of the deep self are a natural epiphany that somehow appears during youth, but later must be sought and sometimes be fought for before being found again. The finding and losing of the golden self is part of an inner alchemy that is unique to each person. Genuine alchemists were working on a level of spirit and soul. Since each alchemist developed their own symbols and methods, most people fail to decipher the forest of strange images and archaic symbols. The confusion of symbols led to the conclusion that the practitioners were delusional and foolishly trying to change common lead into pure gold.

As is often the case, the inner arc of pursuit was overlooked and the message became distorted. The tangle of images and arcane symbols represents the unique efforts made to reveal the hidden gold in the human heart. Since each soul is unique, the symbols and codes within each life also take on unique shapes. What was being sought was the universal gold, yet it could only be figured in uniquely personal images and signs.

Gold is very durable and quite malleable. It can be worked into filigrees and worn as jewelry; it can be used to cover and embellish things and can even serve as illuminated paint. By contrast, lead is dense and dark, a "heavy metal" both difficult to move and resistant to change. Lead lacks the malleability of gold as well as the warm color and soft shine that makes it golden. Whereas gold can be used to cap and protect teeth and even be taken as a medicine, lead is poisonous to the body and can be deadly.

Changing inner lead into gold is a kind of rite of passage on a psychic level. It involves changing that which is dense and base into something noble and illuminating. It also means removing that which can poison the heart and cause it to spread poison instead of golden affection. There is more than one kind of chemistry in this world where one thing does desire to transform into another. Secretly, lead wants to be turned into gold and suffering wants to give birth to some delight not yet recognized. Each soul has its own "gold standard" sewn within it from the beginning and that will remain the standard of one's soul throughout life.

HIDDEN GOLD

The inner organ of the heart holds the dream of life and eventually becomes the genuine place to work for those who would find the treasure hard to attain. The educated heart becomes a place of wisdom and great understanding. This heart within the heart is an invisible and subtle organ that harbors dreams and knows full well what we love and how we need to be in this world. It works the inner alchemy that can turn raw life experience into living gold. All notions of a "heart made of gold" refer to the treasure carefully hidden within one's heart and the innate capacity to turn the lead of life into golden knowledge.

This talk of hidden and timeless things is part of the oldest speech of humankind. The sense of spiritual gold being hidden in the heart and soul permeates all the great religions and most spiritual practices. Golden tabernacles, shining statues of deities, and saints covered with gold all stand as reminders of something hidden inside the prayerful devotees. For we must first see outside ourselves what we would find deep within.

Everyone has at least heard that the heart is the seat of gifts and treasures; the problem involves our inability to truly trust what resides within us. Only after certain bridges of disbelief have been crossed, does the door to the heart within the heart begin to open. The timing of the inner revelation is a mystery that cannot be solved before hand. Gold represents a living spirit that can awaken at any time and inspire the true work and opus of one's life. But, who can say what is required to make the individual heart ready to open.

Meanwhile, the message is sent through many channels because it intends to get through to us. The gold within the heart is a universal and essential truth about individual human life; it is an open secret waiting to be discovered over and over again. When such a secret becomes known it also becomes felt; for the open heart holds and harbors both our deepest thoughts and feelings. There is a deep thought inside each heart, a living knowledge that knows what it feels and feels what it knows. Such felt knowledge needs no proofs and requires no defense. However, until it becomes known within, no proof of its existence will ever seem satisfactory.

A BROKEN HEART

Inside the heart of hearts is a painful beauty that tries to find its way into the world. Heart mysteries have their own sense of rhythm and timing. The problem involves the opening up of the arteries of imagination and the veins of genuine love that alone can deliver the goods and gold we carry within. Awakening in this way involves an inner ripening that requires some genuine heat of lived experience. To become more equal to the dream sewn within us, our heart must break open and usually must break more than once. For only in breaking can it open fully and reveal what is hidden within it.

That's why they say that the only heart worth having is a broken heart. This world is heartbreaking and in more ways than one. Something must crack us apart and break us open to let the spirit that brought us to life emerge more fully. What tries to live through a person is heart-breaking for them. The inner beauty of the soul is always enough to break your heart.

For some, a great loss precipitates a collapse that secretly undermines the inner walls. Others finally reach the top of the heap only to find that there is no "there" there. Only after the little-self loses some of its high assessment of itself does the inner loosening begin; then the time for digging all the way to the bottom of things can arrive. Eventually, like the woman facing the tiger and the fellow with the insult problem, we must find a practice or a way that breaks our heart open without destroying it. If we do, the walls around the heart begin to soften, the mortar of fixed feelings loosens and stones begin to slip and fall away.

THE WHAT, NOT THE WHO

The adventures and dilemmas and even the tragedies of our lives serve to awaken us to the core of imagination that marks us as unique and imbued with meaning. When the heart within the heart opens, the issue becomes not simply "who" I am or appear to be, but "what" is hidden within me. The "what" in each soul is the hidden gold, the interior imagination and core pattern from which the "who" of us grows and from which we draw inspiration and the necessary courage for our intended life.

True freedom means finding the essential "what" within the "who" that we are and learning to live with and serve the divine elements hidden and sewn within. Genuine freedom appears where the heart opens and the inner gifts become available and freely giving from them becomes possible. Then, those nearby also benefit from the self-revelation and self-fulfillment as the inner gold and natural gifts increase from being shared.

Eisik followed the trail of dreams and found the bridge that led him to the gold hidden in his hearth and heart. Having reached the center of himself, he also found his heart-work and core practice. Eisik began to build a big house at the site of his old hut. He didn't build a bigger home to be self-important or pretentious in some way. The point of the larger dwelling was to have a hall big enough for all the people of the village to gather together and talk.

The hall was built around the hearth of the old hut. When it was completed, the local folks would gather there and share their dreams. Eisik would listen to the dream talk and encourage their dreaming. Having found the dream of his life and followed where it led, he became a dream worker who tended the fires of imagination and the dreams of others so that they might also return and find the living word and the inner gold that was in them all along.

CHAPTER 10

GIFTS AND WOUNDS

Each culture, large or small, modern or traditional, must fashion a story that accounts for both the wonders and the conflicts found in this world. Cosmology and mythology are as much a part of human nature as psychology and logic. Each society tries to tell a story of the human soul wandering amidst the great cosmos with its spinning stars and pregnant mysteries. The smallest tribal group must have a story big enough to account for the stars and planets above, the forests and waters all around, and the surprising feelings and dreams found within the soul. Each group must have its own theories and philosophies of life and some story to tell about the nature of the soul, about the inspirations of the spirit, and the presence of the otherworld.

Even the smallest tribe must account for the whole thing, for the real accounts begin in the soul which is the only thing as big as the world. There are many small tribes that live near the longest river on earth. Like many old societies they hold the river sacred and pay great attention to the flow of dreams that come to each person at night. For them, waking up each day involves a sharing of the night messages and communal consideration of what each dream might mean.

Like most traditional groups they imagine the world to be alive and ensouled in all its parts. They consider nightly dreaming to be the vehicle through which the human essence reconnects with the soul of the world. They imagine that the center of each soul remains connected to the origins of life and periodically returns there. Each return to the origins can lead to a renewal of life's vital energies and each visit can also lead to knowledge about individual life circumstances as well as the current conditions in this world.

Like many traditional groups, they consider that the human soul has more than one aspect and imagine that each element of the soul is a kind of living word. They notice how essential language is for people and they seem to follow the sense that "in the beginning was the word." Because they are great singers, they imagine the "word" of creation to be a living resonance, a sound vibration, and intonation of life. Creation is a great sound and song that echoes from the beginning and continues to vibrate inside the soul of each person and in the rhythm of each life.

The elements of the soul are described as three "words" with each playing a critical role in the unfolding of the dream of one's life. The first soul element is called the "good word" or "wise word." It dwells at the center of each soul and is the essential message set within that person, the living word and life song intended to be delivered to life by that individual. The second element of the soul is called the "word placed crosswise" and it resides close to the good or wise word set within.

The two inner words tend to be entwined and always move together, so that each movement of the wise aspect within the soul activates the word-crosswise as a countermovement. From their view, what is wisest within us and most essential to us has a crosswise energy set against it. Each person has an inner capacity to bring goodness to life and a natural wisdom to offer; at the same time, each has something crosswise that can obscure and cancel the goodness within.

Besides the essential opposition of the wise and crosswise within there is a third soul element called the "word held in waiting" or the "waiting word." This third word is the inner charm of each life and the key to unlocking the opposition between the wise word and the word-crosswise. The word held in waiting appears in dreams, visions, and inspirations that can lift and shift the basic opposition and inner conflicts of each person. The waiting-word creates a middle ground of the soul and a pathway for change and healing and learning; especially for learning what the dream messages might mean.

Whether a person becomes conscious of it or not, the three words or elements of the soul interact with each other throughout life. Especially, the word-crosswise repeatedly cancels the wise word at the center of the soul. It creates doubts and acts as an inner critic and darkens the inner light of intelligence and wisdom. Each person has some innate wisdom and something good to offer others, but each has an exacting system for blocking their inherent gifts and knowledge. This helps to explain how it could be that everyone on earth has something valuable to offer, yet most fail to give fully what they naturally have.

The inner dynamic and ongoing struggle between the elements of the soul becomes acted out each night when a person dreams. While the body rests in sleep, the first element or wise-word takes flight into the unseen world. Of course, it is accompanied wherever it goes by the second soul element, the word-crosswise. These two travel together through the dream world and have various encounters and adventures on the way to the center of the cosmos where all things and all dreams share a common origin.

The wise-word seems to receive the dream from the center of the world and the word-crosswise acts as a weight and shadow of gravity that pulls the soul back to the earth. On its own, the good word might just remain in the otherworld and eat the food of dreams. The word-crosswise keeps bringing the soul back to earth and to the project of incarnating. The word-crosswise also functions like fate as it weighs down and restricts the motions of life and creates the need for the waiting word. Wisdom and that which is crosswise to it are the basic set up in the soul and the back and forth of one's inner life. The waiting-word is the creative element through which each life can change and grow and finds its way in the world.

Eventually, the first two soul elements return from the voyage beyond the daytime. They bring back dream messages that they have collected on their night journey. For they have witnessed things in the dream world that have relevance to the dilemmas and troubles found here. The waiting-word receives the dream at the moment of awakening as the dreamer stirs from sleep. Neither completely asleep nor simply awake, the heightened state of true awakening holds a place betwixt and between and the waiting-word has its opportunity to see into the dilemmas of the soul and the conditions of the society.

AWAKENING

In the in-between state of awakening all three elements of the soul are brought together by the presence of the dream. To truly awaken means to experience the wise word within and perceive that which is crosswise on one's soul; so that awakening is both inspiring and therapeutic. If it were not for the word held in waiting, life would become stuck as the light and dark forces might cancel each other and create a stalemate in the soul.

An old Greek word for dream interpreters was *therappe*, for they too saw dreams as messages intended to awaken and clarify and heal. The dream becomes the waiting-word that can penetrate the puzzle and release the vital energy as well as the innate intelligence trying to manifest through us. The word-waiting functions as an inner therapist that attends to dreams, but also develops a capacity to find hidden meanings in the daily events that affect one's inner life. The word-waiting becomes the sage in the soul, the natural counselor that can grow within each person who faces the inner shadows and crosswise patterns within.

Not just the individual, but the whole world lives at the edge of dilemma and continues to exist because of a small bias toward life. Like the word held in waiting, the dawn of each day tips the scales of eternity in favor of life ongoing. There is a natural artistry in each dawn and in this way of receiving the night messages. The waiting-word in the soul seeks wisdom and understanding from the messages in dreams and from insights into daily events. The natural tension between that which is wise and that which is contrary and crosswise creates the crucible in which the waiting, waking word can breakthrough to genuine meaning.

Once a person develops some tolerance for the basic oppositions in life and the shadow aspects of the soul, the waiting-word becomes more evident and available. The waiting-word keeps a person awake and alert to meaning both in the inner life and in events of the outer world. The waiting-word is connected to the level of meaning that can be found just under the skin of any experience. Whatever happens to a human soul happens to both sides of the inner cross and must be reflected upon and dwelt with until the hidden meanings become clear.

Releasing the life-enhancing word and natural speech inside each person depends upon an exposure of all that is placed crosswise and runs contrary in the human heart. As with fate and destiny, a contrary and restricting energy dwells with the intended expression of the soul. Living out the innate wisdom of one's life means living through and cleaning up all that sits crosswise inside oneself. By disentangling the threads both wise and crosswise the underlying meaning and innate intelligence becomes available and grows stronger.

If it were easy to reach the inner wisdom of the soul everyone would simply go there and learn to speak that deep language. If it was simple to learn and express what lies at the core of one's being everyone would be wise already. The road to the center of the soul is always difficult and puzzling like the route one takes to unravel a dream and learn the message sewn within it. On the way to the hidden gold and wise ways of the soul some contrary elements will have to be faced and some issues will have to be disentangled. In the depths of the soul both the gifts and the wounds, both the wise and the crosswise, wait to be found.

MAGGOTS AND GOLD

It's like the old story of a young sister and brother who set out on a journey together. While walking through a wide field in the bright light of day, they suddenly saw their father walking before them and were greatly surprised. The reason for the surprise was that their father had died some time before. Now, he was standing before them and when he gestured for them to follow, they of course obeyed.

The father walked in silence until reaching an opening in the ground where he entered and began to descend. The two children followed him onto a road that drew them away from the light of day and took them steadily down into the depths of the earth. After travelling down for a distance the children could see the shape of a village ahead of them, right there, under the earth.

As they entered the town below ground, they could see that no one else was there. Their father led them to the center of the village and stopped. Suddenly, he began to speak. He instructed them to enter some bushes that grew nearby. He exhorted them to stay hidden and to silently observe everything that happened in the center of the village until the time when he would return. Since it was their father, since he had seemingly returned from the dead, since they were in an unfamiliar place, the sister and brother did exactly what the father instructed them to do.

After they were well hidden in the bushes a crowd of people began to gather in the center of the village. The group seemed to be waiting for something. After a time, a noble looking person appeared and walked directly to the center. The people divided and the chief or king stood quietly amongst them. When the chief turned to one side the brother and sister could see that his body was covered with rotting flesh and crawling with maggots.

The people began picking the maggots from the body of the chief and cleaning off the rotting flesh. They continued cleansing him until he turned and walked away. Soon, all the people dispersed and the center of the village was empty again. After that it became dark and night seemed to swallow all the visible aspects of the place. The sister and brother kept still and remained quiet.

When the light returned they observed the crowd beginning to gather once more. Soon, the chief appeared again and strode to the center where the people made a space for him. He turned the other way and the brother and sister could see that the other side glimmered like gold. The people began to anoint the golden side with oil and they polished it until it shone like the sun itself. After a time the chief turned and walked off and soon enough the entire crowd dispersed and all became quiet again.

The father returned and gestured to the children to come out of the bushes. As they stood in the center of the village under the world, the father asked them to describe what they had witnessed from their hiding place.

They told how the crowd appeared and at first cleaned the side of the chief that was covered with rotting flesh and maggots. They described how the following day the other side was revealed, how it was made of shining gold, how the people anointed and polished that side until it shone like the sun.

The father spoke to them again. He said that because they had come to the village on the day of maggots and rotting flesh their luck in the world would be bad. He stated that it would be their fate to labor and struggle on the road of life, but that little reward would result from their efforts. Had they only arrived on a day when the golden side was revealed, their luck in the world would have been different; their fate would have been much more favorable and the road of their lives much easier to walk.

Then the father turned away and began to walk out of the village. Without saying another word, he went back up the road they had all travelled down together. The sister and brother did not know what else to do but follow him.

When the father reached the place where the road of the underworld opened out to the world above he stood to one side in silence. The sister and brother passed before their father and stepped from the underworld back into the daylight. Neither one looked back as they continued their journey together. The story ends there with nothing further said about what they thought or how they felt about the wounds and blessings they had witnessed. It is left for each of us to decipher the contrasting sides of the chief and the work of those who clean and polish in the village under the earth.

THE INNER VILLAGE

In the human psyche, down and back and within are more or less the same. The psychic village is inside and underneath and behind our daily lives and it contains ancient ideas and images that remain valuable, just waiting to be unearthed and cleaned up and polished. In the deep center of the psyche the living and the dead, the immediate and the ancestral, the wise and the crosswise as well as the gifts and wounds all appear together. All the members of the psychic crowd can meet at the center of the inner underworld and consider what to do with the rotting flesh and golden gifts of life. Like the children observing from the bushes, we are invited to see into the center where the core issues of life wait for our attention.

What is found at the center has a two-fold dynamic, a psychic ceremony in which the waiting-word cleans out that which is crosswise on the soul and polishes the good word and noble lord within the soul. The inner ritual involves both cleansing wounds and polishing up the golden aspects of the deep self. There is an underlying unity of the self where the psychic village tries to heal what is rotten and polish what is golden and needs to shine in each person. For each of us is the inner lord and waiting patient of our own soul.

There is gold to be found in many old stories and this tale of the village under the earth shows the golden side as well as the opposite and contrasting elements. Typically, gold is mined deep in the earth and it appears that the golden side of a person must also be unearthed and separated from the impurities that appear with it. The story makes it clear that the inner gold and wise-word is there to be found and deserves to be recognized and anointed. However, the crosswise and rotten side of life is close to the golden aspects and it needs some accurate attention and careful healing before the inner gold can shine.

The golden self rivals the sun in its brightness and waits to be found and become known. When the golden self is properly attended to, the entire psychic village brightens and shines forth. Each person has access to this deep radiance of the awakened self; but only if the rotten issues nearby are also attended to and cleaned up regularly.

Golden and gifted, wounded and rotten appear together and alternate with each other whenever real attention is brought to the center of one's life. And the same can be said for the life of a community, which is after all an aggregation of souls carrying both wounds and gifts. The deceptive simplicity of the tale reveals a deep psychic truth about the gifted and wounded nature of the soul and about the core problems of each community, each society and every culture.

In order to be a proper ruler of one's own psychic village, a person must face what is rotten inside as well as come to know the ways that they are truly golden within. Imagine the difference in most communities if people realized fully that everyone they meet is both wounded and gifted, both burdened with some troubling issues and gifted with some golden qualities. Imagine the difference if leaders and rulers exposed their mistakes and allowed others to help clean up their inner wounds and cleanse their rotten areas. The inner gold must be revealed and polished until it shines; but first some less golden things must be exposed to the light of day or else the rot deepens and the life of the village becomes sick and ungenerous and unwise.

The inner ceremony conjoins opposite aspects of the deep psyche revealing the intricate relationship between gifts and wounds. The core psychic ritual begins with a careful cleansing and healing of whatever is wounded, corpselike, and rotten. Only after the worst inner issues are resolved can the golden self be restored to the center. Becoming whole involves facing our wounds and inner shadows in order that the innate talents and golden gifts might be given fully.

Just like the sister and brother in the story, everyone has at least a glimpse of their golden side early in life. The problem is that everyone also has inner wounds and most failed to receive healing and help when it was first needed. When left alone, the wounds of the soul fester and deepen and going near them can feel like facing death. It's easy to feel like a helpless child when near the old wounds in the soul; but it becomes necessary to go there if the golden side of one's life would be found again.

OF FAMILY AND FATE

The tale of the young sister and brother implies that visits to the deep psychic village will involve early life experiences. The business of gifts and wounds begins early in life and inevitably involves one's parents. As with the father in the story, parents are a conduit to the core issues of the soul, but they also can be an obstacle to understanding one's own stance and place in life. Through them we first experience love and intimate relationships; through them we often receive our deepest sense of abandonment and most potent experience of misinformation. The father leads the children directly to the center of what life is really about. Yet, the conclusions he draws about life may not serve the dreams or genius of the children or the aspirations of the coming generation.

If the parents fail to deal with their own wounds and allow issues of the family fate to rot in the shadows, they can't help but poison the waters of the soul. Often unwittingly, sometimes mistakenly, but also necessarily, parents mislead and even betray the vulnerable souls of their children. And, they do it with surprising accuracy, so that attending to the earliest experiences of abandonment and wounding will also bring each person close to where their gifts reside.

Each family also has some elements of gold, be it a capacity to shine in public, an inner flexibility that allows emotions to flow, or deeply held values that surface when times become tough. There may be elements of a family inheritance that make life comfortable, humorous, or exciting; but there will also be shadows and inner gravities that descend down the family line. Each family has its "specific gravity," the elements of fate and aspects of psychic weight that cannot simply be swept under the carpet or be left behind or buried or completely ignored.

Each family has its share of human tragedy and psychic residues left over from the dilemmas and dramas of life. The shadow of each family includes some "prima materia," some primal matters and core issues that affect the soul of each child born into it. For each family, at some level, represents an ongoing attempt to struggle with fateful issues, heal certain wounds, and make inner gifts more available.

Each family has elements of fate and energies that run crosswise and contrary to the health and welfare of its members. The inevitability of family shadows and inherited fates are the stuff of the ancient tragedies that were played out on the earliest stages. The fates and shadows of royal and noble families were acted out like the drama in the underworld village so that everyone could feel and reflect upon the dramas and tragedies within their own families and lineages.

Family fate is a weight and specific gravity, a drama that the children silently watch from the earliest time of life. Call it inherited depression; call it anxious tendencies or shared phobias; each family has its familiar, familial traumas and persistent patterns. Each family system also has characteristic ways of avoiding, denying, or glossing over the very issues that need to be faced and cleaned up and healed. When the core issues and inherited fates are too deeply buried or strongly denied, they become a toxic inner lead that can be poisonous to the entire family system.

Family fate can include the leaden shadow, the heavy hand, or poisonous atmosphere that overshadows the natural aspirations of its children and crushes dreams before they fully form. It can also manifest as a cool indifference to both the vulnerabilities and strengths of the children. While indifference may seem preferable to the heavy hand of fate, it will be experienced as a deep blow to the growing psyche of a child. For the expectation for the golden self to be seen and acknowledged and admired is set deeply within each soul. Indifference to the potential brilliance of the growing child resonates deeply within them and adds weight to the crosswise aspect they already carry.

The trusting and inquiring nature of children causes them to directly feel the innermost shadows and wounds of their family. The secret project of the self within can be overshadowed by the unlived lives of the parents as well as the unattended wounds passed down through the family over time.

When considering the events they witnessed in the psychic village, the sister and brother might recall that it was the father who appeared to them at a certain time and called them to follow his lead. He set the timing of the events and brought them to the village of revelations on the day of the maggots and wounds. He first appeared on the unlucky day, so that he is implicated in the heavy fate that he later assigns to them.

Like father's the world over, he feels it his role to interpret what the children see and how they perceive their experiences in life. He invites them into the depths of reality; yet he insists upon determining what their future reality will be. The truth is that it is rare for parents to perceive or understand either the personal fates or the inborn destinies of their children. Parents may lead their children to the doors of knowledge, but what the children see when they open the door is between them and their fate, between them and the thread of their destiny. The story posits a tension between the experience of the children and the beliefs of their father and common life usually reflects the same thing.

The story centers upon the inner gifts and wounds, but it uses the father's attitude and the family fate to arrive there. When the children leave the inner world they must walk past their father and begin their own consideration of what needs healing and what can shine through them. The father was able to lead them to the village but it will be the life-long task of each child to discern what needs to be healed and what must be polished in their own soul.

The old story suggests that a person must go to great depths if they are to break the family spell and awaken to their own fate and destiny. In order to get the whole picture of the inner realm, the children will have to see things in their own unique ways. That's true in the story and true in the world where parents often feel that they know what is best for their children.

THE NOBILITY OF THE SOUL

The sister and brother were still young enough to be projecting the archetypal qualities of wisdom and guidance onto their father. The father represents a knowing authority for them, perhaps more so than otherwise because he has died. However, in order to see the world with their own eyes, each of them will have to pull back the typical projection of their inner gifts and power onto the parents. Throughout life, we project onto others what we need to find and recognize in ourselves. What begins as idolizing the father or mother leads to seeing others as kingly figures and queen-like personages. Each projects their own nobility until finding ways to reclaim it and polish it within.

Sister and brother each view the rituals of cleansing and polishing from the precise angle of their own hiding place. The maggots and the gold are dynamic symbols and it is the nature of a true symbol to be seen differently by each viewer. A symbol serves each person in terms of their own psychic set up; that's how symbols work, that's why stories resonate, and why art can be revealing. The symbolic image manages to be universal in the sense that it speaks to everyone; but also particular at the same time, so that each sees a reflection of their own gifts and precise wounds.

The eye of the self looks out through the window of the soul and the unique shape of each soul provides a specific lens and particular view of the world. If everyone saw things the same way there would be no need for so many people and there would be no urge to individuate and truly become oneself. Each soul has its own wounds and festering issues that need attention and each its unique arrangement of gifts that are needed in the world.

Gifted and wounded, that's how we are from the very beginning. For human life begins with a wound, with a rending of time that lands a timeless soul in this world bounded and hounded by the demons of time and necessity. The dream of one's life necessarily involves both the gifts of eternity and the wounds of time.

Gifted and wounded, that's the innate condition of the human soul; noble in nature, gifted at the core, yet wounded as well. That's the inner state of each soul and the key issue trying to draw the attention of the entire human village. Those who think they are not wounded in ways that need conscious attention and careful healing are usually the most wounded of all. Those who believe they have been cured of the ills of this world have usually not descended deeply enough into it.

Gifted and wounded we are and must be if we are to understand the nature of this world that exchanges light and dark, night and day, life and death. Life is by its nature a gift and a wound; it is a gift that allows us to witness creation and a wound that separates us from the source of creation itself. To be human means to uniquely observe the village of life, to participate in the alteration of gifts and wounds, to grow by healing one and giving the other away.

In the eternal village under the earth the ritual of the deep self waits to be found again and again. The center of the psyche waits to enact the two-sided rite of healing and anointing that preserves the nobility of the soul and grows its capacity to be creative and generative. For each soul grows and each person's individuality develops through the dual process of revealing inner gold and healing inner rot. No matter who a person might be in the outer world they remain gifted and wounded within and in need of both further healing and greater anointing.

Once caught in a dilemma, a person either attends to the wounds that appear or else suffers them without self-knowledge and the inner treasure and meaning of the events become lost again. Each time an inner gift appears an inner wound will need some attention; each time a wound receives the healing touch some golden quality of the self will shine further forth. Healing the wounds, polishing the gold; that's the ritual of the self and soul set within us. First one side, then the other; the inner rite of individuation shifts from opening and cleansing to polishing and unifying again. Each person must become divided again and again so that a greater unity might be forged within.

Each visit to the depths of the soul reveals another level of wounds that need healing and another aspect of the golden presence of the unified self. Some wounds are ancestral ailments that keep trying to surface and be cleansed. The human soul is capable of reaching profound states of healing; yet it can only remember and reach such depths when life makes us vulnerable again, when some new betrayal takes us to the places of healing.

Old wounds and deep losses wait for vulnerable moments in order to reappear and become further healed. Any shock, betrayal, or loss in the upper world can serve as a catalyst that irritates old wounds and tries to instigate healing and clearing in the soul. Only in that way can the suffering and injuries, illness and losses experienced in life truly become opportunities for healing and growth in the soul.

CLEARING THE SOUL

Most people avoid the painful areas and resist the natural inclinations to pick at the wounds and open them to healing. However, there is a maggot capacity in each person. Although they make people queasy and uneasy, maggots are the expert cleansers and instinctive purifiers that remove the rot and precipitate genuine healing. Maggots appear wherever the tissues of life begin to rot; they know instinctively how to cleanse whatever becomes diseased. They will remove all decayed flesh but not damage the healthy tissue nearby. The maggots represent a deep process in the soul that knows that whatever ceases to contribute to a healthy life becomes as if a corpse within that will eke its way toward decay and death.

Secretly, maggots are the agents of life and the natural healers of the earth. In the story they appear deep in the earth and at the center of the noble rites of healing. Those who have the gift of healing know something of the skills of maggots. Although maggots can be seen as the agents of death that eat the flesh away, healers have to have some maggot qualities in them in order to help preserve life. In order for healing to begin, the wound must be opened further. The decayed flesh must be cleanly separated and removed in order for the wound to close and for the living flesh to renew the wounded place.

Maggots are like the waiting-words that know how to distinguish between what is healthy and wise within us and what is unhealthy and crosswise to our spirit. Maggots are whatever attends to our wounds and helps to clean up the inner mess of the psyche. Despite their eerie reputation they can be "exactly what the doctor ordered." As mini-surgeons they symbolize the essential process of healing and making whole in which the corpse becomes separated from the living elements of one's life.

Once healed over the wounded places often become stronger than normal tissue. Healing makes a person stronger than they were before the wounds were found. The ritual of making oneself whole requires the removal of whatever has become rotten and corpselike or else the golden qualities cannot expand. Denying the wounds leads to losing the gifts. Our wounds are next to our gifts and healing them makes us more able to shine and offer what we came to life to give.

The sequence in the story shows the healing before the anointing as if to indicate the steps in the process of sustaining and increasing the nobility that resides in the soul. If a person receives nothing but adoration and reverence they will come to believe that they have no necessary faults or shadowy parts. They will imagine that they have no inner issues that need attention. Such a state of benign neglect or willful denial is the perfect inner environment for the shadow to grow and the decay to spread.

The process of revealing one's gold and pursuing one's destiny depends upon the companion practice of handling elements of fate and healing one's inner wounds. Those who rise to great heights in particular need repeated healing if they are to develop and maintain some inner nobility. Whoever rises closest to the light must cast the greatest shadow; whoever would be anointed must submit to continual cleansing and healing or suffer a fall when the decay becomes revealed. Whoever would become wise must face and resolve what is most unwise within them.

UNITY AND OPPOSITION

Human life, like all things incarnated, manifests through polarities and oppositions. The heart beats with two sides, the lungs double up to breathe, breasts hang side by side, and the testicles as well. This world operates through pairings that both oppose and complement each other. The eyes and ears watch and listen from two sides of the face and people can become two-faced. Sometimes, one hand doesn't know what the other is doing and people have been known to speak out of both sides of their mouth. Humans are part of the doubled world and are most often at odds within themselves.

A person is both a unity and an opposition; so is a marriage, and society works that way as well with opposing political parties and upper classes looking down on those with less to hold. The inner opposition in people is reflected in many outer conflicts and whatever is not faced inside will develop and eventually add to the conflicts in the outer world. Elements of fate that are not made conscious and faced within us become aspects of fate lived out in the world. The wise come to know their own inner conflicts while the unwise keep insisting that all the trouble is the fault of another.

Meanwhile, even our dreams are carried in this two sided way. Expression and repression come together, just as knowledge and ignorance reside in the same person. This explains many things including the common tendency to undervalue and undermine those exact things that are most important to a person. A person feels the presence of inner gifts, but underplays them or defers to others who may be less gifted but more bold. Each soul carries a unique version of the wise-word and each carries the words placed crosswise that can cancel that resonance.

The inherently good and wise-word inside each person is fundamentally and repeatedly opposed by the words placed crosswise upon it. This is the source of real ignorance; not simply a lack of knowledge about oneself and the world, but an inborn and contrary element that obscures wisdom and opposes learning. Each attempt to draw from the well of wisdom is accompanied by a tendency to forget the plan or spill the healing waters being sought. This is the case with everyone, no matter about appearances; it is the universal condition of the soul.

Didn't the old thief enter a great darkness in order to find freedom and release? Didn't Eisik go back and forth when the treasure was near? Didn't Narada first lose and then find the errand god sent him on? The inner dream of one's life exists in a necessary tension held between the wise aspects of the soul and the words set crosswise upon it. That is a cross we bear as humans, as dual beings in this world where things appear on opposite sides and each thing carries its own shadow.

Avidyā is the old Sanscrit word meaning "ignorance, delusion; being unlearned or unwise." It is the opposite of *vidya*, meaning "to see, to know" as in the English words "vision" and "visible." Avidya causes a person to move further away from the knowing self and leads to increasing obscurity rather than to the brightness of one's wiser destiny. The old notions of enlightenment depended upon facing up to and removing specific forms of ignorance and contrary energies set in each soul.

This is the crux of the matter when it comes to wisdom and healing and change. Each person exists with their own inner contradiction long before they face any opposition or enemy outside themselves. Call it avidya or the inner shadow; call it the inner demons or blind egotism; everyone has it to one degree or another. Each has their inner radiance and each has distinct blind spots. Everyone has their cross to bear and some basic wounds that keep them from becoming whole and being wise. Just as the crosswise aspect of the soul can be found in proximity of the wise word within us, the inner wounds always reside in the same place as one's natural gifts.

The intimate connection and close proximity of gifts and wounds explains why many people fail to find or use their natural gifts and share their inner gold. In order to reach the most gifted and wise areas of the soul, a person must encounter and deal with that which is darkest and most contrary in themselves. In order to be near the gift of one's life a person must touch and heal their deepest wounds. Because the inner wounds were first felt during the vulnerable periods of infancy and childhood, going near them makes a person feel childish, helpless, and abandoned. Although the gifts are near they seem far away.

Because the wounds can run so deep, because the resurrection of old pains can be so fearful and painful, stories and images of the inner gold abound. People need to be reminded in many and diverse ways that the inner dream of life, the wise world within, and the inner gold are the natural inheritance of the human soul.

The psychic village exists below the daily world and often appears as the village of the dead. Many people fear to go there and some call it hell. In its older forms it was more like Hades, a place you could visit through any deep feeling. More importantly, the village of the underworld was secretly connected to the source of life. The willingness to go there meant entering the oldest ritual of the world where releasing the corpse of one's life leads to the renewal of the golden self within.

III

The Return of Wisdom

*"The wise person allows universal imagination to
operate through them."*

CHAPTER 11

DIE BEFORE YOU DIE

There's an ancient creation story from India in which the beginning of the world comes as a surprise to the creator. The god Prajapati makes the world from an abundance and exuberant expression of life that bubbles up and flows out somewhat unexpectedly. The universe appears as a sudden inspiration and derives from a hidden excess. It comes into existence full-blown with all its complexities and diversity of life forms, with all its evolutionary tendencies and continuing surprises.

Ever since that original creative eruption the world can be experienced as abundant and bountiful and as a place of constant wonder and awe. Creation continues in the surprise of each dawn that arises and unfolds from the dark reaches of night. It continues in the surprising birth of each child and in the many ways that people all over the world create more life by responding to inspirations, by fashioning art, and making abundant relationships. Prajapati made the world through the surprise of creation and that way of making continues to occur throughout the world each day.

After the world was abundantly born, fully made, and thoroughly elaborated, Prajapati experienced a new feeling and strange sense from within. In the aftermath of the overflow of life, the god of creation began to feel quite empty; he felt sad and lonely, and even fearful. The creator suffered a post-partum depression on a cosmic level as all seemed to grow shadowy and dark. Something else was almost present and Prajapti was the kind of god that did not shrink from the presence of anything. So, the god created the world all over again, this time using the depths of loneliness and longing as the source of creation; this time using fear and trepidation to proceed. To the expanse of being and the overflowing joy of the world Prajapati added a second layer and darker level of creation arising from the depths of negation, and loss, and longing.

What had been made of pure abundance was made again of pure loneliness. What had arisen out of joy and exuberance was followed by fear and by sorrow. Prajapati was so full and so empty that everything that was and all that wasn't came pouring forth form him. Life flowed from a hidden abundance to a manifest fullness and poured from the empty to the void as well. That's the world to which we are born, the world that keeps being born again and again from the overflowing fullness at the center and from the emptiness at the center of the fullness. For fullness harbors emptiness within it and the void turns back into the abundance of the world in the dance of creation and in the secret exchange between life and death.

The second level of creation continues to be felt in this world where night's shadow follows each day as the teeming light of existence dims back to the eternal darkness from which it arises. Light and dark are the partners of existence; joy travels with grief and fear can follow happiness in this ever changing world.

Some believe that god must be far above such "negative emotions" and seemingly faulty feelings; they have difficulty imagining loneliness in connection with the creator. Yet, older ways of seeing considered that a creator must know all aspects of creation. All aspects must be there at the beginning if they are going to exist at all. If loneliness and fear, if sorrow and death are in the world now, they must have been present at the beginning when everything that was going to be began to be.

The old story about the two hands of creation depicts the alternating drama involving light and dark, positive and negative, full and empty from beginning to end. Abundance and fullness only existing in contrast with loss and emptiness; life, as we know it, inevitably leads to loss and death; one following upon the other, both being aspects of the ongoing resonance that echoes from the surprise of creation.

To this day, each person inherits this two-handed, double-sided, back and forth way of being in the world. Each has a hand of abundance and each is empty-handed at times. Each has the surprising gift of life and each life has to come to the end of life's road one day. It's not simply that "death must have its due," but also that death has a place in life. Death and loss must have a place in life in order that the creation of the world might continue. If we treat death simply as an absence of life, something essential to creation becomes lost to our awareness. When seen in the context of an ongoing creation, death can be found to have a place in the midst of life and a hand in both renewal and re-creation.

An old Celtic proverb boldly places death right at the center of life. "Death is the middle of a long life," they used to say. Ancient people did things like that; they put death at the center instead of casting it out of sight and leaving such an important subject until the last possible moment. Of course, they lived close to nature and couldn't help but see how the forest grew from fallen trees and how death seemed to replenish life from fallen members. Only the unwise and the overly fearful think that death is the blind enemy of life.

Placing death only at the end of life causes a kind of existential displacement that makes it seem more devastating and fatalistic than it need be. A healthy awareness of death makes the breath of life more pertinent, more immediate, and all the more precious. Death used to be called the great teacher of life; for in knowing something about death people came to value life more distinctly. The point of considering the role of death in life isn't to be morbid; rather, facing one's own mortality may help clarify one's role in life.

Ancient notions of where to place death might offer surprising hints for how to find the center of our lives. If the issue of death could become more central to life again, then life might become more centered upon meaningful things. When death is in the middle as well as at the end, more than one kind of death can be discerned.

It's like the old story of the fellow who met death unexpectedly and surprisingly right in the middle of the great marketplace of life. He was the servant of a wealthy merchant in the old market town of Isfahan. The occasion began on a fine morning with the sun warming the earth and promise in the air. The servant rode off on his errands feeling carefree. His purse jingled with coins as he anticipated a feast planned by his master. He was ready to see what fresh items the market had to offer on such a fine and promising day.

As he moved amidst the teeming crowd, the servant suddenly saw the figure of Death. In the midst of the great marketplace of life, death seemed to beckon as if about to speak to him. Before a word could be uttered, the servant turned and fled with the utmost speed. He had heard the old belief that once death speaks to you, your life will end. He had no interest in having that conversation at that time, so he raced off on his master's horse striking out on the road that led through the desert to the town of Samarra.

By nightfall he had left Isfahan far behind and arrived on the outskirts of the distant city. Seeing an inn nearby, he drew the tired, sweating horse to the door. Using the merchant's coins, he purchased a room for the night. Exhausted in body and soul, he stumbled to his room and collapsed onto the waiting bed. His fears and fatigue mingled with a sense of relief at the idea that he had preserved his life and had outwitted Death. As the night closed around him, the servant fell into a deep sleep.

In the middle of the night he awakened at the sound of something moving in the room. When he looked up, he saw Death standing at the foot of the bed, smiling at him. "How can you be here?" demanded the servant beginning to tremble with fear again. "I saw you only this morning in the midst of the marketplace in Isfahan?"

"What you say is true," said Death. "When I saw you I tried to speak and say that you and I have an appointment tonight in Samarra. But, you would not let me say a word and only ran away."

The tale ends in silence as the conversation between Death personified and the fearful servant comes to an abrupt end. It's an old tale, one told in many lands and in different ways. The names of the towns change to suit the locale. Sometimes the servant is young, sometimes white of hair. Sometimes Death appears as an old woman, sometimes as a grim old man. There are old folk versions of the tale and more famous literary renderings of it. What remains consistent however is the sense of an inevitable appointment with Death and the irony of the servant trying to escape his fate. He thought he had left his issue with Death far behind him until he found it right before him. In running from his meeting with fate, he ran right into it.

The servant can't escape death by running from it and the listener is left with puzzling questions regarding personal fate and the presence of death in the midst of life. The presence of fate is a great paradox in human life, especially when viewed through its connection with death. From one point of view, it was the fate of the servant to meet his end in Samarra. Thus, his attempt to run away from his fate only led him more directly to it. From another angle it could be said that he had to cooperate in order for the fateful meeting to occur. The servant went to the meeting in the dark inn of his own will and unwittingly contributed to his own demise. Thus, he willed it as much as fate decreed it.

An African proverb states: "on the road where you will meet your death, your legs will carry you and your feet will go." Our fate is unavoidable because it travels with us wherever we might go. The sense of fate as a companion in life was common to ancient cultures. "Death is in the fold of your cloak," they used to say in order to make clear how death is folded into life from the beginning. The modern mind struggles greatly with the paradoxical nature of fate and often runs into it when least expected.

At times, the modern world looks like a harried and confused servant trying desperately to out run the inevitable while claiming to be on the verge of a miracle cure for all that ails life. The presence of death has become a fearful pain in the midst of life as well as something to be avoided "at all costs." In making death a medical occasion more than a metaphysical event, life itself becomes diminished. When the end of life is simply attributed to "heart failure" or "lung failure" death becomes a "failure of life" and dying but a failure to live on endlessly. It's as if we believe old superstitions about the presence of death and even avoid "end of life" conversations because they seem morbid or fatalistic; and because they mention the unmentionable.

Meanwhile, many lose their dignity amidst overly heroic efforts to prolong life "under any circumstances." The marketplace abounds with promised cures for aging, drugs for whatever ails you and pain-killers that will make death's sting almost painless. It's as if death has been separated from its connection with fate and has lost all its meaning as the teacher of dark wisdom and as the metaphysical instructor in the course of life. When death becomes a "final indignity" rather than a necessary element in the human drama, something of the meaning of both life and death has been lost.

A DARKER KNOWLEDGE

In denying death's presence in the middle of life people run the risk of denying life itself. In foolishly thinking that all answers must be found outside ourselves, we too often miss the conversation going on within our souls. For there is a "darker knowledge" that involves a conversation between life and death. It's as if people forget that life is fatal, that agreeing to be born also means agreeing to die one day. Everything that happens to us occurs on the road that begins with birth and ends with death. Without death there is no road of life. We live between Ishfahan and Samarra; between the teeming marketplace of life and the dark inn of death. We run back and forth repeatedly without knowing it.

A genuine life involves more than one brush with death and having a meaningful life requires dying more than once. There are "little deaths" throughout the course of life and attending to them secretly adds to the abundance in the soul as well as to the greater dance of life.

Isfahan was such a renowned market town that people called it "half of life." It stands for the fullness, variety and freshness of life; it represents the endless deals and exchanges that keep the market of life pulsing and thriving. Isfahan is life's diversity and abundance; yet in the middle of the marketplace of endless possibilities and delights, fate and death will also be found. It is important to enter the marketplace and participate in the reckless dance of life; yet it is also important to know the other half of creation and learn how to die a little when the time for true change comes.

In the long run, there is no way to be entirely free of the hand of fate and no way to cheat death; the problem is that most people cheat themselves out of the promise of their own life. In dismissing fate's limitations in favor of seemingly endless possibilities people fail to learn who they are in their own center and how they might be called to a unique destiny. Running from the presence of death and the inevitability of loss can limit the depth of feeling and breadth of understanding waiting to be found at the center of one's own life.

The servant accepts the fearful superstition that any conversation with death means that life is over and done. Meanwhile, his "death sentence" only becomes pronounced after he runs as far as he can from the middle of life. The true point and darker knowledge of the old story may be that running from death also means running from life. When we fail to grasp the nature and shape of our own fate, we become ruled by it.

Many people live their fate unconsciously, failing to sense an inner purpose waiting to be found within the precise limitations of their lives. In trying to escape our fate we inadvertently contribute to the hardening of it. Such is the nature of fate; either it becomes conscious and more malleable, or else it becomes increasingly restricting, and fearful, and finally, fatal. Either we face our limitations and find the meaningful thread that would unwind from within us, or missing our destiny, we blindly live out our fate.

If we stop the story at the point where death first appears but has not definitively spoken, the presence of death may have a different message to deliver. There is no help for the fact that the road of life leads to the door of death; yet the road to a greater life also requires a brush with death. The presence of death is a tactic of life and a little death is needed whenever life would grow greater. Death used to be considered the beginning of all philosophy. *Philosophy* means "love of knowledge" and those that love knowledge will search at the door of death and beyond in order to understand the mysteries of life.

THE HOUR OF DEATH

Where one story ends, another picks up the thread and continues on. Unlike the fearful servant who ran from his fate, there was a learned man who purposely sought an encounter with the angel of death. People called him Luqman the Wise because he was dedicated to the pursuit of knowledge, especially the knowledge of spiritual things. People called him a prophet because he could see things that were hidden from others. However, after years of perfecting his wisdom, one thing seemed to elude him: he had no knowledge of the time of his death. He was wise enough to know that such information was the privilege of god; yet he was also convinced that he could deduce a way to learn the exact hour of his death.

He began a practice of deep meditation and did not stop contemplating until he managed to ascertain the time of his death. On the morning of the day on which his death was expected, the prophet left his home and made his way to a nearby cave. When the angel of death arrived at his door, the wise man was nowhere to be seen. A small boy, whom Luqman had instructed, told the angel how to find the cave to which the prophet had retired.

The angel had an errand to perform and quickly found his way to the mouth of the cave. He stood outside in the broad light of day and looked into the darkness of the earthly enclosure. He called Luqman by name and gave the salutation that begins "peace be upon you;" for prophets were always greeted with respect by the angel of death before their lives were taken from them. That was a courtesy owed to those who become wise in the ways of the spirit and the soul.

"Welcome," responded a voice from within the cave. The angel then stepped from the light of day into the dark interior and became unable to see for a moment. Once his sight adjusted to the darkness, he saw before him, not a solitary prophet but a hundred Luqmans. The messenger of death was completely baffled. "I am commanded to take the life of one called Luqman the Wise; so please show yourself," said the angel.

"I am here," answered a hundred voices.

"Yes, but I can only take one Luqman, which one are you?" questioned the angel.

"That is for us to know," the answer came in a quantity of voices, "and for you to find out."

Luqman the Wise had figured out how to multiply himself and hide within the multiplication of selves. He was there in the cave, but hidden amongst replicas of himself. Not knowing what else to do, the angel of death went to seek some guidance from god. Upon hearing of the cave and the hundred forms of the one prophet, the creator instructed the angel how to proceed.

"Return to the cave and enter it without making any greeting. Once your vision clears, greet the prophet in your customary manner and he will have to reply as his individual self or else offend the holy tradition. Before he completes the reply, take his life."

The angel returned to the cave as instructed, he entered it silently and stood before the hundred forms of Luqman. "Peace be upon you, Luqman," said the messenger.

"And on you, angel of…" one of the figures began in the customary reply. Before he could complete the response, the angel of death took his life.

Shortly after that, both the angel and the prophet appeared before god.

"Dear lord," said the angel, "there is something I do not understand about this strange occurrence. Only you know the time of each person's death. Even I only learn it when you reveal it to me. How did the prophet know when the hour of his death would come?"

Before the divine could have a say, it was the wise prophet who offered an answer to the question.

"I didn't know that my friend. Had I truly known the hour of my death, I would not be here. What my learning revealed was the time of your first arrival. Everything that happened between the time when I first saw you and when you came again was unknown to me. I knew *that* you were coming, but I was taken by surprise in the end anyway."

Now, the conversation with death has become more specific and it extends all the way to god. Instead of an unwitting servant surprised by mortality, we find a wise man seeking to learn all about death and final things. Whereas the fearful servant sought to escape death at any cost, the learned man made the meeting with death the whole point of his life. Where one would run away under any circumstances, the other sought the encounter on his own terms.

After his concentrated effort the wise man found a way to stand before death and not succumb to it. He learned what the wise often know, that here on earth everything has a limit, even death. While standing amidst the army of identical figures, death cannot find him, mortality cannot touch him. For just like life, death can only deal with the particulars. The prophet was able to decipher a limitation placed upon death: that death must come to each person individually. Death is an individual matter and what matters at the time of one's death is one's individuality.

Even in a great catastrophe where many souls are lost, death must come to each one specifically, exactly, and personally. The wise man had discerned an essential truth that underlies the contrasting energies of life and death. The situation of death is similar to the expectation of life: that each person exists as a unique individual and can only be approached that way. Since each person's fate is uniquely threaded to them, their death as well as their life must be specific and particular to them.

The prophet baffled the dark angel by appearing amidst false versions of himself. The learned man was able to turn things upside down so that even death did not know how to act. He kept death in the dark by hiding his true self. In the end, he could not be touched by death except in the unique form of his own life. Since he could only live as Luqman, he could only die as Luqman.

The ruse might have worked, except that god reestablished the basic protocol in which the unique identity of each human soul is addressed at both the beginning and at the end of life. What brings a person to life is unique to them and it is that inner uniqueness that is called back to the divine when one's time on earth is done. Once again, the divine sends the message that the crucial element that unites one world with the other is the uniqueness dwelling in the individual soul.

Meanwhile, the wise man reveals another aspect of the mystery of human existence. Through great effort he had deciphered that death would come on a particular day; yet, he could not penetrate the mystery any further. He could determine when the first meeting with the dark angel would occur, but the final encounter remained in the hands of god. Death must be dispatched at the end by the same divine force that gave life to begin with. When it comes to the human soul, even death must wait for the proper time to arrive. Death is not only the unknown, but is also in some way unknowing.

A BRUSH WITH DEATH

There is an unknown territory, a mysterious area where the presence of death does not equal the end of life. There is an appointment with death that is separate from the final meeting with the dark angel. There is a "little death" before death becomes such a big and defining event in life. Death is the middle of a long life and a little death can lead to a greater understanding of the life one already has. The territory of little-death is where simple knowledge can give way to a deeper revelation. Our little encounters with death and sorrow and loss are inevitable and if engaged honestly can become the darker wisdom from which a greater life can grow.

We are all servants in this life, each having come to life in order to serve something greater than out little-selves. No matter what speed we travel at or what costume we may wear, we are all on the way to the dark inn or the old cave where the dark angel calls to us. The question is whether we can learn something of our true essence from the way death brushes against our lives. The presence of death can be a teacher and guide that unlocks the way of life waiting to be found within.

Remember the story of how the Buddha first encountered death? He was also on the way to the market place when death appeared before him. The one who was to become the Buddha of the age was in the midst of life's fullness when he first saw death and that encounter began his awakening to the greater path of his life. Death was in the middle of the life of the one who would become known the world over for finding a middle way through life's suffering and sorrow.

At the time he was still known as Prince Siddartha. He was the son of a wealthy and powerful family and his given name said as much. *Sidd* or *siddha* refers to achievement and fulfillment; *artha* typically suggests wealth and power in the material world. Prince Siddartha was intended to inherit his father's kingdom and become a powerful and wealthy ruler. Yet, fate always has a say, even if a family is powerful and has distinct plans carefully set in place for its children. Every family has its status and each has its share of fate; yet each child born will have its own twist of fate that can unwind in the direction of a meaningful destiny.

At the time of the prince's birth an ascetic sage mysteriously appeared. The holy man offered a prophecy about the fate of the newborn child. It was a puzzling fate and it became the cause of great concern for the father of the prince. The sage announced that the royal child would either become a powerful king and rule far and wide, or else would become a saint who renounced all worldly power and wealth in favor of a spiritual path.

The father wanted a son who would follow in his footsteps and an heir to carry on the legacy of ruling. In fear that the prince would become attracted to an ascetic or saintly path and turn away from the royal life, the child was raised within walled palaces. The father controlled all aspects of the prince's world and kept him from any influence that might lead him down the road of philosophy or the path of spiritual learning.

Prince Siddartha grew up within a luxurious confinement inside walled gardens that isolated him from the ills and pains as well as the conflicts and troubles of the common world. For many years he remained unaware of the sufferings that plague most people. Yet, fate has its way of entering the garden of each life and something early planted in the soul of the future Buddha began to grow. At the age of twenty-nine, the prince yearned to see and feel the commotion of the great market place of life. Feeling severely isolated and increasingly curious about the outside world, Prince Siddartha eventually received permission to step outside the garden walls and visit the nearby city.

Some say that in advance of the prince's outings, the king ordered that all the old and infirm people and all the dying and suffering folks be removed from sight. They say that no inauspicious object was left in view and only people who appeared young and healthy were permitted to be seen. Yet, these precautions were also in vain; for fate will have its day, just as death will have its due. Despite all the arrangements made by the king, the prince became a witness to the suffering and death so common in this troubled world where light and dark alternate daily and even moment to moment.

The prince left the garden of innocence and rode into the common world accompanied by his faithful charioteer. In quick succession he had four encounters that would alter the course of his life and in due course affect much of the world. The first apparition was an aging man, bent with years and short of breath. The prince asked the charioteer if the poor fellow was in a singular condition. The answer came that this was the common fate of all who grow old in this world. The next figure that appeared before them was someone ill and immobilized with pain. The prince asked if this kind of condition was a frequent experience. The charioteer offered that illness comes to all who live, for that too was part of the fate of the human soul.

Next, they came upon a corpse being carried to the burning grounds. When the charioteer explained that this was a recently deceased person about to be placed in the funeral fires, the prince asked if he too would die one day. The answer sadly came that each person, royal or common, must one day meet their death. When the time comes, the breath of life will expire and each will be carried to the funeral grounds.

The prince was shocked by the presence of death in the midst of life and by the preponderance of suffering and illness that seemed to follow each life like a shadow. After all the years of protection and distractions, the prince had finally entered the marketplace of life and met his fate. He stood at the crossroads where life and death converse and where fate and destiny can become revealed. Those who would live a bigger life and become conscious of their purpose and destiny in this world must somehow face a little death in order to grow, in order to know where there soul would have them go.

Fate is the drama we can't avoid, the puzzle we must consider, the mystery we must attend to or else fail to take our true part in life. In that sense, fate is unavoidable; it waits for each person step onto the road to life and enter the great marketplace. Once the prince began to live his own life, the hand of fate began to unfold. Having left the family compound and stepped beyond the family complex, the prince had arrived at a crossroads where his life had to go one way or the other. The fate announced at his birth became the choice before him in life.

Either he returned to the family estates and took up the role of his father, or he went further along the road marked by suffering and death. Either he became a powerful ruler and king amongst kings, or else became a spiritual seeker and potential saint, a *bodhisattva*, or "Buddha to be."

Before the decision could be made, there was one more fateful apparition awaiting the prince. In the crossroads of fate and destiny, in the crosshairs of life and death, the prince observed a solitary ascetic who exhibited a surprising calm and seeming serenity amidst the palpable suffering and confusion of the common world. The fourth and final apparition came in the form of one who renounces the common desires and usual entrapments in order to find a path through life's suffering. Once the eyes of the prince began to open, the path of his life appeared before him and he both understood the common fate of humanity and recognized the unique nature of his destiny.

Like many a soul in this world, the life of the prince could have gone either way. That was what the prophecy stated at the very beginning of his life; that was the hand that fate had dealt to him. Yet, the one who receives the cards must actually play them. The prince was bound to become a significant person and destined to have an effect on the world around him. What remained in question was whether it would be in the worldly realm or on the spiritual path. Fate weaves a certain pattern, but the soul makes choices when it comes to living out the inner design. Choices must be made and commitments are required despite and because of one's fate in life. And, something must die if a greater path in life would be found.

Often, what must die before a person can truly live is the plan their family has for them. Each child must be born to a particular family; yet the destiny of each soul rises from a different conception and often aims at a different star. There is an innate tension between the family expectations and the destiny bequeathed to each of its children. Even if a person takes up the family business, they must first enter the market of life on their own terms. Some serve the spirit of their life by sustaining or improving a family tradition; others must take a completely different path in order to fulfill a purpose woven deeply within them.

The elements of fate and destiny press from within and also call from outside the walls and doors of the family complex. Unseen threads and inner designs secretly pull each of us into the crossroads where choices must be made as life and death, sleep and awakening hang in the balance. Prince Siddartha would renounce his entire inheritance of power and wealth and seek for a way through and beyond the illusions of life that seemed to only lead to sickness, old age, and death.

The very one who had not been allowed to see the world outside his childhood enclosure would one day spread teachings all over the world. The walls that held him back also compelled him to find the way most suited to his soul. The exact elements of fate that restricted him also set the scene for the revelation of his destiny. For it is the twist of fate's mortal thread that hides and holds the filament of one's true destiny in life.

PATHS OF DESTINY

The tales of saints and teachers and stories of great leaders and great lovers do not exist so that we may simply imitate their actions. The points most worthy of emulation occur when those we revere bow to the presence of fate within themselves and in so doing take up the thread of destiny that leads all the way down the path their soul would take. The prince would have become but a servant of his father's dream had he not found his own path and founded a way for others to follow. How often has it been the case that a capitulation to the expectation of a powerful family has led to a darker fate and greater suffering in this world? The crossroads of history are marred by blind duty and needless suffering; but also darkened by unlived lives and destinies ignored.

Until we accept the hand that fate has dealt us and pick up the inner thread of our soul, we are servants and beggars regardless of our possessions or privileged status. The prince had to renounce his inherited position and become a homeless beggar to find a true way in this world. For the nobility of the soul is grounded in an inner inheritance rather than a received privilege. The fateful encounters with illness and loss, with poverty and death serve to remind us how everything we touch is temporary and all we possess must one day pass. Meanwhile, an eternal thread has also been woven within us. In order to find that holy thread and come to know it we must allow a "little death" to occur.

In the case of the Buddha, the first encounter with death changed everything. Unlike the servant who tried to run from the dark apparition, the prince used it to awaken to his genuine purpose in life. At that point, it was the life he had received and the inheritance shaped by others that had to die in order that the genuine life-calling could be fulfilled. For the "Buddha to be" the recognition of human suffering invoked a profound understanding of the futility of materialistic life. The presence of illness and death provoked an awakening that opened the door of renunciation. In the threshold that appeared before him, he saw a *yogi* whose life was yoked to the unseen and tied to the divine. In that moment, the old life, the received life began to wither and die. From that death a greater life grew forth and a new philosophy for living was born.

The desire to know more of life drove the young prince out of the garden of inheritance and into the marketplace of life. In seeking a greater knowledge of life, the Buddha encountered the presence of death. The path that led to greater knowledge began with death and dying; death was the middle of the long road that has become the practice of Buddhism throughout the world. Buddhism, with its intricate and compelling philosophy of the illusory nature of both life and death, begins in the silent conversation between the budding Buddha and the presence of death in the world. No death, no Buddha; no illness, no Buddha; no poverty, no Buddhism.

The point is not to become a Buddhist; that may be helpful to some; may be off the track for others. Remember great Rama of the Ramayana? He remains the counterpart to the Buddha in many parts of India. Rama also renounced a great throne with its attendant power and wealth. He shed the pricely robes rather than disobey a foolish command from his royal father. He willingly spent years as a homeless seeker. He wandered through forests and learned what he could from a succession of gurus. All the while, he was always searching for a particular sage widely known for his devastating insight and penetrating wisdom.

When he finally found the teacher and asked how he might find the truth, the blessed one responded: "What can I tell you? All truth comes from within. I cannot teach you anything you don't already know. The search for truth is really the search for one's self. When a person truly understands who they are, they realize that they are part of the divine. This understanding cannot come from the intellect. It must come from a place far deeper. Know yourself, my friend, and you will know what you are searching for."

A rare shadow of confusion passed over the countenance of great Rama. Meanwhile, the sage offered that although he couldn't give any other answer, he did wish to give the prince a gift. While the old sage searched his hut for an appropriate gift, Rama imagined the present of a begging bowl or a saintly seeker's walking stick. The sage returned with a diamond-studded bow and a golden sword. While handing them to the one still known as the greatest lord of India, he said: "Know yourself. This is who you are."

Rama had followed the path of renunciation only to have it lead him back to the place of sovereignty. He gave up all power to search for the truth and found again what he could never give away. For Rama ruling in this world was a destiny he will always be remembered for the grace with which he handled the powers of this world. For the Buddha to become himself, renunciation of worldly power was necessary. He will always be remembered for the wisdom of the path that passes between beliefs and beyond all thrones.

The point isn't to blindly follow any path, but to look fate in the eye and see what is trying to be revealed by it. Early encounters with fate and death are intended to awaken a person to the exact value of the gift of life they have been given—not necessarily the life given by one's parents, not the life defined by the marketplace, or even by religious leaders. The point is to find the life seeded in the soul before one came to life. The point is to be willing to undergo a little death in order to find the genuine thread of one's life.

In the marketplace where death and life often exchange places, Prince Siddartha had to die so that the great teacher and spiritual leader waiting within him could be born. The Buddha had a fate waiting for him and a destiny that continues to leave footprints long after those events were said to have happened. Those who follow that path follow it best when they have their own conversation with death and learn how the particular seeds of their lives would grow. It may be part of their fate to be a Buddhist; yet it must be their destiny to become themselves.

Prince Siddhartha only became the Buddha when he left his family complex with its dedication to outer achievement and its fear of imperfection, poverty, and death. For him, death was the great teacher on the road of life. He did not overcome death or run from it; rather he overcame the life he had been given in order to live the life seeded in him from before his birth. We, too, must slip beyond the family complex, whether it be one of servitude or one of dominance and power. Once we enter the great marketplace we are bound to encounter the particulars of our fate in life. If we face what fate shows us rather than run from it, we are bound to find hints of our true calling and eventually our genuine gifts will be revealed.

LIFE, DEATH, REBIRTH

The question isn't whether death will come to us or not; for we will go to it. From the first moment of our birth we began travelling to our death. Death is life's companion all along and at certain critical crossroads is as close as the next breath. That's just the way it is here on earth. The point is not simply that everyone has their appointment with the grim reaper; there is a greater point about living life fully. The death that comes at the very end used to be called Big Death. It was big because it was the final word on one's life.

The death that can be found in the middle of everything carries a different message and speaks more of change than of final things. The failures and losses and mistakes in life are "little deaths" from which the greater lessons of life can best be learned. A little death is necessary whenever life would become bigger. When the little-self suffers a little death, the greater self within can grow and find ways to shine forth. The fullness of life includes necessary brushes with and lessons from the presence of death.

Those who avoid learning something about death wind up knowing less about life. In order to avoid arriving at the door of death full of fears, blinded by anger, and disappointed with life, a person must turn and face death in the midst of their life. Those who fail to attend to the little deaths and sudden endings inevitably encountered will also fail to find the life trying to live through them. Not everyone is destined to be a great teacher or spiritual leader; yet the failure to become oneself removes some pertinent knowledge and some spiritual essence from the world. Remember old Zushya; he was trying to teach about the real question that death has for each us. On the road of your life did you manage to become yourself? Did you open the seeds trying to grow in your soul and branch out from there?

Life occurs between the extremes of birth and death and both extremes are required whenever a renewal occurs. Besides being the final act of life, death is also the transformative agent throughout life. Death is the middle of a long life and it is a necessary ingredient of each big change in our lives. Genuine change requires that something corpselike be put down before the new way can be fully embraced. Life and death secretly conspire in order to make renewal possible. Knowing something about the nature of death leads to knowing more about the essence of life.

Life and death are deeply entwined with one constantly turning into each other. Each transformation in life requires a little death to become complete. In the big scheme and long sense of it, life leads to death and death secretly leads back to a renewal of life. That's the mystery that nature tries to reveal and that fate and destiny depend upon. For those reasons people used to teach young folks about death, so that they might better understand the fateful and inevitable encounters that await them when they enter the marketplace of life, and so that they might better understand the imperative to become oneself.

Our destiny tries to approach in the form of a fate we cannot escape, in conditions that we cannot avoid. Our fate will bring us to a crossroads each time we need to transform ourselves. Fate will ensnare and constrain the vitality of our lives until we turn our face where the wind of destiny would blow us forward. We have an appointment with destiny but must suffer the disappointments of fate in order to arrive there. Fate would stop us in our tracks and strip us to the bone, so that we might discover the essential imagination and seeds of destiny seeded and sown at the core of ourselves.

The mystics say that each exchange of breath with the world has a little death in it. Death right there in the middle of each breath we take in life; each breathing moment silently repeating the pattern of life-death-rebirth. Death situated between birth and rebirth, a little death in the middle of life ongoing. Whatever death touches will certainly transform and those who accept the presence of a little death in life transform the most and are least shocked when the hour of their death comes to them.

In the end, we all go to the dark inn. The true issue is not avoiding our death, but moving our fate. The question concerns what are we serving when we arrive at our meeting with death. Did we run from the knowledge of death and therefore run away from our true life? Death is the shared fate of all who come to life; but it is "a fate worse than death" when those given the gift of life fail to learn what their gifts are for and how they are intended to be used. When we face our fate in life we also begin to move it; and when fate moves destiny can become revealed. Wherever we brush against the limits of our fate we also stand near the doors of our destiny. Facing up to fate allows the doors of destiny to open, at least for a moment.

CHAPTER 12

THE DISCIPLE'S TALE

Modern life takes place within the massive exchanges that constitute the world-wide marketplace. Amidst the great massing of matter and the seeming loss of cultural distinctions there also exists a rapid exchange of ideas and even traditions.

Amidst the great confusion and the torrent of rapid changes, Western ideas and customs flood into the East at the same time as Eastern practices and philosophies penetrate the West. The radical individualism characteristic of the modern West can increasingly be found throughout the East, while ancient Eastern ideas and yogic practices pop up all over Western societies. In the wild exchange two contrasting stories are also spread.

One tale involves the epic sense of progress and discovery as new inventions and ideas of evolution triumph over all obstacles and natural limitations. The other story places more emphasis on inner life adventures and involves a greater acceptance of the limitations found in life and the vagaries and even the tragedies that occur. Both views have archetypal roots and each forms a natural inheritance of human imagination. Both exist at the same time and have always existed together. However, to be alive at this time on earth means to be more exposed to all the uncertainties of life and to be more transparently suspended between the belief in progress and presence of collapse and decline.

The Western view tends to favor an unlimited sense of individual destiny and a drive to overcome all limitations and entrapments of fate in a single lifetime. The Eastern view tends to embrace fate as the rule of "karma" in which each action cause reactions that cannot easily be removed and that can affect even more than one lifetime. The West tends to work at finding meaning and making change by engaging the outside world. The East tends to engage the inner life in order to change all life circumstances. Yet, both views share the sense that the limitations of life, be they fate or karma, can be altered by choosing a proper course in life and suffering the adventures that ensue from it. At the personal level the dynamic of learning and growing and becoming is played out through the archetypal pairing of fate and destiny.

THE BELOVED COW

Whether it be undertaken as a search for progress or as a pilgrimage for greater understanding, a point comes in each life when a person must choose a path and take the first step and learn where it might lead. While we choose at the level of awareness most natural to our orientation to life, something unseen has already chosen us. While we seek a way to go, we are also being called to find a way that already exists within us. No matter where we begin life's journey, certain moments become momentous and time itself opens and we begin to learn who we are intended to be. The true way is already within us, but as you must know, we must go a long way in order to finally find our way in this world.

It's like the old tale of the young fellow in ancient India who had reached the age for choosing a direction in life. He had come to the point where he had to step further into life in order to find his way of being in the world. From an early age he had been the kind of child that asked questions constantly. He wanted to know how things worked and why certain events happened. Although his family were simple folk and lived as peasants in their little village, they encouraged his questioning ways and his pursuit of knowledge.

His mother was wise and patient with him. She would answer his questions if she had truly had an answer to give; but would put the question back on him if she didn't. As a result, the young fellow trusted his mother to be knowing and honest with him. So, he brought the question of what to pursue in life to her. He asked her directly: "What is the best occupation in this world?"

The mother said, "Well, I don't know; except that they say that those who really seek in this world go in search of god."

"Where do I begin looking, then?" asked the questioning son.

"I don't know a practical way to begin," said his old mother; "but, they say there are only two directions when it comes to searching in this world."

The young fellow was relieved that there were only two directions to consider and asked what they might be.

"Well," said the old woman, "there's the way of solitary searching in the great forests of nature or the way of wandering in the centers and byways of culture. I've been told that those are the two great pathways in the world."

The son was satisfied with that view of things, and taking leave of his old mother, he set off wandering and seeking to learn more. Sometimes, he would wander in the wide forests. Sometimes he would search in the big towns and even in the great cities. Sometimes, his patience would become exhausted, or his heart would be broken. Often he would be disappointed. Then, he would return home and visit with his old mother and father. They would care for him, nourish him, and send him back to the world to search again.

During one such visit, the son asked his mother whether there was any other way to go in this world. She said, "Well, I don't know. There are only two ways; although some people say that if you meet a teacher that might lead you to another way."

She asked him if he had seen such a teacher. Well, he didn't know for sure, except he had seen one old fellow in the depths of a forest, surrounded by some pupils. When the time came to leave home again, he went back to the place where he had first seen the teacher.

Upon arriving, the young seeker observed that each student had their own little hut in which to study and meditate. The young fellow desired to join the group and wanted to have a little hut like the others. Since he approached in a humble way and had a pleasing manner, the son of the peasants was accepted and he began to study along with the other students.

One day, the teacher gathered all the students together and asked them to answer a single question: "What do you love most in the whole world?"

Each had to consider in a real way what it was that they loved in this world in which we all love something. The students contemplated the question and began to offer answers. They named all kinds of things, truth and wisdom, love and family, honesty and devotion. Some even named the teacher. In due time, everyone had named what they loved except the son of those village peasants.

The teacher turned to him and asked: "Will you tell us whether you love something in this world above other things?"

The youth said that there was something, but he was embarrassed to name such a humble and foolish thing. The teacher asked again and he had no choice, but to answer. Only one thing had come to his mind, so he said it out loud.

"Of all the things of this world, what I love most is the cow I grew up with. I love the sound of its lowing, the shape of its great back, the swelling of its belly, its great teats, and the sweet milk it would pour out. I love the articulate horns on its head and its deep, dark eyes. Of all things, I love that cow."

The teacher then instructed all of the students to go to their little huts and meditate on the thing they loved the most in this world. The students went off and after a while, began to wander back from the huts and gather again. Soon, all of them were there except the peasant son. The teacher arrived again and asked if all were present. All except the cow lover, they reported. The teacher sent some students to fetch him, but when they called he didn't come out of his hut.

The teacher went over the hut of the son and all the other students followed. Even though the teacher knocked on the door and called out to him, the young fellow did not emerge. Finally, the teacher pushed the door open and looked inside. There, he saw the peasant son sitting quietly in the hut, immersed in deep concentration. The teacher spoke firmly to him: "All right, the exercise is over. You have meditated for a long time. Everyone else finished long ago; now it is time to come out and join the others."

The student answered softly, "I would love to come and join you. However, I'm afraid that the horns on my head are too big to fit through the doorway."

The teacher turned to the other students, "Here is something to truly contemplate; here is the living example of concentration and genuine study, of love and learning. People seek god and don't know where to turn; they work and practice, they argue and dispute and still can't find a path that leads them close to the divine. This one meditates on a cow and becomes the cow. His usual self is lost and he becomes what he loves.

Today, he is our teacher. He has become what he loves and that is the point of all genius and the destination of any real path in the world. Being lost or confused is not the problem; not becoming what we love, that is a real problem. In learning what our souls love we move near the divine, for love is a divine gift. Today, this one is our teacher, for he is not afraid to become what he loves."

The young seeker had found what he was looking for inside the hut of himself. He sat inside his joy and in the wonder of awakening from within. He had wandered far only to come back to a place in his heart where he kept dear the cow he had grown up with. The cow was close to his heart and close to his deeper self because it represented strength as well as sweet nourishment, full embodiment as well as gentle articulation. The object of his affection and concentration might seem strange to others, yet he learned something of his own love of life and his inner orientation from the generous being that nourished him.

Of course, in India cows are quite sacred and having love for a cow could easily be seen as loving the divine. People wonder at the practice of revering cows rather than eating them, especially when so many people lack food and even die from hunger. It could be said that in India the hunger for the divine is greater than the hunger for food. The cow was imagined as the mother of all civilization, its milk the inner nurturing of all populations. In order to make the symbol real, all cows became sacred. In order to make clear that any approach to the divine must be respected, all cows were allowed to roam free. In order to remind that humans help to nourish the otherworld as well as receive sustenance from it, it is still considered good luck to give a bit of bread or pieces of fruit to a passing cow.

When associated with Brahma the creator, the cow was an ancient symbol for the entirety of creation with each part of the sacred animal being related to a deity or some other kind of being. "All the gods are in Brahma as cows in a cow-house," went the saying. The horns, being the highest part and pointing to the bright heavens were especially connected to Brahma. Indra, who sustains all life and order in the world, was the head of the holy cow. Shiva, who can destroy the world with dancing or a sudden blow, was in the hind legs. All the people alive in the world were said to be in the inner organs of the world cow. The mind of each person was connected to the great mind of Brahma and Brahma's mind was in the holy heart of the cosmic cow.

Brahma was considered to be in all aspects of the world as being present in each person. "Soul of the Universe" was another title of Brahma and was used to denote the divine essence and eternal breath with which the universe breathes; the source from which all things emanate and must return to. This eternal essence is immaterial, invisible, unlimited, and all-pervading. It is in the gods as well as in people and all creatures. The source of existence is inside the cow and the cow is a reminder that the divine breath is in the soul of each person as well.

"As above, so below" went the saying that reminds of the subtle integrity and continuity of the universe. Brahma was imagined to be the Great Self, the universal presence, divine essence, and grand thought at the center of all existence. As a microcosmic replica of the macrocosmic arrangement, there is a great self within each person, a breath of the divine in each living soul. Our true self hides within the breath of our life, so sages would attend to each breath and meditate upon Brahma until they reached enlightenment and were absorbed by it.

Certain ancient rites that focused on rebirth involved a return to the womb as a "golden embryo." If a person were being initiated to a higher level of awareness or needed to be purified from some defilement, they would be placed inside a golden replica of a cow. After a period of fasting and meditating inside the cow the initiate would be considered to be reborn from the cosmic cow, but also to be in greater touch with the golden embryo of their hidden self. If the expense of fashioning a golden cow was out of reach, an initiatory hut could be used to replicate the uterine darkness and embryonic state.

On one level, the young son had projected all that he loved and enjoyed in life onto the body of the cow that had given milk for his growth and food for his imagination. On another level, the young seeker had been meditating on Brahma, the great creator and source of consciousness and wisdom. At the same time, he was mimicking in his hut the process of the cosmic birth of the deity as the golden nucleus of life. In concentrating on what he loved he entered a grand imagination and found an inner pattern that could continue to nourish his growth and help guide his search for knowledge. Remember the old idea that each person secretly serves the god that stands behind their destiny in this world. In doing the little exercise, the young seeker had found an image of the deity behind the unfolding story of his life.

FATE INTERVENES

In some sense, the student had found what he was looking for. Yet again, finding and holding can be two different things. At the beginning of a life-long path there will be a revelation that opens the way and reveals the intended destiny. After that, some consolidation is required and some integration is needed. The young student continued with his studies; he learned what he could learn until he felt that he was no longer growing. After much reflection, and after fully expressing his gratitude for what he had learned, he took his leave of the teacher and once again set forth on the forest paths and the byways of the cities of the world.

After a time, a short time or a long time, his fortune or fate led him to the compound of an old sage who lived in the heart of a forest far from the mad reach of civilization. The sage welcomed him and gave him a place to stay, nearby his own hut, next to where the holy river ran and sang its way along.

The young student humbly served the old sage and his wise wife and learned all he could from them. He took his studies seriously and entered each practice with characteristic commitment. He learned quickly and soon became a true disciple of the old sage who also became inspired by all the teaching and learning. Genuine learning makes a person pregnant with knowledge and the presence of a true disciple can inspire new life in the teacher.

For their part, the sage and his wife remained youthful in some ways themselves. They enjoyed certain pleasures despite their age and they soon learned that they were to have their first child. Inner awakening involves a rebirth in one already born to this world. The awakening occurring in the inner world of the student was mirrored by an impending birth in the family of the teacher. The act of truly learning affects both worlds. The student is a new addition to the spiritual realm just as the newborn will add life to the evident world. Each act of awakening is a kind of birth and every birth is secretly related to the original act of creation.

When the pregnancy was far enough along, the sage had a desire to make a journey to the source of the holy river near which they dwelt. He entrusted the care of his pregnant wife to the young disciple and invited the wife of another sage to stay with her in the birthing hut. The sage instructed the student to guard the hut and not allow anyone else to enter there. While he was gone, the sage's wife entered her labor. The woman friend stayed with her inside the hut while the disciple waited outside, protecting the space and praying for a safe birth and a healthy baby.

The old people in that place believed that Brahma, the great creator must be present at each in order to write a fortune on the forehead of the newborn. Brahma was present at the dawn of creation and is the source of creation ongoing. Each birth is a re-creation of the world at the microcosmic level, so Brahma must be present. Being the creator of all things, Brahma must arrive at the moment when each infant leaves the interior world of the mother's womb and enters the common world. In particular, Brahma must be present at the crowning moment and when the newborn takes its first breath in the new life.

Although the god is present at the moment of each birth, he remains invisible to most people as does the fate written on each forehead. However, the young disciple's eyes were no longer those of an ordinary person. The sage had taught him to truly see rather than simply look at what appeared before him. As the moment of birth drew near, the disciple saw what looked like an old Brahmin or priest approaching the hut where the new life was pressing on the doors of this world. With his acute vision the disciple recognized that it was in fact Brahma who was coming to attend the crowning moment of new birth.

The disciple had learned to perceive what others cannot see. For those with eyes to see, the deities pass amongst us and creation continues nearby and within each moment. The young student had gone seeking for knowledge and found himself in the increasing depths of knowing. He had taken up a serious path of learning and had taken on a responsibility to his teacher. He had agreed to protect the birthing hut and guard the mother and the child being born.

"Stop right there," said the disciple to the disguised deity. "What do you think you are doing entering a hut where a woman struggles to give birth? You can't go in there, no one is allowed."

Brahma explained that he was the god of creation, that he had a divine task that he had to attend to immediately inside that hut. The infant was about to leave the womb and there was no time to waste. He had to go in at once or some great error could occur that could imbalance all of creation. The disciple bowed in respect to the god, but would not let the deity enter unless he revealed the fate he intended to write upon the forehead of the newborn.

Pressed for time, Brahma explained that even he did not know what his divine stylus would write. "At the moment the child enters the world, I place the stylus on its forehead and the instrument writes by itself. It draws upon something already existing but hidden within the child. Don't try to stop me; I must go in at once."

However, the disciple persisted. "I too have been entrusted with a sacred task. If I do let you go in, you must tell me on your way out what was written on the forehead of my teacher's child."

Even a god can become trapped when the issue is one of fate and destiny. Whatever he might have felt or thought about the situation, Brahma had to agree to the condition or else fail to perform his divine task. He entered the agreement with the disciple and quickly entered the hut. The child was born and unseen by those involved in the labor, the divine stylus was applied and the fate of the newborn was activated. The first breath we take breathes life into the fate we bring to life.

As the god left the hut, the disciple was waiting with great attention. Brahma spoke to him directly: "As agreed upon, I will tell you what was written. However, if at anytime you tell anyone else the fate inscribed on the forehead of this child, your own head will split into a thousand pieces. The child is a boy and he has a hard life before him. A single buffalo and a sack of rice will be his share in life. He will have to live on that. Don't blame it on me; you wanted to know and I did not choose this; but only raised up what was within him."

"How can this be his fate," cried the disciple, "this is the child of a great sage?"

"What have I to do with it?" said Brahma. "Remember, if you ever tell this to anyone, your head will explode in a thousand pieces."

The god vanished, leaving the disciple bewildered and pained by what he now knew of the hard life awaiting the sage's child. The seeker had encountered the god of creation and learned more of the secrets of life than he wanted to know. Not only that, but he could not share what he had learned with anyone. He had asked to learn about fate and soon found himself bound by it.

Eventually, the old sage returned. He found the mother and child to be healthy and happy. The infant grew rapidly and everyone was delighted to see the prosperity of the old couple. Time went on and the river flowed by. In the course of affairs and with the learned company of the old sage, the disciple forgot his sorrowful experience. He said nothing of his encounter with fate to anyone and continued to dedicate himself to the paths of study and learning.

DEALING WITH GODS

Strangely, the encounter with the god was not glorious, but rather conflicted. The task of the god was at odds with the duty of the disciple and both fell under the rule of necessity and the hidden hand of fate. Fate becomes the issue as the force of creation pushes the child toward the crowning moment and fate is also involved when the disciple compels the god to stop. The crowning moment involves the effort of the mother, the presence of the god of creation, and a mysterious force already present in the one about to be born. Brahma has the magic stylus that writes of its own accord, but what it writes is in accord with a previous condition in the soul and an existing life sentence waiting to be evoked.

There are two forces which even the god of creation seems unable to counteract: the rule of necessity or hand of fate, but also the duty of the disciple. Meanwhile, something is revealed of the path that the teacher and student are following. The disciple has learned to see what most cannot perceive. He has entered a practice of seeing beyond what is evident and obvious to others. This increased knowledge and expanded vision of life turns out to be both a blessing and a curse; it allows the disciple to know subtle things, but it gives him the burden of that knowledge.

In the tension and labor of the impending birth more than one fate becomes revealed. The disciple learns the fate of the child, yet we learn something of his fate as well. The fate, and possibly the destiny, of the disciple involve an ability to perceive and learn unusual things that includes the fate of other people. In addition, after the god reveals the fateful sentence of the newborn, the disciple must accept the fate of not revealing the knowledge given to him. What is revealed in the first deal must remain completely secret in the subsequent agreement. The disciple has entered the precise twist of fate that places him firmly on the path of revelation, but that also puts him in a double-bind.

He now knows something profound about life; in fact, he knows what the god knows. However, unlike the deity, he cannot share what he knows for fear of disintegration. His fate seems to include a hard education about how knowledge can be a burden. Ignorance may be its own kind of bliss, but genuine knowledge can be its own kind of danger.

After the birth the old sage returned to find mother and child healthy and happy. Although he and his wife taught the disciple to see in penetrating ways, neither of them could perceive the troubling fate written on the forehead of their own child. Maybe that was just as well, and a good reason why parents rarely learn the fate of their own children. Despite having holy and revered parents, the child of the sage had a poor cast and a limited lot in life.

Time passed quickly as the disciple continued his deep study and pursued his search for knowledge of the two worlds. Remarkably, the old couple continued their own practices and somehow managed to conceive another child. When the pregnancy was far enough along, the old sage again conceived a desire to visit the source of the holy river by which they dwelt. Once again, the teacher placed the disciple in the position of guarding the birthing hut and protecting the laboring mother and the child about to be born. Once again, the student took the task seriously and brought his full attention to the situation.

Just as before, when the moment of birth drew near, the god Brahma suddenly appeared in the form of an old man. Before he could enter the hut and activate the child's fate, the disciple blocked the door. He refused to allow the god to proceed until he again agreed to reveal whatever fate was written on the forehead of the newborn child. The disciple was hoping to ease his heart by learning that at least one child of his teacher might have a fortunate fate in this world.

Once again, the god was trapped by the devotion of the disciple to his duty and the issues of fate and destiny already underway. In the interest of time, the deity agreed to the terms. Then the god entered the hut just at the crowning moment and applied the stylus to reveal the fate of the infant. Mother and child were both healthy and in the warm embrace of life as the god retraced his steps.

Just as before, the disciple waited attentively to learn the news. Brahma informed him directly: "This time the child is a girl. Don't hold this against me, but the stylus has written that she will have to earn her living as a prostitute and sell her body every night. There's nothing I can do about it. In the meantime, remember the rule, if you tell what is written to anyone, your head will immediately split into a thousand pieces."

The young man was in shock. He was so deeply hurt he couldn't find language to express the pain. Besides, if he could express what he knew and how the knowledge made him feel, he might explode or disintegrate. Where he had hoped to find relief from the sad burden of his knowledge, he found himself instead in a greater and more perplexing situation. He tried to console himself with philosophical considerations and he tried to dismiss what he knew from his mind.

However, neither approach was of any help when he would actually be in the presence of the two children. Although they were obviously healthy and seemed to prosper and grow readily, he could not look at them without seeing the hidden fates that were bound to bring sorrow into their lives. Being near the children and their parents while being unable to speak a word of what he knew made having the knowledge unbearable. He had gained a penetrating insight into the mysteries of human life, but was increasingly filled with pain and anger, with sorrow and anguish over the unfairness and seemingly random cruelty of the whole thing.

How could it be that a child is born into poverty and becomes fated to live that way throughout life with no possibility of redemption or escape? How could it be that another would be born to do nothing but prostitute herself simply to survive in a world where people traffic in bodies and in souls? He knew that poverty was everywhere to be seen and that in many ways prostitution was the oldest profession. But that knowledge did not ease his mind or diminish the pain in his heart when he saw the young children headed for hardships they could not imagine. In many ways, he felt he would rather not know if knowing must come with such a cost.

At first, the seeker desired access to great knowledge expecting that it would be its own reward. Later, he learned that true knowledge can also a burden that can weigh upon the soul and isolate a person from others. He knew the burden of fate that other had and as a result felt his own fate more strongly. He felt the sorrow of this world where people suffer in untold ways and walk toward fates they would never choose. "Every increase of knowledge is an increase of sorrow," they used to say when speaking of the pitfalls and realizations that can be found on the sacred paths.

The local people imagined the river to be the living presence of Saraswati, the divine consort of Brahma and goddess of learning and creativity. Saraswati was "She who flows toward the divine." Knowledge tended to flow easily when she was involved. Saraswati would be invoked to remove the obstacles and create the flow in any course of education. Music and the arts were ruled by her; but also the course of enlightenment flowed best when she led the way. Just as the river flowed to the great sea, Saraswati showed the way to "moksha" or divine release from the troubles of this life.

The old sage had been drawn to pray at the source of the river at the time of each birth. Now, the disciple found himself drawn to the river as he sought some release from the burden of his knowledge. He felt trapped and feared that either he would suddenly tell the secret and explode or else continue to hold it within himself and thereby implode. Try to explain and he would fragment; say nothing and he might collapse with the growing weight of anger and sorrow. He tried to release the burden of his knowledge to the river while seeking a greater understanding of life's pain and suffering.

TEACHER AND PUPIL

Over time, the weight of knowledge grew heavier within him as he watched the children grow up and move unwittingly toward their respective fates. Eventually, he realized that things could only become more painful if he remained as a student of the old sage. The disciple went to the sage and his wife and asked for permission to leave.

The sage was wise enough to see the writing on the wall and sense that there was an unspoken burden on the soul of his student. A true master knows about being a student and has an eye that recognizes pupils as well as an intuition for people's true nature. The old sage knew that genuine teaching and honest mentoring serve to awaken the nature of the pupils as well as the inner authority they have within them. While considering the request, he also considered that the point of learning was to awaken the master within the pupil and help develop an inner compass that could orient one to the proper paths and the true work of the soul.

The pupil in each of us is the part willing to study and learn; it's also the opening in the eye through which we see. The inner pupil is the eye behind the eye, the part that desires to perceive rightly, to pierce the veil of ignorance and find wisdom. The pupil is the first form of the seeker and seer within, both the natural visionary of the soul and the "wide eyed" innocent that must learn to see with a darker eye. For wisdom is a darker knowledge that combines the brilliance of the light with the darkness needed to embrace and hold it.

Disciples are the pupils who become completely transformed, those who take the discipline of learning seriously and take the teachings to heart. Rather than a form of punishment, *discipline* refers to what the students take away from their practices and studies. If the discipline becomes too harsh or the teacher holds too hard to the lessons, the students will take away pain and resentment instead of the light of knowledge that they were seeking. In the long run, learning involves both obedience and disobedience and teaching involves giving freely and letting go.

A discipline can be imposed upon a person or else be freely chosen. Imposed discipline depends upon an outer authority, whereas inner discipline develops fidelity to one's true nature and attunement to the innate authority of the deep self. Unless the inner master awakens, an outer master cannot help transform the student.

The old sage knew that the life-long learning of a true disciple must include the awakening of an inner teacher as well as the nurturing of the inner pupil. He believed that deep within, we are all students and each a master in some way. Each seeks the way of being that is already sewn and woven in the soul, only needing an outer path that will draw it out. He also knew that the presence of the disciple had brought new life to him and to his family. He knew that genuine learning involved love and that love involved letting go as well as holding close. As the old saying has it: "We can't use the feet of a teacher to walk where our own feet must go."

After considerable contemplation, the old sage was ready to grant permission for the disciple to depart. One day, with the blessing of the old couple, the disciple left the forest and the holy river that ran through it. He left the children to their fates and once again became a seeker on the paths of life. He seemed to limp a bit as he walked away bearing the painful knowledge he had found while dwelling with the old sage and his family.

Sometimes, he would wander in the wide forests and sometimes he would search in the big towns. Sometimes his patience would become exhausted, or his heart would feel as if it would break from the weight of unspoken words. Often, he would be disappointed by the suffering that he saw. Just as often, he would think of the old sage and the fates written on the foreheads of the two children.

CHAPTER 13

THE ROAR OF AWAKENING

To know is to be on the verge of being shattered; for genuine knowledge breaks the shell of what existed before. Knowledge can also be a blade that cuts and the disciple had been pierced and cut open by the wound of knowing. His own silence cut him deeply even if it was rightly based in the understanding that revealing knowledge at the wrong time can do more harm than good. In seeking to learn what the wise know he found sorrow, in trying to help others he became helpless himself. His new knowledge may have brought him closer to the divine, but it also separated him from others. Genuine knowledge tends to be isolating until it is integrated more fully.

The disciple carried with him what he learned and found new teachers along the way. As they say, a child has more than one mother, so a student can learn from more than one teacher. Anything that nourishes life can be considered a mother, whether it be a beloved cow or a revered teacher. The disciple had been nourished by both and he trusted that more of the milk of knowledge would come to him. Each time he found a genuine teacher he found more of his own way to be. When he felt that there was no more nourishment to be had on a certain path, he would take his leave and move on again.

He wandered through forests and traversed mountains; he visited towns and walked the busy streets of cities. He noticed how the temples in cities imitated the shape of the mountains beyond and imagined that those entering the temples were also seeking what the mountains held so quietly. He examined the world as he found it and pondered the hidden ways of life. During his wanderings he would sometimes think of the old sage and his wife. He had seen and learned a great deal during the time he dwelt with them and he continued to contemplate the issues of fate and destiny that troubled his heart.

While walking along the banks of a stream in a deep forest, the disciple recalled the time when the first child of the old couple was about to be born. He remembered how the old sage left to visit the source of the holy river while leaving him to guard the birthing hut. The sage had never explained the ceremony at the water's source or why it had to happen while the child was expected. So much had happened at that time, yet so little could be discussed because of the onus of his head splitting into a thousand pieces. However, he had reviewed the scene many times and each time found himself in the depths of sorrow as the burden of his knowledge of fate would return like a stone in his heart.

The condition that troubled his soul began when he stopped Brahma with his magical stylus and errand of fate. It was as if he had interrupted the god and interfered with fate and must now suffer for the arrogance and presumption of that. Yet, he grew tired of simply blaming himself for what continued to be a mystery before his eyes. As he felt his way through the events that continued to live within and as the stream rippled nearby, he recalled an old tale that the sage once told about birth and rebirth, and the nature of awakening.

THE TIGER OF THE SOUL

It seems there was a tiger that was mightily pregnant. She was near the term of her pregnancy and the one inside was pressing ever closer to the doors of life. One was trying to become two and the tiger-mother had to eat for both of them. Food was scarce at the time and the tiger found herself climbing amongst the rocky outcroppings of a mountain in search of a meal. As she hauled herself over some rocks, she spotted a herd of goats foraging in a little meadow down below where she stood.

Looking down, the tiger saw immediate nourishment for herself and for the one about to be born. At the same moment, the goats were looking up and seeing the shape of death in the sharp teeth that can turn one thing into another. There is truth in the notion that life feeds on life and that death connects all things; but that was not the immediate consideration for the goats. As the mother to be leapt at the herd, the goats scattered in all directions. She leapt with the sense of using death to contribute to life; they scattered with the idea of continuing life by avoiding death.

Life and death hung in the balance and in the air as the great tiger descended in the direction of the terrified goats. Yet, as fate would have it, the tiger died before even reaching the ground. She was overcome by exhaustion or hunger and she expired mid-leap. Not only that, but the shock of the leap induced labor and just as the tiger-mother struck the earth, the little life within her was born. Thus, death and life were each born in the same moment, the death of one being the birth of the other. It was a case of life literally growing from death.

All of the goats survived the scare and eventually convened around the lifeless body of the great tiger and the little package she had seemingly delivered to them. Once they felt assured that the great beast could not cause any harm, they became interested in the little presence nearby. The mother instinct is as old and as great as anything in life and the mothers in the herd of goats recognized new life in its delicate and dependent condition. It wasn't long before they were sniffing and nudging the strange shape of the new life. Since for goats as well as tigers loving consists of licking, the mother goats began to lick at the newborn that had fallen into their lives.

A tiger or any other cat will lick every part of the newborn, if not the infant may die. Some say that something similar is true of humans; if a part of them has not been loved and licked into life they will fail to fully live. At any rate, the newborn responded to the love-licking and began to stir. Soon its own instincts were driving it to nurse on something. Having been licked into life, it wanted to nurse and suck on the sweet milk of existence. The goat mothers did not disappoint. After some experimentation, the little tiger was nursing and soon following the goat mothers wherever they went.

Nature has its natural cycles of life and death, and creatures in the animal realm have natural adversaries; but sometimes things are "contra naturum" and the exception must prove the rule. Strange to say, but the little tiger was eventually accepted by all of the goats. It fed on goat milk and like any child in this world began to imitate those around it. Soon enough, the child of the tiger began to act like a goat; it began to sound like a goat, and even feel like a goat. The little one learned the language of goats and acted like any other kid in the herd.

One night when the moon was rising, another tiger found itself hungry and searching or food while climbing amongst the rocks on the side of the same mountain. Coming over an outcropping, it spotted the same herd of goats and began to prepare for the next meal. While looking down, the tiger was shocked to see a little tiger acting like a goat and participating in the activities of the herd. At the same time, the little tiger-goat looked up and found itself gazing into the eyes of a full grown specimen. As all the goats scattered in fear, the tiger-goat stood transfixed, gazing up at the apparition with both fear and awe.

As the great tiger leapt down to the glade below, the tiger-goat thought the end of life had suddenly come. When it felt itself being clenched at the nape of its neck and held in the great jaws, it knew it would be carried off to be devoured elsewhere. The tiger-goat was completely surprised when the grown tiger took it to the edge of a stream and held it out over the waters. Under the illumination of the moon and in the reflection of the clear water, the little one could see that it was more like the image of the tiger than the goats that it knew so well.

In the sudden moment of reflection the little one knew that it was actually a tiger and in the brilliance of that moment, knew it in every cell of its body. Something old and knowing awakened within the young one and it suddenly roared triumphantly. The transformation of a lifetime took place in that single moment as the young one became entirely changed within. The moment before, it believed that it was a goat and that it would die as a goat. In the next moment it had become a tiger and had begun to understand the ways of a tiger in this world. With a little guidance, the little tiger became all tiger and began to prowl the forests and burn with its natural brightness.

As he contemplated the story, the disciple began to see further into the circumstances that surrounded the birth of the children of the old sage and his wife. He had been left to guard the birthing hut in full knowledge that the god of creation would have to make a visit with the stylus of fate. It was his own fate to be present in the moment when life begins and to learn of the mysterious workings of fate. What he was just beginning to realize was how the thread of his own destiny had been pulled to a point of painful awakening.

In a single moment of awakening the would-be goat became a tiger and the world became completely changed. It wasn't a case of the young one learning to see things another way, but more a matter of an inner essence bursting into awareness. The disciple recalled a similar sense of sudden realization that he felt while sitting in the solitude of the hut nearby his first teacher. As he mediated upon the cow that he loved as a boy, he became that cow. As he became the cow, he learned of his own capacity to love the gift of life and discovered something of his own gift of imagination. He would never forget that moment of awakening, for it opened something within him that continued to live with him.

He realized that another moment of awakening had been close when the fates of his teacher's children were revealed to him. If he took the lesson from the tale of the tiger-goat, he could see that those fateful moments carried a deeper revelation that was still trying to awaken something in him. At the birth of each child he had been placed in a position through which he could see his own true nature. It was in his nature to see deeply enough into life that the strange workings of fate might be revealed to him. Although he hoped each time for promising news, a darker knowledge and deeper wisdom was being offered.

His expectation of a glorious fate for the children of the sage had blinded him to the reality of the situation. Afterward his overwhelming disappointment held him in a darkness of his own making. Now, he remembered an old saying that stated how each person was set down at a place by the river that made most sense for their life. It may not look that way or feel that way; yet, a person must in some way be equal to their own fate. If not, then this world would be far more unfair place than even he was willing to contemplate.

Like the goat waking up to the presence of its tiger-self, he had to awaken to something greater within himself. Suddenly, he could see something behind the life sentence written on the forehead of the son of the old sage. Almost as swiftly, he could see behind the cursed fate given to the daughter who had been sentenced to a life of prostitution. He had been shown, but had not seen until the reflection became clear. As he continued to reflect upon those indelible events, as the river ran by singing its endless song, he realized what he must do. He felt a great longing to see his old teacher and knew that it was time to return to the banks of the holy river. The direction being clear, he lost no time setting out on the path of return.

LET GO AND DON'T HOLD BACK

Eventually he arrived in the area of the old compound only to learn that both the old teacher and his wife had passed away. Heaviness grew in his heart again only eased by the sense that they would have been as ready for the arrival of death as they had been for most things in life. He felt compelled to seek out the children of the old couple in order to learn how they were faring and if their fates were as written.

He set off to inquire about the son and daughter of the old couple and soon encountered a poor man walking the road before him. The fellow led a single buffalo on a rope while carrying a sack of rice on his back. Of course, he recognized the son of his teacher and decided to follow him home. After a short distance, the poor man led the buffalo to a rickety shed near a simple hut. There, the poor fellow lived with his wife and two children.

As the disciple watched quietly from a distance, the poor family ate anxiously from the sack of rice seeming to fear that they would run out of food if they ate too much. Once they had finished their simple fare, the disciple approached their hut. He introduced himself and lamented with them over the passing of the old sage and his wife. After introductions all around, the disciple drew the poor man aside and offered him some advice.

"Do not continue in this way, but take the buffalo and the rice to the marketplace and sell them for whatever price you can get. Then, buy whatever you wish to have; spare nothing, hold nothing back and keep nothing in reserve. On the way back, feed the poor as well, and if there is anything left, simply give it away."

The poor fellow was shocked. "If I act in such a carefree and foolish manner, how will I feed my family tomorrow? You disciples and seekers always advise poor people to stop being so desirous and fearful, and simply give everything away. Listen, I can see that you are the ones on the receiving end of this celebrated charity."

The man went on about the difficulties of life and all the injustices and oppressions he experienced and how no amount of effort or prayer seemed to change the conditions of his poverty. He had never been given enough in life and it was all that he could do to survive and provide something for his wife and children. "And, don't get me started on politicians and all the promises they make while they simply line their coffers with gold gathered on the backs of all who are poor and oppressed. Why not take your philosophy of giving freely to those who receive more than their fair share and would benefit from giving some of it away?"

Before he could work himself into a further frenzy, his wife entered the conversation and spoke to her husband. She pointed out that the disciple seemed to have something of the manner of his father, the old sage. She suggested that he might also have some of the wisdom of that wise man. She encouraged her husband to try the radical plan. "Why not try the new approach for one night and one day and see what might happen."

The poor man argued that if it didn't work, trying it just once was the same as trying it for all time. If he gave away all that he had and it didn't change things immediately, he would clearly have nothing left at all. The problem with the whole plan was that it was an all or nothing venture. Just one act of such reckless abandon was all that was needed to wipe them out forever. The wife simply looked at him steadily and waited.

What could the poor man do? Between the disciple's wisdom and his wife's pleading eyes, he felt caught. Besides that, he felt miserable about his life. A part of him simply wanted to roar out his pain and anger at being so restricted. He was barely able to acknowledge that he dreamed at night, much less admit that he longed for something beautiful and more meaningful than his daily rounds. Inside, he felt a deep anguish that his children might never know the true delight of life. All at once, he became strangely unable to refuse the request of his long suffering wife or the startling advice of the disciple.

When daylight came and chased the darkness from the world, the poor fellow took the buffalo and what remained of the sack of rice to the nearest marketplace. Once there, he sold them for whatever he could get. With the money he received he bought enough food for a fine feast. He invited everyone he knew to come to the feast and added a few that he met along the way. He struggled mightily however, when it came to giving what little remained to the poor beggars he passed on his way home. Somehow, he found the depth of his long denied generosity and gave all that he had away.

Soon after he arrived home, all the food was prepared and everyone gathered for the feast. All who came were well served and each ate their fill including his good wife and the children. As on most human occasions, the feasting finally came to an end and everyone retired to the land of sleep.

The poor man awoke sharply before the light of dawn appeared. He was in a state of blind dread. He felt certain that he had foolishly given away everything he had in life. What would he do now with no source of food, no income, and no way to feed his family? How could he face his hungry children? Why had he listened to that weird disciple? What a mistake he had made!

As the sun began to rise in the sky, he went out to the little shed where he had kept the buffalo. That's what he had done on most other days and he didn't know what else to do now. His heart was heavy with the overwhelming sense of loss as he continued to berate himself for being stupid and foolish and reckless. As the sun dropped its light on the bare boards of the old shed, he entered it fully expecting to be greeted by nothing but emptiness and loss and further recriminations.

As his eyes adjusted he was astonished to see a full grown buffalo standing there as if waiting for him. Before he could get over the shock of that presence, he spotted a full sack of rice leaning against the wall. He began to shout with joy. He called his good wife to come and see the wondrous sight before him. He called the disciple to come and see the wonder for himself. The simple joy of being alive overflowed within him. "Life is a gift," he said, "so why worry over it and care so much about what is given or taken away?"

When the man finally calmed down, the disciple asked if he would like some more advice. Of course, the fellow said he would listen to anything and probably try it as well. "Take the buffalo then and the rice and sell them again just as before. Buy what you desire and don't hold back. Feed your family and invite others as before, and whatever is left give it all away."

The son of the old sage was just getting used to the notion of having something when he was told to give it all away again. He gazed at the fine, healthy buffalo; he looked back carefully at the disciple. He looked at his smiling children and at his wife's eyes. This time the poor man did not have to be convinced. He did it all again and he held nothing back. After enjoying the new feast and resting up, he found that the buffalo was back and there was another sack of rice as well. Thus it happened, day after day and night after night. He gave it all away and received it all back again.

The disciple advised him to continue on in this manner, only warning that if he reserved anything or held back from his giving, the good fortune could just as readily desert him. The poor man didn't argue, for something had transformed within him and he saw the entire world with new and brighter eyes.

WHY CHANGE IS HARD

Something had changed in the disciple as well. Whereas he had been unable to face the heavy fates of the children of his teacher, he now sought them out. Whereas he had found the knowledge of fate to be an unbearable burden, he now seemed to find in it a door to prosperity. The poor son had no idea of the fate he carried from the moment of his birth. Being unconscious of the inner situation he became ruled by it. His entire life had become an outer manifestation of the inner sentence. No matter how he slept or what he dreamed, he woke each day inside the limits of a fate that he had not awakened to at all. No matter what time he woke up, his fate was there before him. The inner sentence was on his forehead and it preceded him wherever he went.

What could anyone tell him that might slip past the fateful blinders that kept the world before him narrow and kept his own spirit entrapped within fixed attitudes. He was like many others who wake each day within a prescription that they carry within them but never understand. "That's the way I am," they say; as if there were no other way to be. As if the point of life was to never change, but simply be just the way they happened to be and defend their right to always be just that way.

Until some hint of awakening occurs a person can simply be a tiger acting like a goat. There's nothing wrong with goats; they have their own stories in which it is *their* essence that triumphs. However, they are known for being hard-headed and for always taking the hard way, even if a broader path is nearby. The poor son's insistence upon the narrow path of his life kept him in the goat world where the restrictions of his fate decided everything before hand. The poor son was not truly himself; he was one-sided in his outlook and as a result, he felt continually blind-sided by life. He became unable to imagine any notion of genuine change, much less the idea of having a deeper self within that needed to find its own voice and learn to roar.

He was a poor and unfortunate man and that was a fact that he could demonstrate and prove. However, in the bigger story of his unlived life it was as if the literal poverty of his fate had become an emotional and spiritual poverty as well. The same thing can happen to an entire community or a country that loses the big story and becomes impoverished on more than one level. It can also happen to those who have great wealth; for wealth on the surface can hide greater forms of poverty within. Until the inner poverty turns to generosity no real change will happen even if there are piles of bread on the table.

The son of poverty could not accept the greater notion of giving freely or even of receiving something from an unseen bounty. He was stuck in a firm belief that he had never been given enough in this life. It wasn't just that he didn't trust that his life could change; the poor son had convinced himself that he couldn't trust the world at all. How could he trust the world if he had no real trust in himself? His habitual fear and continual need to control became part of his inner poverty. The poor son had decided to remain small and control the little life that he had. He put his little goat-self in charge and denied that there could be a greater self within.

In remaining unconscious of his own internal life he must remain impoverished in relation to the world around him. It's not to say that poverty doesn't exist or that it can't crush the spirit and turn one's heart bitter. More to say, that a person can become ungenerous and secretly punishing to themselves. Something had to wake the fellow up or else he would live his entire life inside a story that kept his spirit small and threatened to turn him bitter. In holding so tightly to his narrow fate he would fail to find the natural generosity of spirit that was also born with him.

People continually approach life with habitual attitudes while expecting outcomes to be different. Changing one's fate means awakening to some other way of being. Not simply "doing things differently," but becoming as a different person, both more aware within and more alert in life. Such an individual awakening doesn't happen simply because a person joins a movement or converts to some form of faith. Those things can help; they can widen one's perspective and bring one to the banks of the flowing river of life. Yet, the baptism takes place under the water and no one actually sees the change that occurs. An immersion of some sort is required as well as a genuine reflection that allows the inner nature to rise to the surface.

The poor son must give away all that he has to move past the sharp constrictions and hidebound restrictions of his fate. He must step beyond his usual ego attitude and cease to be so cynical and controlling. In order to change his life and alter his fate, he must let go and not hold anything back. In order to find the blessing hidden in the curse, he must enter the fate more fully before letting it go completely.

His real safety, his health and growth can only be found in the opposite direction of his well-defended ego and self limiting attitudes. He must change from the inside out if he would have the world around him change. He must change both his idea of himself and his world view and risk everything on a destiny as yet unseen. Only by letting go and not holding back can his fate shift within and allow him to find a joy in life that has been trying to reach him all along. For the point is not simply life improvement, nor is it a change in status. The point of change is to become as another, to become as the other hidden inside that ever waits to be revealed. In order for such a change to happen a person must let go of who they think they are.

In ancient India hunters developed a proven method for catching monkeys. The monkeys were quick by nature and clever enough to dismantle all kinds of traps set for them. The trap that they couldn't dismantle involved a simple trick that trapped them in their own nature. A big coconut would be found and hollowed out. Then a hole would be made in it; just large enough to allow a monkey's paw to pass through. The coconut would then be pinned to the ground and some tempting, fragrant fruit would be placed inside the hollowed shell.

Inevitably, a monkey would approach the shell full of desire for the fragrant food it could smell and almost taste. As soon as the paw of the monkey had slipped through the hole and grasped the food inside the trap, the poor fellow would become caught because the fist holding the food was too large to pass back through the hole in the shell.

In order to become free of the trap all the monkey had to do was let go of the prize that it coveted so much. More often than not, the hand that held the desired fruit would not let it go. Thus, the monkey was trapped by what it desired and held onto no matter how near freedom might be. Release from the entrapment was right at hand and just within their grasp. However, most would stay trapped and imprisoned, caught by a narrow desire, but also by a fierce and blind unwillingness to simply let go of what they held to be necessary or important.

People can be just that way. Many take hold of something and refuse to let go, even when they become stuck in one place, even if they can't taste the sweetness they first reached for in life. Some hold onto another person and refuse to let go, even when each part of the relationship becomes a trap. Others take up an idea, a political belief or a religious notion that was supposed to set them free. After a time, they become trapped inside narrowing ideas or rigid rules. Next thing you know, they are caught in a trap made of their beliefs.

Change is hard because we hold onto what keeps us from changing; because freedom feels like losing something that we are used to clinging to; because real change means that we would no longer desire what others insist upon and no longer restrict ourselves to the game at hand. Fate may be what we wish to deny when claiming that we are free; but it is also what we unconsciously cling to in order to avoid letting go of who we think we are.

Genuine change involves pain just as birth involves labor. Many come to prefer a pain that they know to a birth that they can't control. That's one reason why there are teachers in this world. A true teacher can help stop the pain once the student finds the familiar to be unbearable. After all, a healer can't begin the work of healing until the patient indicates that there is a wound. Until there is some indication of the nature of the pain nothing will be done to stop it.

THE CURE IS IN THE PAIN

In India, where cows are sacred and allowed to wander freely; people often keep water buffalo to do various kinds of work as well as to give milk and cream. Certain buffalo have horns that spiral out from their heads only to curve back toward their ears. Over time, the horns can begin to grow right into the ears causing the buffalo to bellow in pain and roll on the ground amidst tremendous suffering. If left alone the horns will continue to grow inwardly until they penetrate the brain and the buffalo dies from piercing itself.

Even at the height of its pain the animal can't stop the process; for it has become the cause of its own torture and torment. The piercing pain comes from its own unconscious way of being and it is powerless to do anything about it. Such a condition is brutally painful and potentially fatal, yet the cure is simple and instantaneous. If someone simply saws off the offending horns the entire descent into pain and suffering stops in a moment. For the animal, the moment of healing and release must seem a miracle and a wonder as all the pain and suffering suddenly stops.

Those who tend the buffalo naturally step in before the piercing goes too far and the animal becomes the victim of its own unwitting behavior. Naturally, they also draw some analogies to the presence of pain and suffering in all human beings. For, humans can also be seen to be afflicted with troubles and torments, with compulsions and obsessions that seem to have no cure and that surpass all understanding. Innocent children suffer and even well intentioned people fall into depressions and despair. Whatever cause the suffering may be attributed to, the question remains of how to stop the daily pain and the unconscious suffering of blind existence.

Humans can act as blindly as a herd of buffalo and often do. Humans can also withhold the kindly cut that could stop the suffering of others nearby. Usually, the blindness and denial that keep the level of suffering constant come from conditions that people can't simply stop on their own. Meanwhile, any redemption must come after some rolling on the ground in pain. "The cure for the pain is in the pain," as they used to say when people understood better the role of pain in change. Until a person realizes what hurts and harms them from within, they are unlikely to call out for someone to help stop the pain.

There are many religions and philosophies that promise to end the piercing troubles and deadening habits if you only believe in them. However, belief in the spiritual experience of others can only act as an inspiration. In order to truly change we must let go of our habitual ways of being and cut off that which otherwise seems natural and common to rest of the herd. Saints and teachers and holy ones can point to the dangers of allowing our horns to grow and can present examples of awakening to the dangers that are as close as our self-involvements or self-indulgences. However, the release cannot simply come from outside oneself. Humans may bellow in pain and decry their circumstances; but humans are not buffalos and no one will come to simply cut off the behaviors that threaten death and deliver anguish.

Wisdom is always valuable because it remains hard to find; it hides where most people prefer not to go. Wisdom and true freedom are found where we submit to the way we are intended to go and surrender to the mysterious ways we are intended to grow. Wisdom involves a necessary descent into the depths of life, for that alone can produce "lived knowledge" and a unified vision. In finding a way through his own pain and suffering, the disciple had come to understand the nature of the pain as well as the need to cut off the habits that allow it to keep growing. They say that a person truly becomes a healer when they heal something in themselves. Until then, they have more of an interest in healing than a capacity to bring the real energy present.

The disciple couldn't take the buffalo and rice to market and sell it in order to change the situation. All he could do was cut off the usual conversation and offer some accurate advice that could reverse the curve of the fate that impaled the poor son. In order to help him the disciple had to move him closer to the pain and hope that he would have the insight and the courage needed to let go of what he had learned to hold so tightly. All he could do was try to cut through the resistance and stop the pain for a moment. The poor son had to let go and learn to not hold back and thereby make the change himself.

The pain we feel comes from the crosswise energies that keep curving back and cancelling the wise self and the good word that waits to be expressed from within us. That is the usual human fate and the common predicament. Either we find a way to reach the tiger-self hidden within or we fail to know the roar of awakening that can alter our way of being in the world. Either we remain a part of the herd and suffer in ways that become common to us, or else we find a way to face that which causes the suffering and learn to awaken from it.

The rule of destiny has a tiger in it in the sense that each person's deeper nature includes a right way of being. Once awakened, the tiger nature knows exactly how to proceed in the world. People call it a "natural law" or an inner "dharma." It is a law in the sense that it has been laid down within us; it is a dharma in the sense that it is a holy power that indicates our true role in life and our capacity to become ourselves. It lays within us as an inner gradient or interior way that seeks to manifest through us at each critical turn in life.

This inner gradient plumbs a through line that can offset whatever inner faults and heavy burdens a person might have. The true gradient shapes a pathway of intrinsic value that leads to an awareness of our genuine self worth. The disciple had finally awakened to the intrinsic value within himself. As soon as he saw the reflection of his own tiger-self he knew that he had unfinished business with the children of his old teacher. For it was in his true nature to trust what he saw in others and to try to assist them to find true value in themselves.

Once he grasped the tiger presence behind his own stubborn and goat-like ways of carrying his own disappointments, he not only had a clear direction, but also had the vital energy he needed. The tiger image suggests the deep vitality that can become available to us through the unseen channel of the inner gradient. It carries the vital current of one's life and it has a deep capacity for renewal. Each re-alignment with the natural law of our being and inner gradient of our life produces a greater sense of imagination and meaning at the same time that it provides a renewal of the flow of vital life energy.

The natural way of being within us is a creative force that shapes both the inner pupil and inner sage. When we find and follow the gradient within we learn what we need to know and naturally become a helper to others who suffer along the way. The disciple had awakened to a deeper sense of self and had found a key that could unlock the tangled relationship between a person's fate and their greater destiny. Whereas he had despaired of being able to help the ill-fated children, he could now see where the limitations of their fates might be aimed.

It wasn't that he could cancel the fate of the poor son or remove all obstacles from his life. Rather, he found within the exact limitations that trapped him, the inner motions that could release him. The disciple had learned to roar in the way that made most sense in his life. He didn't pounce on the poor son like a tiger on a helpless goat; that was not his nature or way to assist change. Rather, he studied the situation until he could see how the inner thread of destiny might be pulled from the exact twist of the fate that had confounded and entrapped the poor son of poverty.

He found a way to use the dark knowledge that seemed to be an essential aspect of his own tiger-self and he shared in the roar of joy that came when the soul could finally express itself in its full form of generosity and delight in life.

CHAPTER 14

PEARLS OF THE FIRST WATER

For years the disciple had carried the burden of his knowledge of fate within himself. He had struggled mightily with the impulse to tell the whole thing and with the concern that his head would break into a thousand pieces if he said a single word. At first, the condition of his soul irritated everything in him and frustrated his attempts at seeking further knowledge. Eventually, he held the unwanted knowledge as a secret and it became a seed around which other knowledge formed. By keeping the troubling truth to himself, he was able to polish it and hone it like a gem or a jewel.

They say that a true teacher offers knowledge in a form that is palatable for the student. This leaves those who are called to teach with the dilemma of having to relieve themselves of the burden of knowledge on one hand and having to deliver it in a digestible form on the other. Often a teacher can only go as far as the student's capacity to learn. Information may be transferred readily; knowledge can be communicated with care; but wisdom will test the patience of the teacher as well as the capacity of the student.

Despite all that had happened with the buffalos and the rice and the great feasts, the disciple could not explain the inner workings of fate and destiny to the son of the old sage. All he could do was share the fruit of his hard-won knowledge in a way that the son could understand and use in his own life. The disciple was relieved that the burden of the poor son's fate had been shifted. He felt he had fulfilled a duty and performed an act of dharma or "right action." The son and his family were enjoying the fruits of destiny and embracing the abundance of life with a newfound joy. After celebrating with the family and accepting their gratitude, the disciple knew that it was time for him to depart again.

Before going on his way, the disciple asked what had happened to the daughter of his old teacher. The sage's son choked with tears at the mention of his sister, but he didn't wish to speak a word about her. When the disciple waited in silence for some kind of answer to be offered, the son admitted that she lived nearby in the next town over. He stated sadly that she had become the town prostitute; that's all he knew about it. At that point, he became overwhelmed with shame and would not say another word on the subject. Once again, knowledge can be seen to divide before it can unify. The disciple did not need further explanations; he took his leave of the son and his family and set out for the town where the sister was said to be.

Although the distance between the brother and sister had grown quite wide, the distance between the towns where they lived was minimal. The disciple found the town readily and only had to ask where he might find a prostitute in order to learn the exact location of the sister's hut. People thought it odd that what appeared to be a holy man would be looking for a prostitute; but then again, there are stranger things in life. When it comes to love and sex everyone must deal with their needs and desires in some way; so they pointed him in the right direction.

The disciple arrived at the sister's hut in the evening as the shadows grew longer and night began to fall and chase the light from the world. He knocked on the door of her little house and waited. Without asking who it might be, the poor woman pushed the door open and left it for him to enter. She thought it must be her first customer of the night arriving a bit earlier than usual. So, she was thoroughly surprised to see that it was a disciple or holy man standing at the threshold. It was an unusual sight; but she was used to seeing all kinds of men appear at the edge of night, so she simply invited him the rest of the way inside.

When he explained who he was and that he had been looking for her because of the old connection to her mother and father, the daughter of the old sage began to weep. When he reminded her that he had been there at her birth, tears poured from her eyes. She cried bitterly and became overwhelmed with the depth of shame she felt. Here she was, the daughter of a great sage, reduced to being a common prostitute. She tried to explain how poverty had punished her, how easily a woman could be reduced to nothing in the eyes of men, how she felt that she had nowhere else to turn.

Although the lament didn't change the situation she was in, she felt some relief in being able to express how utterly miserable and trapped she felt. She knew that no one in the village respected her and that she had lost most of her self-respect as well. The disciple listened carefully; he consoled her and after a time asked if she would like some advice. She said she would like anything that might change the way she lived and alter the way she felt about it.

"Well then," said the disciple, "keep your door closed tonight. No matter who or how many come knocking upon it, tell them that you will only open to one who brings you a bag of pearls of the first water. Do that for just one night and I will return and visit you in the morning."

The poor daughter was used to making deals and making them quickly so as to not lose what little opportunities might come to her. But, this was an agreement of a different order. On one hand the poor young woman was afraid that if she said no to anyone at all she might lose everything. She might hate the life she had, but she also feared falling into a deeper hole. She wished to change, yet feared that any change might make the disaster worse. On the other hand, she felt ashamed and anguished enough to be willing to try anything.

She considered that the disciple wouldn't take an interest in her welfare if she were completely devoid of all value. She decided to do it. She took the bargain and accepted the deal such as it was. The one who repeatedly gave herself away for practically nothing at all, now agreed that she would hold out unless the finest pearls were offered. She told the disciple that she would try her best; he said that was all that anyone could do. He left her to it and repeated that he would return in the morning to see how she fared.

It was an exciting idea for the sister to consider and at the beginning of the night it gave her a sense of confidence and a feeling of hope where she typically felt resignation and a touch of despair. Her customers came calling as usual and they came with the usual needs. However, no matter how many came knocking at her door, she refused to open it to anyone unless they brought with them a bag of pearls of the first water.

Upon hearing the outrageous conditions being required by a common prostitute, they thought that she had lost her mind and all quickly went away. As the night drew on, and became deeper with silence and isolation, the sister of sorrow became truly despondent. Toward the close of night when the darkest hour spread over the land, the daughter of the old sage began to feel that she had made a huge mistake. She became overwhelmed with an old anguish and the familiar fear that no one would ever come to her door again. She felt completely alone and certain that she would wind up with nothing but her empty self and her own pile of regrets.

This is a strange world where mysterious things happen all the time, and happen especially when the issues of fate and destiny are afoot and when the time has come for one thing to change into another. In the small hours before dawn, a beautiful and noble young man knocked upon her door. He stood at the threshold as the poor daughter of misery uneasily made her demand for fine pearls one more time. To her great surprise, the latecomer responded that he had a full measure of pearls of the first water and desired nothing more than to spend the remainder of the night with her. This time, she opened the door wide and stood wide-eyed herself as the noble fellow placed a bag of stunning pearls before her.

Nothing more is said of what passed between them; suffice it to say that delight replaced fear and beauty replaced shame and that which was torn and divided became healed and united again. This world can be but a string of moments hung precariously against the eternal darkness; yet certain moments can reveal a hidden wealth and beauty that secretly sustains life. Certain moments can open wide and break time apart and in draw down enough grace to redeem even the darkest past. In this world ruled by necessity, but sweetened by delight, time can be stilled and remorse can be softened and even the deepest pain can be relieved.

According to Brahma, the god of creation, fate must be fulfilled in some manner. It was her fate to be a prostitute and "sell her body each night." That much had already proved to be true. However, nothing had been said or written about the price to be asked or about the role of love in the exchange. In this world made of nights and days, the fate had to be fulfilled, but the bargain could be made in many ways. The anguished daughter had stated her terms and waited her wait. She held the tension between the old bargains and the new agreement and that was enough to change the entire deal. What started in the first fateful moment of her life now found remarkable fulfillment at the end of the long night of waiting and wondering if change was indeed possible.

When the daylight returned and chased the darkness from the world, the disciple arrived again at the sister's door. She told him of the long night of loneliness and anguish and of the surprise that came at the end of it. When he asked how she had fared throughout the night, the daughter of the old sage explained how she struggled in the darkness with an old loneliness and familiar feeling of worthlessness. As she refused to admit those who knocked at her door with the usual offers, she felt herself sinking and feared that she would give in to her desperation at any moment.

THE RIVER OF CHANGE

Surprisingly, she began to meditate as her father or mother might have done. She found herself remembering times when as a child she played by the river that ran through her parents compound. She loved the sound of the rippling water and the play of light on the surface. She began to recall what she had learned of the river as a girl. The water was always treated as sacred because the river represented the bounty and fertility of life. It was also the source of purity and the model for how life continuously renews itself.

The river was named Saraswati after the ancient goddess who was the source of learning and speech, especially wise speech. Saraswati was the "flowing one" through whom knowledge and wisdom as well as music and the arts find their true course. Saraswati was the source of a different kind of longing called *anurāga*. The longing of anuraga included a love for rhythm and music that could be a vehicle for all the emotions and feelings that can ever be expressed in speech or in music.

The sister of sorrow had forgotten something of her natural and divine inheritance, but now it came flowing back to her. She had long forgotten the importance of devotion and how she had felt the stirring of it when she was young. Instinctively, she began to say the old name of the goddess as she learned it as a girl. She repeated the sounds and the meaning over and over to herself: *sara* means essence and *swa* means self; *sara* means essence and *swa* means self. She tried to hold to the essence of herself in a way that she had not felt since she was young and innocent and blessed by the river nearby.

Saraswati is the river and the essence of the self. In that way she was able to calm herself and become strangely centered in the midst of her aloneness. In the depths of the night she recalled old stories in many of which Saraswati appeared as a disinherited daughter or as an estranged wife. Although representing the essence and self and despite being the original consort of Brahma the creator, Saraswati lived alone.

Although she had long felt herself unworthy of the old traditions, they now came flooding back to her. She remembered that Saraswati at times would enter a self-imposed exile and she drew from that primal sense of self-preservation. She recalled the old idea that the goddess could focus her calm gaze upon the past and wash away feelings of anger and resentment, sorrow and despair. Saraswati was the source of the flow of genuine knowledge as well as the purifying powers of running water. Whoever desires change must enter the deep waters; why couldn't she remain present in the depth of night?

The act of deep purification that leads to renewal was Saraswati's greatest gift. Throughout the night the daughter of sorrow kept company with the one who could cleanse the soul and bring its deepest intelligence into the light. The daughter of the old sage kept calling on Saraswati as a reminder of the hidden value of the soul immersed in its own truth. Only when the new morning came with its profound sense of both release and fulfillment did she remember that the river goddess would be shown with a string of pearls in her left hand.

The disciple listened to all that had transpired in the dark night of the soul and found his own memories of the sacred river flowing back to him. He had learned to honor Saraswati as the source of learning and wisdom himself. She was said to be the inventor of Sanscrit, the ancient language of so many seekers until this day. But, he had not thought of the role of the goddess in purification and renewal rites for a long time. He considered from a new angle why the old sage might have gone to the source of the river when the time for the birth of the children drew near.

Although the old sage could not see the fate of his own children any more than other parents, he may have had the intuition to seek blessings for them from the deity that bestows wisdom and can cleanse anguish and heartache from one's soul. It now seemed that the old sage had been seeking the blessings of Saraswati for them. Now, the disciple wondered if the sage had somehow seen the writing on his student's head.

After thinking his own thoughts for a while, the disciple spoke to the daughter again. "Now, you are of the purest of people. For, you were faithful to yourself and few in the world can say that after knowing the difficulties of life and sitting in the broken depths of darkness."

He then asked if she would like some more advice. When she said that she would love further guidance if it led her in the same direction, he explained that whoever brought the pearls one time must bring them every time.

"Don't open your door to any other," he said. "Only wait each time for the true worth to appear no matter what feelings or hauntings might precede it. In the meantime, spend the value of the pearls and give freely to those caught in the teeth of misfortune. Continue to cast out everything in yourself that diminishes the value of life and the importance of love."

The young woman was happy enough to do that each day and she waited each night for the beautiful visitor to arrive with the gift of pearls. Her life had changed completely and she knew more joy than ever she had before.

For his part, the disciple took his leave and contemplated the complexities of life and the differences between the fate of the sister and that of her brother. For the two children of the old sage not only lived in separate villages, they had opposite attitudes toward life. The poor son held onto everything he had no matter what, while his sister gave herself away and often to the lowest bidder. Each lived their fate unconsciously, believing that they could only live a certain prescribed way. In order to change and find their connection to the deeper self the unconscious deals had to be turned inside out.

The brother had to learn how to give and become generous despite and because of his impoverished circumstances. The sister had to learn to love herself and wait for genuine recognition of her inner worth. Each had trust in something unseen and beyond their usual way of being. Each had to become conscious of the way that their fate held them back and kept them blind. Only after facing fate fully could the hidden deal become conscious and the inner destiny and secret blessing become revealed. Destiny is one's fate in life turned inside out so that the inner pearl is discovered where it has been all along, seeded within and trying to grow inside the shell of one's life.

THE OLDEST PROFESSION

The unconscious fate of the poor sister continually caused her to "sell herself short." It wasn't simply that she sold her body for small change; she gave herself away before learning what true value she had within. Hidden inside the word *prostitute* is the sense of one's innate stature and true standing in life. Prostituting oneself means to indiscriminately give up one's "stature and standing." In that sense, it is the "oldest profession" in the world and it is the most common contemporary condition as well. Prostitution occurs whenever a person fails to stand for and stand with their genuine self. Destiny is the opposite stance where a person is seen standing with their own genius and on the ground of their true nature.

Everyone prostitutes themselves in some way until they learn their own true worth. Think of all who rise to power on the promise of justice and reform only to succumb to back room deals and shadowy arrangements. A genuine sense of justice might have called them to the public arena to begin with, but an unconscious fate and lack of courage soon has them adding to the common state of injustice. Soon enough they are crusading to punish those who offend in one way or another, while steadily forgetting what drew them to seek power in the first place. Inside justice is mercy, but that can't be found until a person becomes both honest to themselves and forgiving of their own failures.

People say that power corrupts those who hold it and that's true as far as it goes. Power corrupts the little-self which has so much desire for it. The deeper self has its own power and its own sense of purpose. The point in life isn't to avoid power, but to open and loosen the grip of the little-self so that the greater self within can use power and love in ways that enhance life. The problem is that those who remain unconscious of their own fate and fail to awaken to a greater sense of self will always give power to those in a similar state.

People look down on those who prostitute themselves openly partly because the shame of inner prostitution is so common and widespread. People make distorted agreements all the time that increase the distance between their little-self and the great self within them. It is the golden self within and the pearl at the center of the soul that is continually sold cheaply in this world where people hope to simply survive or just get by. The same situation occurs where people insist that one more business deal or one more conquest will make everything right.

Power, wealth, and love all converge each time the deep self is prostituted for some immediate gain. Everyone sells themselves short to one degree or another. Often, those most willing to condemn the actions of others have long lost touch with their own essence; otherwise they would have more compassion and understanding. In the darkness of night many deals are made that cannot stand the penetrating light of day. Wherever power aggregates, where wealth accumulates, and even where love is being sought, there will be shadows and deals, clumsy manipulations, and all kinds of power plays. When it comes to self awakening everyone must enter the deep waters and risk drowning in order to learn how to swim.

THE ACT OF TRUTH

It's like the old story of the realm that was almost destroyed because no one high or low seemed able to face the truth or state it openly. The situation came to the surface when a mighty river began overflowing its banks and threatened to flood the entire land. In India, all the rivers are considered sacred, each being an embodiment of the divine feminine. The river Ganges was only an exception in the sense that it was more revered as Ma Ganga, the "mother river." The Ganges was long considered the sacred source of the flow of life on earth.

Although considered to be the primal model for both the milk of nurturance and the clear waters of compassion, even the Ganges could become dangerous. Too much of anything can overwhelm a situation and the holy river had become swollen and soon threatened to overflow its banks.

At the time, the king of the realm was a powerful ruler who had become the first Buddhist emperor. He lived in a magnificent palace in the center of a royal city through which the holy Ganges flowed. When a storm of torrential rains came and fell upon the city in sheets, the river began to rise. When the winds would not relent and the downpour continued, it became clear that the rising river was about to flood and the entire city would be destroyed.

Everyone feared for their lives, but no one wished to leave the royal city and lose all that they had in it. Eventually, the trouble reached the ears of the emperor who ordered everyone in the city to gather at a high point on the bank of the swollen Ganges. The crowd gathered along the river bank and watched fearfully as the waters continued to rise. Everyone stood in the miserable rain, while ministers consulted and officers commanded and the water kept rising nonetheless.

Finally, the emperor asked out loud: "Can no one make an Act of Truth that could change the situation and cause the waters of the Ganges to flow back upstream?"

He was calling upon an ancient idea that stated that a person who had fulfilled their life duty could draw upon something deep in themselves and make an act of complete truth. Whoever had found a way to live in accord with their deepest self would also be in accord with the sun and the moon that rise and set in accord with time and the seasons. On the basis of such a deep inner accord, they could make a request that could alter the immediate conditions of life.

The idea of an act of truth rested upon the ancient notion: "as above, so below." The sense that the essence of each person was part of the living organism of the universe served to connect the center of one with the center of the other. A person who could draw upon their own essence could also draw upon the essence and power of the universe. That person could become a conduit for the primordial energy of the source of life; thus, they could produce change in the moment. If what they said was true in essence the action that they requested would occur.

Apparently the emperor was unable to make an act of truth and it soon became evident to everyone that none of the members of the royal court could manage it either. The depth of silence became profound as the ranks of the military officers were quiet and not a word came from the leaders of the various religious groups. The silence spread through the crowd as the merchants and bankers went quiet and even the common people fell into a collective hush. Amidst the soaking rain, the threat of loss and the lack of available truth, the great Brahmins and the lordly nobles as well as the ranks of warriors and the throngs of merchants all hung their heads.

As word of the request of the emperor passed down through the ranks and reached even the outcasts a cloud of silence spread behind it. At the end of the line, farthest away from the royal host above, there stood an old prostitute named Bindumatæ. She was considered the lowest of the lowly and a life-long outcast. She was avoided by most people if she was noticed at all. Yet, she was the one person who spoke into the swelling silence and quietly said to those around her, "I have an Act of Truth."

The silence grew deeper again as the old woman closed her eyes and entered a state of profound concentration. As the old prostitute stood deep in the depths of herself at one end of the quay, the emperor at the high end of the crowd noticed that the waters of the holy river were beginning to slow their rushing pace. As people watched in awe the waters appeared to reverse their course and begin to flow the opposite way. As the waters reversed and receded a roar began to rise and spread through the crowd.

Once the miraculous situation became clear, the emperor asked who in the world had performed the act of truth. No one in the immediate area had any idea. Everyone looked at each other, but gained no knowledge on the subject. Only after a time did the rumor that was flowing through the crowd reach up to the level of the royal court. Amidst the growing amazement the emperor was informed that of all people, it was an old prostitute who managed to make the act of truth.

At that point, the great ruler himself went down the long line of people standing in descending ranks until he reached the area where the outcasts were gathered. People moved aside as the emperor approached the old prostitute who remained in a state of internal reflection.

"You!" the emperor exclaimed. "A wicked old sinner and disgrace to the community! Am I to understand that you have an act of truth?" "Your majesty," she answered, "I possess an act of truth and I performed it at your request and for the direct benefit of everyone here."

The emperor became quite curious and requested that the old woman explain how it was that she of all people could manage an act of truth when so many above her could do nothing of the kind. The old prostitute replied: "Whoever offers me something, be he a high Brahmin, and their have been some of those; be he a merchant or a warrior, and their have been many of them; be he a person down on his luck or another outcast, I treat each one the same.

I make no distinction in favor of those who happen to be powerful, or in favor of those whose fate has put them in a lowly condition. Being in this way free from both pretension and contempt, I have learned to serve in the way that I know best. Since I treat no one better or worse than another, I have learned to treat myself in the same way. It is from this inner sense of worthiness, your majesty, that I am able to perform an act of truth and alter the desperate condition of all involved."

The emperor was satisfied and even instructed by the explanation and everyone had something to contemplate regarding their own inner state.

On that day the old prostitute became the teacher of everyone else. Despite what people thought of her, she had found a truth inside and she was able to draw upon that essence. When the hard time came, she used the truth that she carried in her heart and soul for the benefit of everyone. That meant that she had cleared whatever resentments and disappointments, angers and conflicts might have developed within her. Of all those present, the lowly prostitute was closest to the pearl of the self and therefore nearest to the source of life's energy and flow. She had found a way to reverse the fate within herself and that made her capable of reversing the course of events that threatened others.

PEARLS BEFORE SWINE

A deep connection is being drawn between those who seem lowly and valuable pearls from the depths of the ocean. Those who desire pearls must dive into deep waters and risk darkness and the confusion of the depths. Similarly, those who would find the pearl of the soul must enter treacherous waters as well and face the darkness within them. They must crack the shell of their little-self and come to know themselves from inside out.

The daughter of the old sage had to dwell in darkness and sit in the depths of her soul before pearls could be brought to her door. She had to find and secure a genuine sense of the inner value of her soul as well as refuse to sell herself short. Like the old prostitute making the act of truth, the sorrowful sister had to reach the center of herself; she had to learn the truth that resided there before the current of her life could change. No one is truly empty inside, but there can be a lonely wilderness in the soul that must be crossed before the center of the self can open and renew the flow of one's life.

Beyond that, each arrival at the doors of truth requires that we descend to the depths and immerse ourselves in the troubled waters of the soul. Those who seek for pearls must dive deep time and time again. Each descent involves some inner adjustment and learning to see more clearly. In the depths things can appear differently than on the land above. People think that a prostitute cannot have any inner value, that outcasts live in the shadows because of something distorted in their nature. Yet, the innate destiny of the soul also hides in dark places. The soul itself is a light that grows from darkness.

Doesn't a pearl begin as an irritant inside the life of the oyster? The rare gem that eventually emerges as the gift of the deep waters begins as an alien presence inside its host. The same situation exists with the human soul; that which can become the most valued aspect of the self is just an irritant to begin with. All the carping on the part of the poor son had to do with poverty and a lack of resources. The pearl that was deeply hidden inside all the laments and complaints turned out to be his native generosity. It was the inner irritant of unrecognized generosity that the disciple spoke to when giving his advice.

As fate would have it, the inner seed of great value is not valued at the beginning of life and it will ever be overlooked by those who only see with conventional sight. People expect beautiful things to come with an attractive wrapping; but the soul has it another way. Remember the necessity of imperfection and having a weird and un-adaptable foot that keeps a limp in each life. The weird foot keeps in touch with the inner depths that hold the forgotten essence. Genuine pearl-fishers know exactly that formula. They seek shells with an irregular shape or stunted growth; for those are most likely to yield pearls.

In the depths of the sea the divers after natural pearls learn the old lesson that the greatest gifts are found where life leaves its fateful mark as irregularities and deformities, as wounds and even as woeful conditions. Unless a person goes deep enough within themselves and faces the worst deformities and anomalies, they can't find the pearl of the self. Those who claim to be perfect or pure are like manufactured pearls; their glow does not come from the mystery of the soul's depths. In the deep waters of life one thing can become another and what seemed worthless can turn out most valuable. The brightness of the tiger-self hides inside the dull determination of our goat-like attitudes. Some deep soul searching and genuine reflection are necessary if the shining self would be found.

The calling already seeded in the heart must wait to be called forth and something hard must be cracked open. People fear the cracking and breaking open process, yet that which tears at the shell doesn't harm the pearl within. People fear that in breaking open they will turn out to be the vacant oyster that has little value and becomes cast aside. In nature that may be the case; but this soul search goes against nature and beyond it. The inner pearl is the result of the irritation of fate; it is the seed of fate that becomes the jewel of destiny. As with a pilgrimage, arriving at the appointment with destiny means arriving at the center of the self-soul.

The pearl being sought began as a foreign body within one's life. Over time and with the troubled attention of its host, the inner seed begins to lose its abrasive contours. Eventually, it becomes smooth and round like the drop of a tear. Old traditions describe the pearl as "the child of lightning" that originates in the opposite place and distant from the watery depths. The foreign element strikes and penetrates the interior of the shell of one's life like the first agreement of the soul. The organism responds by covering the light with layers of its own secretions. The pearl must grow as a secret within the secretions that both hide it and protect it until the time for cracking open arrives.

What is seeded within us tries to grow all along. It irritates us from within like strange dreams that trouble us after sleeping. It appears in strange desires that resist being dismissed. Until it becomes clear that what irritates our life is an inner pearl trying to grow, it feels as if something is wrong and out of place. Yet, all along it is the hidden union between light and darkness, between fire and water that is trying to develop. Pearls were called "tears of the divine." Although made of water, tears are produced by heat and are warm when they flow. The pearl of the deep self represents a unity formed of the fires of longing and the waters of peace. Finding the pearl of the deep self reveals the ancient longings of the soul as well as the iridescent peace of the self.

The inner pearl develops from cultivation of the hidden spirit of one's life; but it also incorporates that which is most foreign within and unfamiliar to us. Since ancient times, the pearl has been a symbol of beauty and richness that rises from the unseen depths of life. To the ancients, pearls were a symbol of the moon that also rises from darkness and shines opalescent in the night. Both the moon and the pearl were considered to have magical powers. Both had to do with water and each has a revelation to make. The moon pulls the tides and shifts the seas and in doing so uncovers what was hidden and reveals the abundance of life underneath the waves. In the same way, a pearl could reveal the hidden alchemy taking place in the depths of the waters and tides of the human soul.

When the revelation takes place the pearl does not need to be cut or reshaped in order to be valuable. Unlike gemstones that must be cut and polished to bring out their beauty, a pearl can be worn in its natural form. An old word for pearl also means "unique," attesting to the fact that no two pearls are identical. A "pearl of the first water" is translucent and possesses a unique iridescence or "orient." Such an inner glow and specific orientation are characteristics of the self within the self.

Since pearls appear fully formed with each having a unique iridescence and orientation, the pearl became an ideal representation of the uniqueness as well as the completeness of the deep self. The great self in each person has a unique shine and character, yet it also represents the cosmic pearl at the center of existence. As cosmic center it can offer calmness and clarity; as unique essence it offers the creative energy necessary for continuing life.

DESTINY TURNS FATE UPSIDE DOWN, INSIDE OUT

In order to be properly valued in this world a person must find the pearl of the first water in the depths of themselves. Everyone enters this world with such an inner seed or hidden gem worth "more than gold." The problem remains that the inner gold or hidden pearl must reside and usually hides near the most wounded and most rejected parts of ourselves.

The poor daughter of the old sage is the sister of the soul stuck at the point where she can't imagine that there is something truly valuable within her. Her fear of being empty is so great that she sells herself short each day. Meanwhile, the only deal that can make things right and open the way of her inner life is a return to the first agreement that her soul made. Her fate placed her in a desperate condition and the only genuine way out was to reconnect to the agreement made before the moment of her birth. She had felt her inner nature in her early connection to the flow of music and art. In finding that current again, she became ready to receive the pearls.

The poor sister had to learn to wait inside the tension between loneliness and awakening. Before she could understand the great value in her deep self, she had to refuse to make herself worthless before others. She had to find the pearl within the shell she believed she was and begin all future negotiations from that point.

The deep self is a natural epiphany, a shining through of the gold sown and hidden within the personality that both knows of it and again does not. The little-self is itself a creation of the great self within; yet it cannot know that until something breaks the shell which hides the inner spirit. The little-self is both shell and spell, it protects and it hinders; it both hides and reveals. Especially, it hides the radiance of the deep self which only occasionally shines forth; yet it can eventually learn to turn to that deeper self for solace and calmness, for clarity and power if needed.

Consider the old prostitute again. She didn't proclaim what she knew or try to be paid for it. Yet, when the true presence of the inner self was needed, her regular personality knew exactly where to turn. Some insist that the ego must be removed for the deep self to appear; yet the little-self can also learn to work with the greater source of its own presence.

Pearl fishers are known to work in pairs: one must dive deep into the sea while a partner stays above to hold the other end of the lifeline. Both are required to bring the pearl of great value from the depths to the surface. Some say that the deep swimmer represents the greater self, while the surface partner stands for the little-self that remains in place in the common world. Seen that way, the little-self or ego-self has a value and a function when it comes to bringing the pearl of the deep self to the surface of life. The ego can be seen as a double agent that both hides and can reveal the presence of the deeper self within. The issue then is not the complete removal of the little-self as much as the need for it to awaken to the inner process and learn to serve the deep presence to which it is tied by life.

When a life situation will no longer abide compromise and something deeper and more meaningful must be faced, the little self can learn to bow to the greater presence and innate knowledge of the deep self within. When the shell of the little self can be cracked open, the inner radiance and iridescence of the soul can shine through. That shining through and revealing of the deep radiance of the self is both creative and healing and it has a mysterious affect on other people. Once a genuine path has been found the little-self can become the agent of the deeper self within. The trick in this life is to become aware of the wise self within before the little-self hardens too much and becomes a fixed fate and crosswise ruler.

THE TWO VILLAGES: GIVING AND RECEIVING

Feeling that his work was done, the disciple prepared to depart from the place where he had studied and learned from the old sage and his wife. Before leaving he returned to the river and reflected upon the two villages nearby and the kinds of fate that he had encountered in them. In one town lived the son who believed he had too little and worried endlessly that life would never give him more. He became cynical as people do in the haunts of poverty where there seem to be no second chances and no reversals of fortune.

In the village of internal poverty and growing cynicism everyone fears losing what little stability they might have. Yet, there can be no growth in one's outer life when there is no sweetness and generosity within. Altering the fate of inner poverty depends upon finding a generosity of spirit toward oneself. Life has hidden abundance and an endless capacity to renew itself from the ashes; but a person can only learn the truth of that by letting go of restricting attitudes and self-defeating practices.

Meanwhile, the inhabitants of the next town fearfully accept whatever role in life they first find. They wait for scraps of attention to be thrown to them. They become orphans of love who dwell in constant loneliness and continually sell themselves short. Fearing that they must quickly accept what little attention they are offered, they wind up starved of all genuine love and affection, while increasingly losing affection and respect for themselves.

The poor daughter had given up on herself and on life. She only clung to the barest sense of existence. In forsaking herself she could not imagine that anyone could care for her and she didn't know how to truly care for herself. He despair made change seem impossible; yet she had to enter despair and face her fate fully for change to occur.

The poor son who clung blindly to his meager possessions had to learn to let go and give all that he had to life. The poor daughter who gave herself away too cheaply had to learn to hold herself dear and wait until she was treated as a noble soul. Letting go and not holding back was the secret to the destiny for one, while holding back and containing herself was the secret for the destiny of the other.

The poor son had to learn to give like a king. The poor daughter had to learn to demand what she was really worth. In doing so they each found the inner nobility of the self. By making a practice of such self awareness and self respect they were able to shift the onerous elements of fate in the direction of the destiny hidden within them. Holding back one's deepest nature keeps the spell of fate in place; so does the mantra of excessive self deprecation or the torment of self loathing.

Most people spend time in each village; some run back and forth between fears of letting go and impulses to throw oneself away. Some days a person is like the poor son who must learn to let go of things in order to find the hidden generosity within. Some nights a person finds themselves in the village where love is abandoned and they must become like the sister who refused to prostitute herself because she learned how to wait for the pearls.

It seems so naïve to give all one has away, yet when done at the right time it leads to a pattern of abundance. It can feel terrifying to insist on one's self worth and core value; yet when done with sincerity and humility such self recognition can erase shame and attract genuine love. The practice of giving all one has and fully valuing what one has to give seem to be essential to breaking the spells of fate. Each must arrive at the edge of their knowing, take the next step and cast their fate upon the wind. Fate may set exact limits on each life, yet there are also limits on fate. Each must risk learning what story truly lives inside their heart. Finding one's destiny requires becoming whole-hearted, both willing to give all that one has to live, and willing to trust that life has something valuable to give to them.

CHAPTER 15

THE RETURN OF WISDOM

The disciple was satisfied that he had helped the children of his old teacher and that their fates had been moved. He decided to begin another pilgrimage and learn what the roads of life could teach him. He woke well before dawn and could see the moon hanging in the dark sky like a pearl on the ocean floor. He took it as a good sign for setting out and began to walk. He was not far along when he perceived someone walking the night road before him. As he drew closer he could see that it was young man in fine clothes with a noble bearing. However, he was leading a buffalo and carrying a sack of rice on his head. The fellow looked overburdened with a bag slung over his shoulder as well.

"Who are you sir," asked the disciple, "that you walk the lonely road at night and carry heavy burdens?"

The man gladly stopped, threw down his sacks and almost wept with frustration, "Look, my head has become almost bald from carrying a sack of rice every night to that poor man's hut up ahead. Night after night I must lead a buffalo to his empty shed. Then I must dress up and carry pearls to his sister's house in the next town as well. I'm worn out with the burden of these tasks and it is your fault that I suffer in this way. Granted, it was my stylus that brought their fates to their foreheads; but, because of your guidance, I must supply what was secretly promised at their birth but hidden from view. You ask who I am, when you can see with your own eyes who it is that carries these burdens and walks the night roads. The question now is whether you will relieve me of the burden of the fates of those children?"

And Brahma began to weep, for even a god can weep at times, and it was surely Brahma in the guise of the young man. The god of creation was walking on the dark side of the road of existence. He was feeling the weight of the second hand of creation that knows loneliness and sorrow and even fear.

The disciple spoke again, "If it is has become my place to change the deal that was made in the moments before the fates of the newborns were revealed, then I will gladly make a new agreement. I will absolve you of any need to fulfill their destiny. They have faced their fates and learned the nature of their original life agreements; they can find their own way now. I readily agree to that, but I have two requests to make of you."

Brahma was quite willing to make a new agreement with the disciple and asked what the requirements might be.

"I ask that you grant both the sister and brother some regular happiness in this world and a continuing share in the joy of being alive." Brahma was quickly agreeable and asked what else.

The disciple then asked that the deity relent with regard to the condition that threatened the explosion of his head into a thousand pieces for speaking any of what he had learned regarding fate and birth and knowledge. Brahma agreed to that as well only stating that such talk of fate and hidden things must be done artfully and could not be used for simple gain. The new agreement was made and the disciple bowed and expressed his gratitude to the god. He continued on his way as the subtle rays of dawn began to slip back into the world. With a feeling of lightness in his heart and relief in his mind he began to consider his next pilgrimage toward the unseen.

THE FINAL DEAL

At the birth of each child the disciple had agreed to the deal that required his silence with regard to the hidden dynamics of fate. He had carried the burden of that agreement until his own understanding cracked open the puzzle and revealed the nature of the dilemma of fate as well as the solution for it. In order to shift his own fate he had to move knowledge in the direction of wisdom; he had to be wise enough to guide the sister and brother to the destiny hidden in their fate without simply telling it to them.

Having come far along the road of his own fate, it was time for the disciple to renegotiate some things. The original situation had turned all the way around. Whereas it was the disciple who first became burdened with the fates of the children, it became the deity who had to bear the burden later on. Fate had held both children captive and had entrapped the disciple as well.

Once fate had been turned inside out and the hidden destinies had been revealed, the burden shifted back to the divine. At that point, even the gods want some relief, for the necessity of fate can compel them as well.

Destiny means to stand apart, to be seen standing in a unique relationship to one's spirit, to be in the proximity of the divine aspect originally seeded in the soul. The disciple was on the ground of destiny for he was a servant of great Brahma before he ever became the student of others. He was able to converse and even could negotiate with the deity that stood behind his own destiny. Brahma had been there in the form of the beloved cow and had been there again at each fateful moment of birth. Brahma had been near all along the way and was closest when the agreements of the soul were being attended to.

The disciple had learned something of the nature of the agreements that keep the world turning and keep each life returning to its crucial issues and original agreements. He requests some simple happiness for the sister and brother, for a little joy can go a long way in this world that can become so dark with suffering and torn with conflicts. Besides, both gods and humans delight in moments that relieve the excess burdens of fate and even the drive of destiny.

INNER NOBILITY

Old stories often bring the gods and humans together in surprising ways. Since each destiny was considered to be connected to a divine source, it made sense that the gods would become closely involved in human adventures. At the same time, the animal realm also had closer associations with human experience. Humans inhabit a middle ground between the animal world and the divine realm. But not just in the sense of having our feet on the ground and our heads in the air. For it is human nature to draw inspiration from the natural world as well as from the super-natural realm. Both realms present images of complete beings with noble bearing and integrity of being.

Only in modern times does it seem that the animals are far below us while the gods remain high above and far away. Being modern can mean being more isolated as well as feeling less able to truly change. The stories of fate all involve radical changes that may take time to develop, but then suddenly allow life to leap forward. In the story of the tiger-goat the first leap of fate left the little tiger in the world of the goats. The little one found a way to fit in, but its true nature was obscured even from itself. The second leap brought the tiger-self to awareness and everything transformed rapidly.

They say that a tiger can't change its stripes; but the essential markings on the human soul are hidden from sight. Our essential identity can be completely overlooked by others and the tiger-self can be sleeping within. When it does awaken such a primal and vital self can come as a shocking revelation to the goat aspect of ourselves as well as to those who believe they already know who we are. The birth of new awareness and awakening to the original agreement can make it seem that we were living with the wrong species.

The tiger stands for the compelling vitality and inner nobility of the deeper self. The roar of awakening is also the song of the self; it intones the original speech of the soul. Rather than being "blood curdling," the roar comes from the great relief that the true nature within can become manifest in the world. It is the roar of existence that clears the soul of basic confusions and residues of shame that otherwise obscure the innate brilliance of the self.

Don't think in terms of zoology here, for this is the tiger of the true self. It may seem dangerous, but even if you mistreat it a little, it will pretend not to notice. Remember the young woman who had to grasp a whisker from a living tiger? She was seeking a remedy for love and her search brought her face to face with the tiger. She had to feed the tiger to make a cure possible. She feared that she might never find love again and had to learn of her own tiger-self. Since the tiger-self knows instinctively how to act and where it fits in the grand scheme of existence, it doesn't fear that it might be empty or essentially mistaken or have no meaningful role to play.

Until we become awakened to the story trying find its way into life through us, we can become trapped in a half-life with an ever growing distance between the little, goat-self and the primal self within. At first, it is necessary to fit in somehow and make all the adaptations and second agreements required for survival and for getting along. Later in life, the tiger-self tries to get our attention and bring us to an awareness of the stunning nature of our dream laden and gold-threaded selves.

Meanwhile, the entanglements of fate and the words set crosswise on the soul conspire to keep the primal self and our original agreements hidden from us. The goat-self will resist the exact intelligence and specific longings that exist within us. Unfortunately, it remains much easier to develop societies that cater to the goat nature of the little-self as opposed to primal nature and inspired presence of the inner nobility of the soul. Typically, something dramatic or tragic is required for the little-self to become so shaken that it relinquishes its hold on us and allows the true and noble nature within us to come to the surface. Each time that happens, there is a potential act of truth as well as an opening for a destiny to appear.

POISON AND TRUTH

It's like the old story of the boy who was playing with a ball, as children do in this world that is itself a sphere rolling through eternity. As fate would have it, the ball rolled into the hole of an old ant-hill where a poisonous snake had taken up residence. Not knowing the situation and desiring to reclaim the ball, the boy put his hand into the hole. Before he could retrieve the ball, the snake bit his hand. No sooner did he pull his hand out in pain, than he fell into a faint because of the strength of the snake's poison.

By the time the boy's parents found him, the poison had spread throughout his body. Realizing the danger he was in caused both parents to act with uncommon awareness and great speed. Since there was no doctor in the vicinity and no time to travel, they quickly carried the unconscious boy to the hut of a nearby monk. Laying him at the feet of the ascetic, they implored him saying, "Sir, religious people are known to have potions and charms; please cure our son."

"I know no cures; I am not a physician by trade," said the holy man.

"Well, you are a man of religion; you follow a spiritual path. Have pity on the boy, have compassion and perform an Act of Truth for him."

"I know the truth of my own life and can only draw upon that," said the ascetic.

Laying hands upon the head of the boy, he composed his words of truth, "Seven days serene in my heart and pure of purpose I once lived while seeking spiritual merit. Since then, for fifty years apart and self-absorbed, I've lived against my will. By this truth, health! Poison be struck down! May this truth be as a blessing and the lad be revived!"

No sooner had this act of truth been made than poison came out from the chest of the boy and soaked into the ground. The lad opened his eyes; then lay still again.

The monk said to the father, "I have used my power; now is the time for you to use yours."

"I will make an act of truth as well," he said. And laying a hand upon his son's breast, he spoke aloud, "For gifts and goods I have cared not at all, and have entertained whoever came calling. Yet, even the good and wise visitors knew not that I was my true self restraining. I was unwilling within all the while that I gave; may this truth be a blessing, may the poison be struck down, may the boy revive!"

After this act of truth, poison came from the small of the lad's back and sank into the ground. The boy sat up, but could not stand or move from the spot.

The father said to the mother, "I have used my power; now it is your act of truth that is needed for our son to arise and walk again."

She said, "I too have a truth to tell, but in your presence I cannot declare it."

She looked to the monk as if pleading for an intercession, but he stood silent.

"By any means make our son whole; don't think of me or of anyone but our son," said the father.

"Very well," she said and she spoke the truth she carried in her heart, "No more, my son, do I hate the venomous snake that came and bit you today, than I hate your father! May this truth give a blessing; may the poison be struck down; may my son revive and live."

No sooner was this act of truth performed than the remaining poison flowed out of the son and sank into the ground. Rising whole again with all his body purged of poison, the boy took hold of the ball and began to play again. While the young one played with the roundness of life, the older folks each had something rougher to consider.

After a period of silence the father asked the holy man how he could live the life of an ascetic for so long in such an unwilling mood. The monk explained that after taking the path of sanctity a part of him kept looking back. "At first there was the excitement of making a choice and dedicating myself to spiritual disciplines. After a week a voice within began to say: You fool; you idiot. You have left the world behind before you ever learned what it was and what it meant to you."

Ever since that time the monk had lived the life of ascetic practices and renunciation, all the while longing to know more of the sensate world. When the father asked him why he didn't simply release himself from his vows and pursue his true nature, the monk explained that he feared being called a sinner and a fool and losing the admiration of learned people. Despite feeling untrue to what he knew of himself, the monk kept up the appearance that others expected of him.

The monk then asked the father how he, a well respected and dutiful man, could pretend to host the learned, the holy, and the wise while all the while withholding his true feelings and dismissing his genuine self. His house, so widely esteemed for nobility and considered by many a model of generosity, was in truth more like a common tavern than a true refuge.

The father responded that he simply followed in the footsteps of his father and in the traditional ways of his family. He was born into wealth and high status and although the trappings and practices seemed empty to him, he feared creating a scandal or ruining the family name. He felt he could not face being considered a failure by others. He feared that they would judge him to have a perverse and degenerate nature.

Having somewhat explained himself, the husband asked his wife how it was that she so hated him, yet never informed him of the matter. How had she lived so long unfulfilled and with hatred so close? Why had she not acted in accordance with her true and loving nature?

After a pause, the wife responded that it was against the custom of society and of their families for a wedded wife to take a newer mate. She feared that she would be condemned and punished for desiring what she did not deserve. Fear of recriminations caused her to keep things as they were and live with him in an unloving way. Only for love of their child had she finally said what had been so long unspoken within her heart. She only knew love in the form of her child and spoke the truth because of that. Receiving love herself and being "in love," that was another matter and one not easily attained or understood.

All three became quiet again, each thinking their own thoughts and feeling what they must feel. When the husband broke the silence it was to forgive his wife for any hatred she felt toward him and to ask forgiveness from her for his own ignorance and callous behavior. Under the unusual conditions and in the aftermath of the act of truth, she found it in her heart to make peace with her husband. Turning then to the monk, the father of the boy said that he hoped that he could find a way to walk in holiness with a tranquil mind, but he also wished him a heart full of joy. Anyone who could bring forth such a painful truth in service of a stranger must have a great heart and such a heart should find a way to live its fullness.

Then, the three who had come together over the poison that troubled and endangered the life of the boy parted ways. Each had something essential to consider and a life change to contemplate. Each, in their own way, had come to understand that those who fail to act in accord with their deepest sense of self not only fail there own spirit, but become a danger to others as well.

In this world, where poison can appear at any moment and a small wound can fester until life it self is threatened, it is important to know that the truth also hides where the pain is deepest. The fate of the boy became dependent upon the honesty and truthfulness of everyone involved. Each had to reveal a hidden pain and a specific lack of fulfillment in order for the life to flow back into the young one. But it wasn't just the child that needed the acts of truth. Life had become stuck inside all the false exteriors and poisons were growing wherever people pretended to righteousness and justice and love. Even seemingly innocent acts of omission produce a contrary energy that weakens the collective resolve to live meaningfully.

An act of truth doesn't have to be strictly positive or a statement of completion. Truth is found where a person truly finds themselves; where they can't help but be. No one can help but be who and where they are at a given moment. Acts of truth are like the ceremonies of cleansing and polishing that remove the rotten flesh and burnish the golden presence of each soul. Such radical rituals are needed to reverse the flow of poison once it gets into the system and becomes a danger both to the youngest part of the soul as well as the younger generation.

Being true in such a revealing way clears the soul and creates a turning point that can turn even a drastic situation around. The ascetic monk turned away from the sensual world and found a brief period of awakening. He discovered a golden part of himself, but there was something left unfinished. Despite his ascetic practices, the fragrance of the sensate world followed him on the inside wherever he went. Had he faced his fate more fully he may have found the true gradient within his life sooner. Had he trusted the way already in him he may have turned toward a genuine destiny instead of entering a half-life in a kind of spiritual limbo.

Remember the old thief, he found truth in a dried plum pit and understood what was behind all the prisons even the ones constructed of privilege and power. He found the prison behind the prison and revealed the poison behind the throne. The most secure prison is the one a person builds inside themselves. Sometimes it is enough truth and enough wisdom for people to simply admit the poison they harbor and pronounce the longing hidden behind it. Wisdom is the truth of the moment; once the edifice of denial has crumbled the ground of truth will be near at hand. Everyone would like to plant the seed that instantly grows the golden fruit and produces a miraculous blossoming; but a certain darkness and culpability must first be faced.

The problem isn't that there is no antidote available for what poisons the joy of life. When the monk claimed that he was no physician and had no remedy to apply, he had to be reminded of the deeper pharmacy. "Physician, heal thyself," is a old remedy that always applies. The problem isn't the lack of soulful medicine; rather it is an issue of being unwilling to pay the price. Think of the maggots and the gold—an opening of the wounds and cleansing of the rotting areas precedes the polishing and shining of one's true nature.

The healing begins when the patient announces the nature of the suffering; that is the price of admission to the place where the soul finds healing. Didn't the poor son of the sage have to face his fears and lack of courage when going to the marketplace? His miserly attitude poisoned the well for his wife and children as well as himself. The fact that his parents had wise practices didn't provide him with the specific remedy that he needed. He had to find the kind of generosity that kept opening wider until it became a benefit to others as well as remedy for himself. He found the hidden generosity by going to the marketplace of life and entering the great exchange, not by avoiding it. The hesitant monk could follow in those footsteps.

Didn't the poor daughter of the sage have to learn how to love all over again? She too had to learn generosity, but from another angle. She had to become generous to herself. Having been trapped at the bargain level of love, she had to revalue herself and no longer "give herself away." The mother of the snake-bitten boy could learn something from that. When the poor sister became willing to face her loneliness and lack of love, she found a way to love herself. She began to wait for the right situation to develop.

Soon, the divine had to come to her. There is no certain way to go, except a person finds the way already seeded within them.

Brahma was compelled to bring pearls and increase the love quotient once the hidden destiny became revealed. The god was compelled by the presence of fate at the beginning of her life and he became compelled again when she aligned with the thread of her destiny. The divine came to her both by fate and by destiny. Although seemingly a lowly prostitute, she demanded such a high price that something divine had to pay. If the prostitute sister and the miserly brother could find a remedy within the limits of their lives, can't those with a better status try looking in similar places?

THE WISE SELF

Remember the prostitute who saved the royal city? She placed respect on another level when she revealed her essential nature. She reminded everyone that the truth hides in low places, exactly where most people decline to look. Most look outside in hopes that the answer will simply appear at an affordable price. In the marketplace people will pay a high price for a pearl of the first water. They recognize that rare things are mostly hidden and wrapped in darkness and even in danger. For those reasons they prefer that someone else do the diving and practice breaking things open. On the paths of healing and the roads of destiny however, each must enter the deep water on their own and learn to swim for themselves.

The true wisdom of one's life lies with the deeper self within and appears when the truth of the situation is faced. When a person acts from the deep self they tend to be considered "selfless;" yet such selflessness begins with self-recognition and self-revelation. That was the wisdom of the moment that appeared when there was no other remedy to be found. The deep self within has access to our innate gifts even if they have been denied for most of our lives. Like water from a stone, the deep self can flow out once the hardness of the little-self cracks and allows some opening to begin.

In acceptance of the fate of the moment, a threshold forms and change becomes possible. True attention is part of the remedy and genuine attention is a form of love. When the monk and the parents turn their real attention to the wounded boy, they also shower him with love. While sending the poison back to the earth, they call blessings down on the boy. Once again, the two-sided ceremony cleanses and polishes the self back into health.

People keep forgetting the uniqueness seeded in the soul and the primary agreement that tries to awaken again and again. The poison develops where the inner seed goes to rot and where the original agreement of the soul is dismissed in favor of conventions or poor bargains with life. Once the ascetic and the parents began naming the poison in them, the boy was on the road to recovery. At the same time, something essential in each of them began to revive and find at least some expression. There was an unlived life within each of them and that kind of holding back stops the internal growth and blocks one's basic vitality. Eisik became both younger and older once he allowed the dream inside his life to lead the way. He became foolish in the right direction and eventually wise enough to help others.

The deep self beckons to us continually, yet the little-self fears a loss of common power and superficial prestige. The little-self believes that letting go will lead to a great emptiness and a "loss of self." Believing itself to be the only self, it imagines life to be empty without it. The little-self is a necessary imposter and a fore-runner of the deeper self within. There is some accuracy even in our mistakes. Didn't the poor sister receive beauty and love after trading away just that? Didn't her brother become the epitome of generosity once he gave up his hoarding?

The ascetic monk lived in the shadow of all that he had denied in life and in himself. The father had to truly give for once in order to stop the poison from spreading. And, the mother had to bring her need for love out in the open or else lose the only one she did love. That's why they say that the cure for the pain is in the pain. Many medicines are made of substances that are pure poison when taken in the wrong dosage or for the wrong ailment. What is poison for one person can be a remedy for another.

The whole thing trembles on the verge of recognition; yet it often takes a great failure or a tragic circumstance for the little-self to begin relinquishing its rule. The story written within the soul requires a drama of self-realization and self-revelation. On such occasions, the veil between the little-self and the deeper self thins, and a meaningful self-adjustment becomes possible. If a person doesn't become paralyzed with fear or frozen in hatred, the deep self will rise to the occasion. It is in that sense that most ordeals encountered in life are also occasions for learning. The continual lesson involves the awakening of the deeper self and the living of the truth it already carries. When a situation feels like a matter of "life and death" the deep self is close at hand and it already carries inner medicine and its own life remedy.

When the deep self does manifest we feel truly empowered, especially empowered to be ourselves. In becoming more ourselves we fulfill a destiny even if it is only in the moment. For the moment of fulfilling opens to the eternity behind it and the release of the inner medicine draws some poison out of oneself, out of those we love and out of the world. None of this can be proven, unless a person risks themselves for the love of life whether that be in the form of a wounded child or a threatened town or a cow whose horns keep turning in on itself.

When the knowing self takes charge, a surprising sense of peace can be experienced even amidst chaotic circumstances. At the same time, inner resources previously unknown become available. The deep self harbors the core imagination that drove our soul to life to begin with. In that sense, the exact knowledge so often sought in the outer world can be found dwelling within the soul all along. We are always close to the source of wisdom because it dwells within us; yet some fateful events are needed for the little-self to let go and wake up to the true situation.

THE TWO ARCS

Consider again the boy who was bitten and filled with poison. He had an awakening after a brush with death. Everyone receives a least one free experience of waking up and tasting the sweetness of life. However, the rolling ball of his life will find other holes in this world and his particular fate will put him in the darkness again. He has had a golden moment, but will find himself falling asleep again on the roads of life. Like old Eisik he will forget the voice speaking in his dreams and fall asleep to the story trying to awaken in him. One day he will have to travel far into the world before the ball of his youth can become the pearl of his life.

His fate waits for him along the arc that will carry him out into the world where he will trade his ball for a book or an instrument, for an idea or for a person he can love. He will rise and fall amidst the times and tides; he will succeed and fail to one degree or another. The point isn't to conquer all and succeed at any cost; the point isn't even to find the right career or marry the right person. The point is to step onto the path of life and try to find one's way.

Along the way, there are bound to be pitfalls and holes where everything goes dark for a time. Eventually, he will face a poison of his own making and will have to find the medicine within himself. Then, the second adventure will begin. The second adventure leads back to the first agreement of the soul but only after a person has weathered some storms and faced some fears and become wet with life.

The first adventure of life traces a path through the daily world. We enter the market place of life; we buy and sell. We buy into a life and live it up or fall down trying to do so. We become a part of the living exchange in the market where life recreates itself each day. We rise in the world and rule the day or stumble in some alley or waste away in a prison of our own making. We become part of the great exchange and the endless deals of day-in, day-out market where life is cheap and truth is rare. This is the "real world" where anything can be measured and everything has a price. There are no free lunches and all the deals have strings attached.

Seen from the hustle and bustle of life's marketplace, the second adventure and first agreement seem unreal, not just foolish but irrelevant. What's the point, where's the payoff, how can you value what you cannot count or hold in your hand? In the modern world, and in all places where mass culture has become the way of life, the inward downward ways are less appreciated; they have become undervalued and less understood. For the value of life is increasingly measured by the literal yardsticks of the outer world and by the rudiments of success found on the first arc of life.

For many people the inner spark and seed of self that makes all of life possible remains obscure even at the very end. Yet, all the while, the second adventure with its mysterious dreams and wild projects sings at the edges of all the deals and continues to hum when the wheels threaten to fall off the wagon that keeps the market of life in motion.

The old idea of the second adventure also involved the road of release along which a person could step out of the strict adherence to collective rules and social attitudes. Even if most of life was spent in the back and forth of the daily world or in upholding an unfulfilling life, the later years could be given over to slowing down and growing down, and deepening one's soul. In the second arc the soul leads the way and the way of the soul involves deeper forms of both sensuality and spirituality. For the soul is connected to both body and spirit and would have us live our life to the fullest. It would have us fulfill the inner longings where they ascend to the heights of spirit as well as plummet to the depths of love.

The second adventure follows the inward, downward roads where the story seeded in the soul waits to be found and followed and lived fully. It is along this inner arc that we each become a disciple in our own lives and learn the nature of our fate and the shape of the destiny that calls us on. Ultimately, the second adventure leads back to the first agreement of the soul, but it takes a circuitous route that passes through the village where the maggots clean the rotten flesh and the friends of the self polish the gold of whoever shows up. There are two sides of the self to attend to and two arcs of life to wander on. There are two worlds that come together when we respond to what truly calls to us.

THIS WORLD AND THE OTHER

A part of us desires the natural delights of this world and a part longs for the unseen and the realm beyond all embodiment. Notice that the acts of truth affect both realms and that love is involved each time some poison is removed. People used to say that without love the real work cannot progress. Love is essential when the cure for one's life is being sought. Meanwhile, we are a friend to the otherworld as well as a friend of this world. In troubled times we must be a friend of nature as well as a devotee of our inner nature. We must live in both worlds or else learn when it is too late that we have wasted our time.

It's like the old story of two friends who meet on a street in their village. They were headed in opposite directions. One was going to a rendezvous with a lover, while the other planned to attend a spiritual meeting. The fellow heading to the spiritual gathering said: "Why do you want to go in that direction? You know that love and sensuality are always temporary. Come with me instead and hear the words of spirit and the wonderful tales of the lives of saints and stories of god. Come with me and improve yourself."

His friend said: "Why don't you come where I am going? There is great delight in loving and it can bring a deep joy that continues to live in the soul. Simple happiness may come and go on a whim; but you should know that joy is also a portion of eternity. You can just as easily waste your time at a spiritual gathering if the transcendent moment fails to appear or if the teacher relies on orthodox ideas and dogmatic approaches."

Neither could persuade the other because each had made up their mind regarding the direction in which the unseen could be found. So, each went their own way; however, the one who went to the spiritual meeting found that he could not concentrate on spiritual matters that day. All he could think about was the wonder of beauty and love and the time he might be having had he followed his friend's advice. He felt that he was wasting his time listening to sermons when he could be learning the lessons of love and deepening his understanding of the meaning of pleasure and the joy of delight.

Meanwhile, the fellow who was in the arms of his lover could not fully enjoy the occasion. He could only think of the spiritual meeting where his good friend was learning of lofty matters and probably enjoying the edification of songs and stories of those on the spiritual path. He had to admit that there was a temporary quality to his desires and joy seemed out of reach at the time. The possibility arose that he was wasting his time and that he had chosen the wrong path to follow.

Who can say which of the friends is right? In a way, they are both correct. Part of us remains anchored in this world even when the other realm is nearby. For some, the sensual way of going and knowing *is* the spiritual path. Not only that, but as a person grows in spiritual terms, the desire for pleasure and beauty also increases. Why else would so many preachers and spiritual leaders fall into scandal?

We are beings of both worlds and must serve each of them or fail to have lived life fully. Both directions involve darkness as well as light; reaching for one can easily lead to embracing the other. The issue isn't so much one of choosing which way to be; rather, the point is to be whole-hearted in direction that is being followed. In making love a person may follow a manual or adhere to instructions from those more experienced. Yet, the real love making begins when a person puts their whole self into the act. In doing so, they forget all the rules and even forget their usual self. Inside that forgetting they begin to remember something unseen; they begin to find the "other" that is quite near. They move closer to the act of creation and can feel the creator's breath.

For a true lover, each act of lovemaking is unique and unrepeatable, especially for those who know something of the uniqueness within themselves. Love, like life, requires that we become ourselves, at least for a moment. People say: "I thought I had died and gone to heaven." Notice the intimate connection between death and the divine state even when the occasion involves delight and joy. There's something to the pattern that has the gates of heaven following upon the doors of death.

Meanwhile, wisdom involves both worlds and knowing that there is more than one way to die and in dying find the middle of one's life. Those who fear too much to embrace either direction whole heartedly will fail to learn the little ways of dying that lead to a greater life. Those who put the lessons of love and the trials of the spirit off until the end will not do well when the divine does the testing.

Remember old Zushya? He tried to state the real diagnosis and indicate the remedy with his last breath. He tried to point the disciples in the direction of genuine becoming and real healing. With his last act he tried to hold open the door between life and death so that those willing to see could learn what the divine was interested in. We are all students at the door where life and death exchange. We are each disciples of our own lives and it is the acts of truth within us that change the angles of fate and draw the interest of the divine energies that sustain our destinies. The awakening of the greater self within is the aim behind all the quests in life and is also the object of the question waiting for us at the end of our unique adventure.

THE SONG OF THE ROAD

Like old Eisik we have little choice in the end; either we follow the dream that calls us to a greater life or we succumb to the village where people keep forgetting what life is all about. Those who never leave the village of discontent find hundreds of ways to dismiss the dreams and desires of others. They use common sense or logic, fixed beliefs or appeals to one's age to dissuade the disciple from setting forth and to keep the dreamer from awakening to the living dream.

Waking up involves an uncommon sense and a willingness to trust something as yet unseen. Each day has moments of eternity waiting to be found and the opportunity to return to the original agreement of the soul is continually at hand. How else could it be when the two worlds exist at the same time and interpenetrate each other at every step of the way?

In the unique projects of the soul's second adventure we open the doors and windows that let eternity back into the world. Then, the issue becomes one of learning to tune to the song carried in the soul and the rhythm kept by the heart. In ancient Greek, the word for road and the word for song are almost the same: *oimos* and *oime*. Song and road arise from the same roots and in the depths of things they are connected by way of origins. The ancient notion of a song included the sense of a journey, especially a journey that brings one closer to the eternal realm.

The inner wisdom of one's life shapes the road that must be followed; but it is also carries a song-line that runs all the way through. The "song of the road" involves the pattern and tune set within the soul before it was born into common time. For some it takes the form of a sacred chant, for others it's a love song or even a battle song that reminds them to not give up and what to keep fighting for. Beauty and truth tend to travel together as each polishes the other's essence. Wisdom involves both finding the genuine way of one's life and learning the lyrical song of one's soul. Both are needed when it comes to staying awake and drawing the poison out of life's inevitable ailments.

"Pearls of wisdom" may be a common saying; yet wisdom itself is an uncommon thing. Wisdom requires more than common sense; it depends upon the uncommon sense of the divine being woven into this world. Wisdom is wise because it combines aspects of the immediate with elements of the divine. That's why it's rare and less available than simple knowledge. Wisdom draws upon the origins of things and returns things to their original condition. Wisdom remembers what keeps being forgotten and what keeps being lost in the knowledge already seeded in the individual soul.

OUR FATE IN TIME

It may have been the fate of the boy to be bitten by a snake and have his life hanging in the balance. Clearly there were poisonous circumstances all around him. Those capable of helping him must at least face and name their own fateful conditions or the young one is abandoned to a fate not completely of his own making. If those old enough to know better fail to at least admit the true state of affairs, the child may never have a chance to find a calling or seek a destiny of his own. Denying the truth at the center of one's soul produces a poison that can fester and grow and affect the lives of those around us.

Here on earth, life can't be neutral. Those who fail to face their own pain and fateful restrictions put themselves and others in danger of some kind and they leave the ball of the world unattended and headed for another hole. People worry over the fate of the world and there is good reason for that. There is great concern over the question of whether we have poisoned the water and polluted the air enough to endanger the entire planet. Increasingly, people see ways in which those with the power to help others indulge instead in their own greed or poisonous obsessions—not to mention the spread of wars and terrors. Amidst all the confusion it becomes easier to forget that the real battle is inside; that the struggle everyone takes part in happens in one's own heart and soul.

We live in radical times surrounded by tasks that seem impossible. It has become our collective fate to be alive in a time of great tragedies, to live in a period of overwhelming disasters and to stand at the edge of sweeping changes. The river of life is flooding before us and a tide of poisons affect the air we breathe and the waters we drink and even tarnish the dreams of those who are young and as yet innocent. The snake-bitten condition has already spread throughout the collective body.

However, it is in troubled times that it becomes most important to remember that the wonder of life places the medicine of the self near where the poison dwells. The gifts always lie near the wounds, the remedies are often made from poisonous substances, and love often appears where deep losses become acknowledged. Along the arc of healing the wounds and the poisons of life create the exact opportunities for bringing out all the medicines and making things whole again.

Meanwhile, fate keeps troubling the soul and even endangering the world until people accept that some deep truths must be faced. When the time for healing comes, those who are closest to the wounds will be better able to face the truth and start the healing. When there's no time for sending out for physicians or waiting for magical antidotes, the medicine must first be found within and it only requires an act of truth to activate the cure. Each soul has something to contribute in terms of the inner truth and each has a part of the remedy that is needed.

It may be our mutual fate in life to be present when the poisons that have long festered become undeniable. The child of the future has already been bitten by the snake of the past. If so, the question that everyone faces is similar to the one asked of the holy man and the mother and father of the fallen child: Can you face the painful issues within and make an act of truth that helps remove some of the poison from the current situation? Can you become yourself in a way that adds a blessed roar to life? Can you make a leap and land on the feet of your soul?

It's the same question that has always hung in the air, just as the condition of the world has always hung in the balance between the fate and destiny born within each soul. It's the same question that the divine asks several different ways at the end of each life's unique adventure: In the midst of all the confusion in the great marketplace of life, did you live the life seeded in your soul to begin with? In the twists of fate did you find the thread of destiny intended for you? Did you become weird enough and finally wise enough to become yourself?

ACKNOWLEDGEMENTS

Many people helped to bring this book to life and to light. I am grateful to: my aunt, Florence Sullivan for the right-wrong gift of the book of myths that first opened my eyes to the world of stories; to James Hillman for advising me to value my thoughts of fate and destiny some decades ago. Jacob Lakatua gives his all to the work with stories and soul and this book could not reach fruition without him. Peter Fedofsky brought a keen eye and a deep attention to the making of this book as he does for all Mosaic work. Christina Zanfagna has been invaluable as an editor and guide and as an inspiration for the writing. Thanks to Lisa Thompson for timely and artful contributions and to Rick Simonsen for many cogent suggestions. Gratitude to Jack Kornfield for careful comments and Luis Rodriguez for encouragement and spiritual support.

Select Bibliography

Cole, Joanna. *Best Loved Folktales of the World*. Garden City, NY: Anchor Books, 1983.

Commarswamy, Ananda and Sister Nivedita. *Myths of the Hindus and Buddhists*. New York, NY: Dover Publications, 1967.

Cowell, E.B. *The Jataka; or, Stories of the Buddha's Former Births*. Cambridge: Cambridge University Press, 1901.

Greene, Liz. *Astrology of Fate*. Newburyport, MA: Weiser Books, 1984.

Hamilton, Edith. *Mythology, Timeless Tales of Gods and Heroes*. Boston, MA: Little, Brown and Company, 1942.

Hamilton, Edith. *The Greek Way*. New York, NY: Time, Inc., 1930.

Hillman, James. *The Soul's Code*. New York, NY: Grand Central Publishing, 1997.

Kornfield, Jack and Christina Feldman. *Soul Food*. New York, NY: HarperCollins Publishers, 1996.

Ramanujan, A.K.. *Folktales from India*. New York, NY: Pantheon, 1994.

Zimmer , Heinrich. *Philosophies of India*. Edited by Jospeh Campbell. Princeton, NJ: Princeton University Press, 1969.

Zimmer, Heinrich. *The King and the Corpse*. Princeton, NJ: Princeton University Press, 1948.

Related Titles by Michael Meade

Meade, Michael. *Fate and Destiny, the Two Agreements in Life*. Mosaic Audio, Two CD Set.

Meade, Michael. *The Eye of the Pupil, the Heart of the Disciple*. Mosaic Audio, Two CD Set.

Meade, Michael. *The Water of Life, Initiation and the Tempering of the Soul*. Seattle, WA: Greenfire Press, 2007.

Meade, Michael. *The World Behind the World, Living at the Ends of Time*. Seattle, WA: Greenfire Press, 2008.

Index

ABOUT MOSAIC

Mosaic Multicultural Foundation is a 501(c)3 nonprofit organization, a network of artists, social activists, and community builders. Mosaic formed to create cross-cultural alliances, mentoring relationships, and social connections that encourage greater understanding between diverse peoples, elders and youth, and those of various cultural and spiritual backgrounds.

Mosaic means putting essential pieces together; forming a whole from separate, divided, even estranged parts. The process of finding, fitting, and weaving together divergent, yet necessary pieces involves making new social fabrics from existing ethnic, spiritual, psychological, and political threads.

Mosaic events draw inspiration from the traditions of many cultures and incorporate knowledge learned in the trenches of contemporary community work. Efforts at problem solving rely on locating the genius of the situation, as the unique spirit of each individual becomes a key to understanding issues and fitting the pieces of community together in new ways.

Mosaic's nationwide youth and mentoring projects help veterans return from war, assist addicts in recovery, and inspire youth to find their way in life. Current projects involve homeless and at-risk youth, high school and college students, combat veterans, tribal communities, as well as those in detention and on probation. The practice of mentoring offers the oldest, most natural, and most effective method for awakening genius in youth, creating mentors, and developing elders.

GreenFire Press and **Mosaic Audio** are imprints of Mosaic Multicultural Foundation that serve to foster cultural literacy, mythic education, and multicultural community development. Proceeds from sales of books and recordings directly benefit Mosaic's work with at-risk youth, refugees, and intercultural projects.

For more information or to order additional titles contact Mosaic:
4218 1/2 SW Alaska, Suite H Seattle, WA 98126
(206)935-3665, toll free (800)233-6984
www.mosaicvoices.org ~ info@mosaicvoices.org

Books by Michael Meade

The World Behind the World: Living at the Ends of Time

The Water of Life: Initiation and the Tempering of the Soul

Mosaic Audio Recordings by Michael Meade

Alchemy of Fire: Libido and the Divine Spark

Branches of Mentoring

The Ends of Time, the Roots of Eternity

Entering Mythic Territory: Healing and the Bestowing Self

The Eye of the Pupil, the Heart of the Disciple

Fate and Destiny: The Two Agreements in Life

The Great Dance: Finding One's Way in Troubled Times

Holding the Thread of Life: A Human Response to the Unraveling of the World

The Light Inside Dark Times

Initiation and the Soul: The Sacred and the Profane

Poetics of Peace: Peace and the Salt of the Earth

Poetics of Peace: Vital Voices in Troubled Times, with Alice Walker, Luis Rodriguez,
    Jack Kornfield, Orland Bishop

The Soul of Change

Books edited by Michael Meade

Crossroads: The Quest For Contemporary Rites of Passage,
    edited by Louise Carus Mahdi, Nancy Geyer Christopher, and Michael Meade

The Rag and Bone Shop of the Heart: A Poetry Anthology,
    edited by Robert Bly, James Hillman, and Michael Meade

Books including contributions by Michael Meade

Rites and Symbols of Initiation, Mircea Eliade

Teachers of Myth, Maren Tonder Hansen

ALL PURCHASES FROM MOSAIC AUDIO AND GREENFIRE PRESS SUPPORT
WORK WITH AT-RISK YOUTH, REFUGEES, AND INTERCULTURAL PROJECTS.

For more information or to order additional titles contact Mosaic:
4218 1/2 SW Alaska, Suite H Seattle, WA 98126
(206)935-3665, toll free (800)233-6984
www.mosaicvoices.org ~ info@mosaicvoices.org